W9-BMH-445

Using the *Teach Yourself* in 24 Hours Series

Welcome to the *Teach Yourself in 24 Hours* series! You're probably thinking, "What, they want me to stay up all night and learn this stuff?" Well, no, not exactly. This series introduces a new way to teach you about exciting new products: 24 one-hour lessons, designed to keep your interest and keep you learning. Because the learning process is broken into small units, you will not be overwhelmed by the complexity of some of the new technologies that are emerging in today's market. Each hourly lesson has a number of special items, some old, some new, to help you along.

Minutes

The first 10 minutes of each hour lists the topics and skills that you will learn about by the time you finish the hour. You will know exactly what the hour will bring with no surprises.

Minutes

Twenty minutes into the lesson, you will have been introduced to many of the newest features of the software application. In the constantly evolving computer arena, knowing everything a program can do will aid you enormously now and in the future.

Minutes

Before 30 minutes have passed, you will have learned at least one useful task. Many of these tasks take advantage of the newest features of the application. These tasks use a hands-on approach, telling you exactly which menus and commands you need to use to accomplish the goal. This approach is found in each lesson of the *24 Hours* series.

40 Minutes

You will see after 40 minutes that many of the tools you have come to expect from the *Teach Yourself* series are found in the *24 Hours* series as well. Notes and Tips offer special tricks of the trade to make your work faster and more productive. Warnings help you avoid those nasty time-consuming errors.

50 Minutes

By the time you're 50 minutes in, you'll probably run across terms you haven't seen before. Never before has technology thrown so many new words and acronyms into the language, and the New Terms elements found in this series will carefully explain each and every one of them.

60 Minutes

At the end of the hour, you may still have questions that need to be answered. You know the kind—questions on skills or tasks that come up every day for you, but that weren't directly addressed during the lesson. That's where the Q&A section can help. By answering the most frequently asked questions about the topics discussed in the hour, Q&A not only answers your specific question, it provides a succinct review of all that you have learned in the hour.

What's New in This Edition

Teach Yourself HTML 4 in 24 Hours has been updated for the newest breakthrough in Web publishing, HTML 4.0. Also included are

- ☐ Lessons to help you take advantage of cascading style sheets
- ☐ Enhanced coverage of JavaScript
- ☐ Many new ideas and hints for Web page layout and design
- ☐ Improved organization
- ☐ Examples which have been checked and updated to conform to the HTML 4.0 recommended specifications.

Teach
Yourself
HTML 4

in 24 Hours
Second Edition

Teach Yourself

HTML 4

in 24 Hours
Second Edition

Dick Oliver
Molly Holzschlag

201 West 103rd Street
Indianapolis, Indiana 46290

Copyright © 1997 by Sams.net Publishing

SECOND EDITION

International Standard Book Number: 1-57521-366-4

Library of Congress Catalog Card Number: 97-68549

2000 99 98 97   4 3 2 1

Interpretation of the printing code: the rightmost double-digit number is the year of the book's printing; the rightmost single-digit, the number of the book's printing. For example, a printing code of 97-1 shows that the first printing of the book occurred in 1997.

Composed in AGaramond and MCPdigital by Macmillan Computer Publishing

Printed in the United States of America

Trademarks

President   Richard K. Swadley
Publisher and Director of Acquisitions   Jordan Gold
Director of Product Development   Dean Miller
Executive Editor   Beverly M. Eppink
Managing Editor   Brice P. Gosnell
Indexing Manager   Johnna L. VanHoose
Director of Marketing   Kelli S. Spencer
Product Marketing Manager   Wendy Gilbride

Acquisitions Editor
David B. Mayhew

Development Editor
Scott D. Meyers

Software Development Specialist
Patricia J. Brooks

Production Editor
Mary Ann Abramson

Copy Editors
Kimberly K. Hannel
Colleen Williams

Indexer
Johnna L. VanHoose

Technical Reviewers
Karen Clere
Will Kelly

Editorial Coordinators
Mandie Rowell
Katie Wise

Technical Edit Coordinator
Lorraine E. Schaffer

Editorial Assistants
Carol Ackerman
Andi Richter
Rhonda Tinch-Mize
Karen Williams

Marketing Coordinator
Linda Beckwith

Cover Designer
Tim Amrhein

Cover Illustrator
Eric Lindley

Book Designer
Gary Adair

Copy Writer
David Reichwein

Production Team Supervisors
Brad Chinn
Andrew Stone

Production Team
Rick Bond, Jeanne Clark,
Brad Lenser, Carl Pierce

Overview

Contents

Dedication

This book is dedicated to my mother, Darlene Hewins (`http://netletter.com/hewins/`), *who had to teach herself HTML without this book.*

—Dick Oliver

Acknowledgments

This book would almost certainly not exist today were it not for this author's loving family, who brought enough fresh carrot juice, tender popcorn, and buttery kisses to sustain him through the long hours of its creation.

Special thanks must also go to the folks at the Buffalo Mountain Food Cooperative in Hardwick, Vermont, for providing the carrots, popcorn, and butter.

—Dick Oliver

Much of the HTML 4.0 additions and rewrites of this book would not have been possible without the vast knowledge and true-blue friendship of my research assistant, Lee Anne Phillips. Thanks, Lee Anne, for always coming through for me! I'd also like to thank my teachers and students, who keep me on my toes when it comes to Web design, HTML, and life in general. As ever, all my love to my family: Mom, Ollie, Morris, and Linus.

—Molly E. Holzschlag

About the Authors

Dick Oliver (dicko@netletter.com) is the tall, dark, handsome author of lots of great books and software, including *Web Page Wizardry, Netscape Unleashed, Create Your Own Web Page Graphics*, and *Tricks of the Graphics Gurus*. He is also the president of Cedar Software and the warped mind behind the Nonlinear Nonsense Netletter at http://netletter.com (and several other Web sites). When he isn't banging on a keyboard, he's usually snowboarding, sledding, skiing, or warming up by the woodstove in his cozy Northern Vermont home (where they celebrate a day of summer each year, too). He likes writing HTML, eating killer-spicy Indian food, and waltzing wildly around the office with his daughters—not necessarily in that order. He also thinks it's pretty cool that authors get to write their own "About the Author" sections.

Molly E. Holzschlag is the author of multiple Web design books, including *The Laura Lemay Guide to Sizzling Web Site Design* and *The Laura Lemay Web Workshop Guide to Designing with Style Sheets, Tables, and Frames*. She is a Contributing Editor to *Web Publisher Magazine*, where her monthly column, "The Web Designer" teaches design professionals how to design better. Molly also writes feature articles about Web design for a variety of publications, including Microsoft's Net-based Start Reading. Holzschlag brings her enthusiastic voice to the classroom, teaching new media design, theory, and techniques in the Graduate Media Studies program at the New School for Social Research. Holzschlag's design can be seen peppered about the Web and on various sections of the Microsoft Network. Visit her Web site at http://www.molly.com/.

Tell Us What You Think!

As a reader, you are the most important critic and commentator of our books. We value your opinion and want to know what we're doing right, what we could do better, what areas you'd like to see us publish in, and any other words of wisdom you're willing to pass our way. You can help us make strong books that meet your needs and give you the computer guidance you require.

Do you have access to the World Wide Web? Then check out our site at `http://www.mcp.com`.

If you have a technical question about this book, call the technical support line at 317-581-3833, or send e-mail to `support@mcp.com`.

As the team leader of the group that created this book, I welcome your comments. You can fax, e-mail, or write me directly to let me know what you did or didn't like about this book—as well as what we can do to make our books stronger. Here's the information:

Fax: 317-581-4669

E-mail: `mset_mgr@sams.mcp.com`

Mail: Beverly M. Eppink
          Comments Department
          Sams Publishing
          201 W. 103rd Street
          Indianapolis, IN 46290

Introduction

In the next 24 hours, approximately 100,000 new Web pages will be posted in publicly accessible areas of the Internet. At least as many pages will be placed on private intranets to be seen by businesspeople connected to local networks. Every one of those pages—like the over 100 million pages already online—will use the Hypertext Markup Language, or HTML.

If you read on, your Web pages will be among those that appear on the Internet in the next 24 hours, and this will be the day that you gained one of the most valuable skills in the world today: mastery of HTML.

Can you really learn to create top-quality Web pages yourself, without any specialized software, in less time than it takes to schedule and wait for an appointment with a highly-paid HTML wizard? Can this thin, easy-to-read book really enable you to teach yourself state-of-the-art Web page publishing?

Yes. In fact, within two hours of starting this book, someone with no previous HTML experience at all can have a Web page ready to place on the Internet's World Wide Web.

How can you learn the language of the Web so fast? By example. This book breaks HTML down into simple steps that anyone can learn quickly, and shows you exactly how to take each step. Every HTML example is pictured right above the Web page it will produce. You see it done, you read a brief plain-English explanation of how it works, and you immediately do the same thing with your own page. Ten minutes later, you're on to the next step.

The next day, you're marveling at your own impressive pages on the Internet.

Before you go any further, there's something you should know from the outset. Professional Web page authors talk about three kinds of HTML pages:

- ☐ *First-generation* pages use old-fashioned HTML 1.0, and are mostly text with a hokey picture or two stuck in the middle. They were the best you could do in 1989, but having a first-generation page today marks you as more technologically backward than having no Web page at all.

- ☐ *Second-generation* pages use a few HTML 2.0 and 3.2 tricks, such as putting a pretty (or garish) background behind a page, arranging text in tables, and offering an online order form. They can look nice, but rarely match the quality that people have come to expect from paper documents.

- ☐ *Third-generation* pages are what the world is talking about now that HTML 4.0 is the standard. They use creative layout, custom color, fast graphics, fonts, and interactive feedback to make your Web site more engaging than anything on paper.

The goal of this book is to help you skip past the first and second generations, straight into the exciting world of third-generation Web pages. So don't expect to learn obsolete HTML or create boring pages with no visual interest. Fortunately, if you start with a third-generation mindset, learning HTML can be faster, easier, and more rewarding than ever.

How to Use This Book

There are several ways to go through this book, and the best way for you depends on your situation. Here are five recommended options. Pick the one that matches your needs.

1. *"I need to get some text on the Internet today. Then I can worry about making it look pretty later."*

    ☐ Read Chapter 1, "Welcome to HTML."

    ☐ Read Chapter 2, "Creating a Web Page."

    ☐ Read Chapter 4, "Publishing Your HTML Pages."

    ☐ Put your first page on the Internet! (Total work time: 2–4 hours.)

    ☐ Start with Chapter 3, "Linking to Other Web Pages," and read the rest of the book.

    ☐ Update your pages as you learn more HTML.

2. *"I need a basic Web page with text and graphics on the Internet as soon as possible. Then I can work on improving it and adding more pages."*

    ☐ Read Chapter 1, "Welcome to HTML."

    ☐ Read Chapter 2, "Creating a Web Page."

    ☐ Read Chapter 9, "Putting Images on a Web Page."

    ☐ Read Chapter 10, "Creating Web Page Images."

    ☐ Read Chapter 4, "Publishing Your HTML Pages."

    ☐ Put your first page on the Internet! (Total work time: 4–8 hours.)

    ☐ Start with Chapter 3, and read the rest of the book.

    ☐ Update your pages as you learn more HTML.

3. *"I need a professional-looking business Web site with an order form right away. Then I can continue to improve and develop my site over time."*

    ☐ Read all four chapters in Part I, "Your First Web Page."

    ☐ Read Chapter 9, "Putting Images on a Web Page."

    ☐ Read Chapter 10, "Creating Web Page Images."

    ☐ Read Chapter 13, "Backgrounds and Color Control."

- ☐ Read Chapter 19, "Creating HTML Forms."
- ☐ Put your pages and order form on the Internet! (Total work time: 6–12 hours.)
- ☐ Start with Chapter 5, "Text Formatting and Alignment," and read the rest of the book.
- ☐ Update your pages as you learn more HTML.

4. *"I need to develop a creative and attractive 'identity' Web site on a tight schedule. Then I will need to develop many pages for our corporate intranet as well."*

- ☐ Read all four chapters in Part I, "Your First Web Page."
- ☐ Read all four chapters in Part II, "Web Page Text."
- ☐ Read all four chapters in Part III, "Web Page Graphics."
- ☐ Read all four chapters in Part IV, "Web Page Design."
- ☐ Put your pages on the Internet and/or your intranet! (Total work time: 8–16 hours.)
- ☐ Start with Chapter 17, "Using Style Sheets," and read the rest of the book.
- ☐ Update your pages as you learn more HTML.

5. *"I need to build a cutting-edge interactive Web site or HTML-based multimedia presentation—fast!"*

- ☐ Read this whole book.
- ☐ Put your pages on the Internet and/or CD-ROM! (Total work time: 12–24 hours.)
- ☐ Review and use the techniques you've learned to continue improving and developing your site.

It may take a day or two for an Internet service provider to set up a host computer for your pages, as discussed in Chapter 4, "Publishing Your HTML Pages." If you want to get your pages online immediately, read Chapter 4 now so you can have a place on the Internet all ready for your first page.

No matter which of the above approaches you take, you'll benefit from the unique presentation elements that make this book the fastest possible way to learn HTML.

Visual Examples

The text you type in to make an HTML page is shown first, with all HTML commands highlighted. The resulting Web page is shown as it will appear to people who view it with the world's most popular Web browser, Netscape Navigator. You'll often be able to adapt the example to your own pages without reading any of the accompanying text at all.

Special Highlighted Elements

As you go through each chapter, sections marked "To Do" guide you in applying what you just learned to your own Web pages at once.

Whenever a new term is used, it will be italicized. No flipping back and forth to the glossary!

Tips and tricks to save you precious time are set aside so you can spot them quickly.

Crucial information you should be sure not to miss is also highlighted.

Q&A, Quiz, and Activities

Every chapter ends with a short question-and-answer session that addresses the kind of questions everyone wishes they dared to ask. A brief but complete quiz lets you test yourself to be sure you understand everything in the chapter. Finally, one or two optional activities give you a chance to practice your new skills before you move on.

Coffee Breaks

In every chapter, you'll find a "Coffee Break" section that takes you to an extensive Internet site called the 24-Hour HTML Café (http://www.mcp.com/info/1-57521/1-57521-366-4). I built and opened the café especially to provide readers of this book with oodles more examples and reusable HTML pages than I could ever picture in a short book.

At the 24-Hour HTML Café, you'll find every example in this book and many more complete Web pages designed to reinforce and expand your knowledge of HTML. In fact, you'll see how I developed the 24-Hour HTML Café Web site itself, step-by-step, as you go through the book.

You'll also get to have some fun with whimsical "edutainment" pages and break-time surprises. You'll find links to a wide variety of Internet resources to help you produce your own Web pages even faster. See you there!

PART
I

Your First
Web Page

Hour

Hour 1

Welcome to HTML

If you've been totally confused about where to begin learning HTML, you're not alone. Many people want to build a home page, learn about HTML in order to improve their job skills, or have serious intentions about becoming a professional Web designer. Yet, book after book is laden with exciting but intimidating titles. Fear not! You can learn HTML with relative speed and ease.

But before you begin creating your own Web pages with HTML, you need some background knowledge about what Web pages are, how they work, and what you can expect to achieve with them. This hour provides you with that knowledge by focusing in on the following issues:

- [ ] What you need to get started
- [ ] A brief history of HTML so you can understand some of the theory that makes it tick
- [ ] What Web browsers are and how they work
- [ ] Why learning to code HTML yourself first—before going out and buying an expensive program—is going to help you in the long run

Getting Started

There's no time like the present to take stock of what you have and what you'll need to have, in order to create HTML pages.

Here's a review of what you'll need before you're ready to use the rest of this book:

1. A Web-ready computer. I used a Windows 95 computer to build the HTML pages in this book, but you can use any Windows, Macintosh, or UNIX machine to create your Web pages. The critical issues are that you have a video monitor that can display at a resolution of 640×480 (the standard Web viewing resolution), supports *at least* 256 colors (and preferably more—thousands or millions are best for individuals working with Web-based content), and enough disk storage and memory to run Web browsing software.

2. A connection to the Internet. You should be able to get one through either a modem or the local network of your school or business. An old UNIX *shell* account won't do the trick; it has to be a modern PPP (Point-to-Point Protocol) connection, which most Internet service providers (ISP) now offer for about $20 per month, depending upon where you are geographically. Some providers, such as Geocities, offer free access. The List, which is a comprehensive database of ISPs, can provide more information (`http://www.thelist.com/`). Your access speed should be at least 14.4Kbps, though faster is better—28.8Kbps and even 36.6Kbps modems are popular and inexpensive items these days. The ISP, school, or business that provides your connection can help you with the details of setting up your connection properly. Along with connectivity, you should receive some Web server space, which is where you'll put your HTML pages and associated media if you want to make them live on the Internet. Again, your source should have information on how it manages this service.

3. A copy of Netscape Navigator and/or Microsoft Internet Explorer (version 3.0 or higher). Together, these two Web browser programs are used by over 90 percent of the people who look at Web pages, so it's a good idea to get them both. You can buy them in software stores, or get them free through the Internet at `http://home.netscape.com` and `http://www.microsoft.com`.

4. The next step is to surf the Web and begin building a sense of what pleases you about various pages that you see, what confuses you, and what you find unattractive. Make notes about what frustrates you about some pages, what attracts you and keeps you reading, and what makes you come back to some pages over and over again.

Now you're ready to think about how you'll be using HTML.

HTML at Work and Play

Once upon a time, back when there weren't any footprints on the moon, some far-sighted folks decided to see whether they could connect several major computer networks together. I'll spare you the names and stories (there are plenty of both), but the eventual result was the "mother of all networks," which we call the Internet.

Until 1990, accessing information through the Internet was a rather technical affair. It was so hard, in fact, that even Ph.D.-holding physicists were often frustrated when trying to swap data. One such physicist, the now famous Tim Berners-Lee, cooked up a way to easily cross-reference text on the Internet through hypertext links. This wasn't a new idea, but his simple Hypertext Markup Language (HTML) managed to thrive while more ambitious hypertext projects floundered.

NEW TERM HTML stands for *Hypertext Markup Language.* It is essentially a scripting language (as opposed to a programming language, which performs more complex activities) that *marks up* a page with formatting commands. These commands are then interpreted by a Web browser and sent to your screen.

By 1993, almost 100 computers—mostly based in educational, research, and military facilities throughout the world—were equipped to serve up HTML pages. Those interlinked pages were dubbed the *World Wide Web* (WWW), and several text-based Web browser programs had been written to allow people to view Web pages.

NEW TERM A *Web browser* is a computer program that interprets HTML commands to collect, arrange, and display the parts of a Web page.

Because of the power of the Web, a few programmers soon wrote Web browsers that could view graphics images along with the text on a Web page. One of these programmers was Marc Andreessen. His early contributions as a Web browser developer moved Web pages from a text-based medium into one that supported graphics, and eventually, a wide range of media. This helped to push the Web out of the work-based environment and into the popular culture. Thousands of people began building their own pages for the sheer fun of working in this new environment.

Today, HTML pages are the standard skeletal system of the Internet, and span a wide range of applications, from the personal home page (see Figure 1.1) to the professional business service (see Figure 1.2). Web sites may include animated graphics, sound, and video, and complete, interactive programs as well as good, old-fashioned text. Millions of Web pages are retrieved each day from thousands of Web server computers around the world.

The Web has become a mass-market medium. In fact, hardly a commercial goes by on radio or television these days that does not sport an associated Web address for the product. Even most non-commercial media, such as news shows, newspapers, and magazines, have companion Web sites. As high-speed Internet connections through TV cables, modernized phone lines, and direct satellite feeds become commonplace, this trend will continue to expand. Media analysts suggest that these various media will eventually converge; you can already browse the Web using a $300 box attached to your television instead of using your computer, and the cost of such devices is likely to fall sharply over the next few years.

Figure 1.1.

A personal home page.

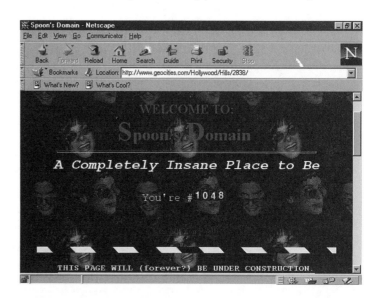

Figure 1.2.

An example of a professional, corporate Web site.

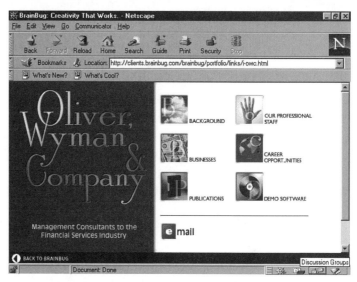

1

1

Yet the Web is no longer the only place you'll find HTML. Most private corporate networks now use HTML to provide business information to employees and clients. HTML is now the interface of choice for publishing presentations on CD-ROM and the new high-capacity digital versatile disc (DVD) format.

With the release of Internet Explorer 4.0, Microsoft has made HTML the language that is binding the browser to the Windows operating system. Add to that HTML integration for suites of products such as Microsoft Office and the results are powerful. HTML becomes a significant interface aspect of the entire PC.

In short, HTML is everywhere. Fortunately, you're in the right place to find out how HTML Web pages work and how to create them.

Pages and Browsers, Oh My!

When you are viewing Web pages, they look a lot like paper pages. At first glance, the process of displaying a Web page is simple: You tell your computer which page you want to see, and the page appears on your screen. If the page is stored on a disk inside your computer, it appears almost instantly. If it is located on some other computer, you might have to wait for it to be retrieved.

Of course, Web pages can do some very convenient things that paper pages can't. For example, you can't point to the words "continued on page 57" in a paper magazine and expect page 57 to automatically appear before your eyes. Nor can you tap your finger on the bottom of a paper order form and expect it to reach the company's order fulfillment department five seconds later. You're not likely to see animated pictures or hear voices talk to you from most paper pages either (newfangled greeting cards aside). All these things are commonplace on Web pages.

There are some deeper differences between Web pages and paper pages that you'll need to be aware of as a Web page author. For one thing, what appears as a single page on your screen may actually be an assembly of elements located in many different computer files. In fact, it's possible (though uncommon and unwise) to create a page that combines text from a computer in Australia with pictures from a computer in Russia and sounds from a computer in Canada.

Figure 1.3 shows a Web page as seen by Netscape Navigator, the world's most popular software for viewing Web pages. A Web browser such as Netscape Navigator does much more than just retrieve a file and put it on the screen; it actually assembles the component parts of a page and arranges those parts according to commands hidden in the text by the author. Those commands are written in HTML.

Figure 1.3.

In this figure, the Netscape Navigator browser assembles separate text and image files to display them as an integrated page.

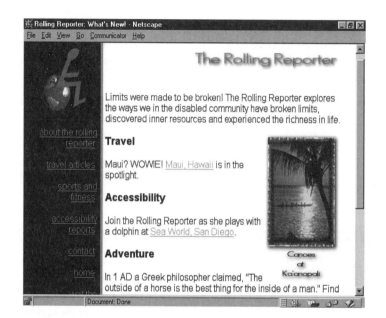

Figure 1.4 shows the text of this page, including the HTML commands I typed to create the page in Figure 1.3. This text file can be read and edited with any word processor or text editor. It looks a bit strange with all those odd symbols and code words, but the text file itself doesn't include any embedded images, boldface text, or other special formatting. The HTML codes in this file tell the browser what to do and where to go to get the attributes I want.

Figure 1.4.

This is the text I typed to create the page in Figure 1.3. The words between < and > are HTML tags.

```
Limits were made to be broken! The Rolling Reporter explores the
discovered inner resources and experienced the richness in life.
<p>

<img src="images/mi-canoe.jpg" width=136 height=244 hspace=5 bord
<h3>Travel</h3>

Maui? WOWIE!  <a href="rr-mi1.htm">Maui, Hawaii</a> is in the sp

<h3>Accessibility</h3>

Join the Rolling Reporter as she plays with a dolphin at <a href=
<p>

<h3>Adventure</h3>

 In 1 AD a Greek philosopher claimed, "The outside of a horse is
you on horseback through the total Ranch Experience of <a href="r
<p>

<h3>The Rolling Reporter Live!</h3>
Join the Rolling Reporter in regularly scheduled events in <a hre
</font>
```

1

All the images and formatting you see in Figure 1.3 are interpreted by Netscape Navigator. It reads the coded HTML commands in the text, which tell it to look for separate image files and display them along with the text itself. Other commands tell it which text to display in boldface and how to break up the lines of text on the page.

To see the HTML commands for any page on the Web, select View | Document Source in Netscape Navigator or View | Source in Microsoft Internet Explorer. This is a great way to get an intuitive idea how HTML works and learn by other's examples.

You'll learn how to understand and write HTML commands soon. The important point to note right now is that creating a Web page is just a matter of typing some text. You can type and save that text with any word processor or text editor you have on hand. You then open the text file with Netscape Navigator or Microsoft Internet Explorer to see it as a Web page.

JUST A MINUTE

Looking "under the hood" at a Web site's code is a great way to get a feel for the way other people write HTML. However, just because you like or don't like a particular Web page doesn't mean its code is going to be well or poorly written. Browsers tend to be forgiving, sometimes ignoring bad code. Look at the way others write code, but until you are well-versed enough to separate the good, the bad, and the ugly, be sure to study how HTML is properly coded and avoid picking up bad habits along the way.

When you want graphics, sound, animations, video, or interactive programming to appear on a Web page, you don't insert them into the text file directly, as you would if you were creating a document in most paper-oriented page layout programs. Instead, you type HTML text commands telling the Web browser where to find the media files. The media files themselves remain separate, even though the Web browser will make them look as if they're part of the same document when it displays the page. For example, the HTML document in Figure 1.3 refers to three separate graphics images—a background, a header, and a photograph. Figure 1.5 shows these three image files being edited in the professional graphics program Photoshop.

You can use any number of graphics programs to modify or replace these images at any time. Changing the graphics might make a big difference in how the page looks, even if you don't make any changes to the HTML text file. You can also use the same image on any number of pages while storing only one copy of the graphics file.

You'll learn much more about incorporating graphics files into Web pages in Part III, "Web Page Graphics."

Figure 1.5.
*Though text and graphics
appear integrated in
Figure 1.3, the graphics
files are actually stored,
and can be edited,
separately.*

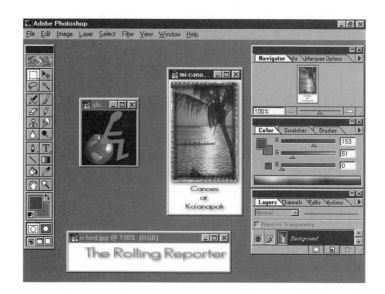

Browser and Platform Considerations

Different browser types, different versions within a browser, and different computer
monitors, video resolution, and computer platforms will all influence the way a page coded
in HTML will be seen.

Furthermore, individual users look at pages differently, setting up their browser interface and
default properties to match their own desires. Both Netscape Navigator and Microsoft
Internet Explorer allow users to override the background and fonts specified by the Web page
author with those of their own choice, altering the end results of the page. You can't even
assume that people will be viewing your Web pages on a computer screen. The page in Figure
1.3 might also be read on a low-resolution television screen or a high-resolution paper
printout (see Figure 1.6).

One thing you can do right away to avoid most common problems is to plan on viewing your
work using different browsers, changing the default appearance on those browsers, and—if
your computer supports it—looking at your browser in a variety of screen resolutions
(640×480 and 800×600 are the most common for Web browsing).

In Part IV of this book, "Web Page Design," you'll find many tips and tricks for ensuring that
your pages look great in the widest variety of situations.

Figure 1.6.

This image shows how the Web page in Figure 1.3 appears when printed out on paper.

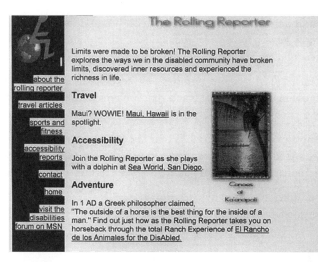

Knowing the Code

Now that you have a good background as to what HTML is, how it is used, and how it is viewed, it's time to begin the actual learning of the language.

There are three methods of coding HTML. The first is what I humorously refer to as the "abacus" method. This is using a plain text (ASCII) editor such as Notepad in Windows. As with an abacus, you'll do everything by hand. It's an excellent way to learn!

A middle-of-the-road option is what's known as an HTML editor. These editors—examples include Allaire HomeSite for Windows 95, and Pagespinner for the Macintosh—offer an ASCII editing environment but have plenty of support for various HTML codes. They are a nice choice for beginning HTML coders, because you can use them as a plain-text editor *and* begin employing some of the power-features once you are more confident with HTML.

A critical lesson I like to impress upon individuals who, like you, want to understand what HTML is and how to use it well, is to put aside the third HTML coding option, WYSIWYG software.

WYSIWYG (pronounced wiz-ee-wig) software packages are "What you see is what you get" programs. These are often important choices for larger production companies working with HTML, so it's good to become familiar with them. Titles in this category include Microsoft FrontPage, Adobe PageMill, and Claris HomePage. This type of software is good to consider later on, *after* you've become skilled at HTML basics.

Why is it so important to do this? Well, a metaphor I've used before seems to force the point home. If you're driving from Tucson to Phoenix, Arizona, in 115-degree heat with nothing but miles of desert around and your car breaks down—well, your're sure going to be glad you know how to look under the hood and troubleshoot the problem. Not only will it save you time and money, but it will prevent those hungry, circling buzzards from landing next to you!

Learn HTML before learning how to code in a WYSIWYG program, and you end up knowing how to identify and fix problems as they occur. This avoids time hassles, and, if you're creating HTML pages for work, loss of valuable resources.

Another point to mention is that HTML is an evolving language. New tags and attributes are added as time goes on, and complex software cannot be rewritten and distributed in time to manage new features you might want to implement today.

For now, stay focused on learning the code, and you'll be well on your way to a happy, long-term relationship with HTML.

COFFEE BREAK

In this book, you'll encounter many sample Web pages. The accompanying 24-Hour HTML Café Web site (`http://www.mcp.com/sites/1-57521/1-57521-366-4/`) has even more sample pages for you to explore.

In addition to all these examples, you can follow the development of a complete, sophisticated Web site from the ground up as you go through the book. You might like to preview this "construction site" now at

`http://www.mcp.com/sites/1-57521/1-57521-366-4/`

Doing so will give you an overview of how this book presents HTML and help you plan the development of your own pages. It will also help you see which hours cover the aspects of HTML you're most likely to use in the pages you plan to build.

Summary

This hour introduced the basics of what Web pages are and how they work. You learned that coded HTML commands are included in the text of a Web page, but images and other media are stored in separate files. You also saw that a single Web page can look very different, depending on what software and hardware are used to display it. Finally, you learned why typing HTML text yourself is often better than using a graphical editor to create HTML commands for you.

Q&A

Q I'm still not quite sure what the difference between a Web page and an HTML page is.

A If you want to get technical, I suppose a Web page would have to be from the Internet instead of a disk on your own computer. But in practice, the terms Web page and HTML page are used interchangeably.

Q I've looked at the HTML source of some Web pages on the Internet, and it looks frighteningly difficult to learn. Do I have to think like a computer programmer to learn this stuff?

A Though complex HTML pages can indeed look daunting, learning HTML is several orders of magnitude easier than other computer languages, such as BASIC, C, and Java. You don't need any experience or skill as a computer programmer to be a very successful HTML author.

Q Do you need to be connected to the Internet constantly while you create HTML pages?

A No. In fact, you don't need any Internet connection at all if you only want to produce Web pages for publication on a CD-ROM, Zip or floppy disk, or local network. You produce the pages right on your computer, and can test your work in the browser of your choice.

Quiz

Questions

1. Define the terms Internet, Web page, and World Wide Web.

2. How many files would you need to store on your computer to make a Web page with some text and two images on it?

3. Should you create Web pages with a WYSIWYG editor?

Answers

1. The Internet is the "network of networks" that connects millions of computers around the globe.

   A Web page is a text document that uses commands in a special language called HTML to add formatting, graphics and other media, and links to other pages.

   The World Wide Web is a collective name for all the Web pages on the Internet.

2. At least three files: one for the text (which includes the HTML commands) and one for each graphics image. In some cases, you might need more files to add a background pattern, sound, or interactive feature to the page.

3. Not for now. Down the road you might want to look at a variety of editors and software programs, but knowing HTML *before* learning to use such programs will help you be a much more productive and flexible HTML coder.

Activities

☐ Survey your materials. Do you have a Web-ready computer? Have you downloaded the latest version of a good Web browser? How about an HTML editor? If you have these tools, you're ready to begin!

1

Hour 2

Creating a Web Page

This hour will guide you through the creation of your first Web page. Don't feel too nervous about jumping in; I'm going to work right alongside you each step of the way. Create the Web page as you read, using the sample page I've developed here in the book as a model. You might want to read this hour once to get the general idea, and then go through it again at your computer while you work on your own page.

In this hour, you'll learn to

- ☐ Prepare simple content for the Web
- ☐ Understand the structure of a basic HTML page
- ☐ Clearly define paragraphs
- ☐ Add headings to an HTML document
- ☐ Save your HTML document in the proper format

As mentioned in Hour 1, "Welcome to HTML," you can use any text or HTML editor to create HTML Web pages. Though you'll eventually want to use an editor specially designed for HTML, for this hour I recommend you use the editor you're most familiar with. That way you won't have to learn a new software program at the same time you're starting to learn HTML. Even a simple text editor such as Windows Notepad will work just fine—that's what I'm going to be using!

Preparing Simple Content

Later in this book you'll learn how to work with more complicated text and graphic styles, but no matter the complexity of an HTML project, you need to have the *stuff* of your Web page. For the purposes of this hour, you'll begin with simple text as your *content*.

NEW TERM When it comes to HTML pages, *content* refers to all of the elements that communicate your intent to the people interacting with those pages. In most instances, this will be in the form of text and graphics, although with advanced media options becoming commonplace, content can also refer to any other media that expresses your project's intent. Examples would include interactive multimedia built with Shockwave, programmed events using Java or JavaScript, and database-intensive operations such as site searches or secure, online financial transactions.

Your first step, then, is gathering and preparing the content for your page.

To Do

You'll want to find or create a few paragraphs of text about yourself, your company, or the intended subject of your Web pages. Be sure that the writing is straightforward, clearly written, and has no grammatical errors. I know you want to get right to the code, but trust me, learning to take the time to look over your content for problems now will save you hours of frustration in the long run.

Here's an example of the text I've been persuaded to use:

Welcome to Tara's Web page!

Meow! I'm Tara. I felt compelled to build this page so people can bask in my beauty and acknowledge my great feline prowess.

More About Me

I'm an 8 year old Abyssinian fabulous female feline. My main interests are keeping watch over my home, my human, and of course—authoring books on HTML and Web design. Really! Don't let that silly human fool you. I happen to be the one doing all of the work!

I know you'll be back soon,

▼   *Tara*

2

▲ Now that you've selected your content, place it aside for a few minutes as I go over the necessary information you'll need to turn it into a real, live HTML page.

HTML Page Foundations

There are several HTML tags that are absolutely necessary for an HTML page to work. These tags should be considered the foundation of any good HTML page. In this section, I'll cover what these tags are and then show you how to combine them with your content.

NEW TERM A *tag* is a coded command used to indicate how part of a Web page should be displayed.

You can identify HTML tags easily. They are the words starting with < and ending with > and are considered coded commands. These coded commands are called HTML tags because they *tag* sections of the HTML page and tell the Web browser what to do with that section.

Most, but not all, HTML tags have two parts: an opening tag (<), to indicate where a piece of text begins, and a closing tag (</), to show where the piece of text ends. As you can see, closing tags start with a / (forward slash) just after the < symbol.

Here's a look at the critical structure tags and their companion closing tags:

<HTML> **and** </HTML> You will normally see these at the very top and very bottom of an HTML page, respectively. The HTML tag tells the browser, "Hey, I'm an HTML page!" You should always be sure your beginning and HTML tags are in place.

<HEAD> **and** </HEAD> The <HEAD> tag is the section of an HTML page where any HTML tags and related information that refer to the entire page is placed. In a simple HTML page, there's only one such tag to be concerned about:

<TITLE> **and** </TITLE> This tag names your page, and the title will appear not within the field of the page itself, but rather at the top of the *browser's* interface. This is also the title that will show up in the bookmark file if a visitor chooses to bookmark the page.

<BODY> **and** </BODY> The <BODY> tag (I know, it sounds morbid, but it's really a wonderful tag!) defines both the area of body text, and—as you'll learn in later hours—controls various visual aspects of the body of the page, such as background design, text color, link colors, and even margins.

Now I'm going to lay out the HTML as it should be within Notepad (see Figure 2.1), and then copy my text into the area between the <body> tags. Note in Figure 2.1 how I've also titled the page, "Tara's Home Page."

Figure 2.1.

Here you see all the necessary HTML tags, plus the text pasted between the <BODY> tags.

```
<HTML>

<HEAD>
<TITLE>Tara's Home Page</TITLE>
</HEAD>

<BODY>

Welcome to Tara's Web Page!

Meow! I'm Tara. I Felt compelled to build this page so people can bask in my
beauty and acknowledge my great feline prowess.

More About Me

I'm an 8 year old Abyssinian fabulous female feline. My main interests are
keeping watch over my home, my human, and of course--authoring books on HTML
and Web design. Really! Don't let that silly human fool you. I happen to be
the one doing all of the work!

I know you'll be back soon,
Tara

</BODY>

</HTML>
```

Adding Basic Formatting

What happens if you look at your current work in a browser? I did just that, and the results in Figure 2.2 demonstrate that an essential element is still missing. See how all the text is forced together with no line breaks anywhere?

Figure 2.2.

Without formatting, my page's text is all forced together.

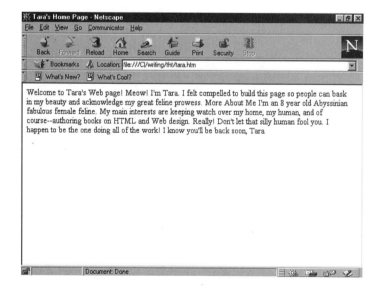

This problem is easy enough to fix, if you use the following tags:

<P>   This is a paragraph tag, and it breaks paragraphs by adding what would amount to two carriage returns on a typewriter or word processor, providing a line break and one empty line to separate the paragraphs.

JUST A MINUTE

Paragraph tags deviate from the common structure of HTML tags. While you can use a start <P> and end </P> tag to define paragraphs, many coders choose not to do so. Instead, they place the single, plain <P> at the point they wish the paragraph to break. This is the most simple method, and it's perfectly legal. I'm going to teach you this method, because it best suits your needs. However, I want you to be aware of the alternative code for paragraph text so that you'll recognize it when you see it, and have it in mind should you be inclined to study more advanced applications of HTML, which sometimes require you to use the other method.

**
**   This is the break tag, which calls for a line break. Use breaks when you want to have one carriage return but no space between the text.

In Figure 2.3, you see my example with paragraph and break formatting applied. Figure 2.4 shows the results, which are much neater than before!

Figure 2.3.

In this example, my code has paragraphs and breaks applied.

```
<HTML>

<HEAD>
<TITLE>Tara's Home Page</TITLE>
</HEAD>

<BODY>

Welcome to Tara's Web Page!<P>

Meow! I'm Tara. I felt compelled to build this page so people can bask in my
beauty and acknowledge my great feline prowess.<P>

More About Me<P>

I'm an 8 year old Abyssinian fabulous female feline. My main interests are
keeping watch over my home, my human, and of course--authoring books on HTML
and Web design. Really! Don't let that silly human fool you. I happen to be
the one doing all of the work!<P>

I know you'll be back soon,<BR>
Tara

</BODY>

</HTML>
```

Figure 2.4.

This figure shows the results—a nicely formatted page!

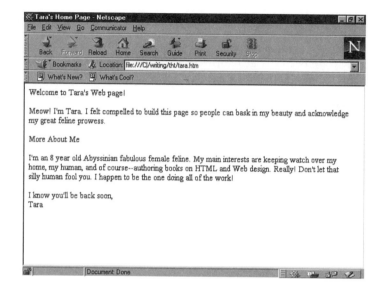

Adding Headers

When you browse through Web pages on the Internet, you can't help but notice that most of them have a heading at the top that appears larger and bolder than the rest of the text. Headers help to call attention to important sections within the body of text.

The HTML to create headings is very simple. For a big level 1 heading, put an <H1> tag at the beginning and an </H1> tag at the end. For a slightly smaller level 2 heading, use <H2> and </H2> instead, and for a still smaller level 3 heading, use <H3> and </H3>.

You'll see many Web pages using the <H1> heading tags, but I'm not a big fan of them because they are out of proportion with the default size text. I recommend sticking to <H2> and <H3> tags for the best results.

You can also use <H4>, <H5>, and <H6> to make progressively less important headings. These are not used very frequently—particularly now that HTML has many more options to reduce font sizes where necessary.

Figure 2.5 shows where I've added the HTML to the code, and Figure 2.6 shows how the code affects the resulting page. You'll see that I removed the paragraph breaks wherever I placed a heading. This is because headings add a line break without the need for a paragraph.

On many Web pages these days, graphical images of ornately rendered letters and logos are often used in place of the ordinary text headings discussed in this hour. You'll discover how to create graphics and put them on your pages in Part III, "Web Page Graphics." However, old-fashioned text headings are still widely used and have two major advantages over graphics headings:

☐ Text headings transfer and display almost instantly, no matter how fast or slow the reader's connection to the Internet is.

☐ Text headings can be seen in all Web browsers and HTML-compatible software, even old DOS and UNIX programs that don't show graphics.

Figure 2.5.

My code with headers added.

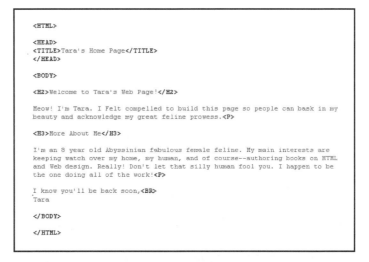

Figure 2.6.

The resulting page. Note the different size and boldness of the two headers.

JUST A MINUTE

It's important to remember the difference between a title and a heading. These two words are often interchangeable in day-to-day English, but when you're talking HTML, `<TITLE>` gives the entire page an identifying name that isn't displayed on the page itself. The heading tags, on the other hand, cause some text on the page to be displayed with visual emphasis. There can only be one `<TITLE>` per page, but you can have as many `<H1>`, `<H2>`, and `<H3>` headings as you want, in any order that suits your fancy.

Saving Files

You want to save all of the HTML you're writing as plain, standard ASCII text. Notepad and most simple text editors always save files as plain text; you'll want to be sure that this is true for the software you're coding with.

Your file extension name, however, is not going to be `.txt` or `.asc`, which tend to be a text editor's defaults. You will manually name your file using an `.html` or `.htm` extension (both are legal, just be consistent).

It's Your Turn!

Now I want you to try out the entire process!

To Do

Take a passage of text you have on hand and try your hand at formatting it as proper HTML:

1. Add `<HTML><HEAD><TITLE>My Title</TITLE></HEAD><BODY>` to the beginning of the text (using your own title for your page instead of `My Title`).

2. Add `</BODY></HTML>` to the very end of the text.

3. Add `<P>` tags between paragraphs, and `<BR>` tags anywhere you want single-spaced line breaks.

4. Save the file as `mypage.htm` (using your own filename instead of `mypage`). If you are using a word processor, be sure to always save HTML files in plain text or ASCII format.

5. Open the file with Netscape Navigator or Microsoft Internet Explorer to see your Web page!

6. If something doesn't look right, go back to the text editor or word processor to make corrections and save the file again. You will then need to click on Reload (in

▲ Netscape Navigator) or Refresh (in Microsoft Internet Explorer) to see the changes you made to the Web page.

Peeking at Other People's Pages

If you've even taken a quick peek at the World Wide Web, you know that the simple text pages described in this hour are only the tip of the HTML iceberg. Now that you know the basics, you may surprise yourself with how much of the HTML you see now seems logical! As mentioned in Hour 1, you can see the HTML for any page by selecting View | Document Source in Netscape Navigator, or View | Source in Microsoft Internet Explorer.

Don't worry if you aren't yet able to decipher what some HTML tags do, or exactly how to use them yourself. You'll find out all that in the next few hours. However, sneaking a preview now will show you the tags you do know in action, and give you a taste of what you'll soon be able to do with your Web pages.

COFFEE BREAK

> The HTML goodies at my 24-Hour HTML Café are specially designed to be intuitive and easy to understand.
>
> The HTML used in the main entrance page at `http://www.mcp.com/sites/1-57521/1-57521-366-4` may look a bit intimidating now, but you'll see how I developed this sophisticated site step-by-step as you work through each hour of this book.
>
> You can uncover the humble beginnings of the 24-Hour HTML Café at
>
> `http://www.mcp.com/sites/1-57521/1-57521-366-4`
>
> which uses only the tags introduced in this hour.

Summary

In this hour, you've been introduced to the most basic and important HTML tags. By adding these coded commands to any plain text document, you can quickly transform it into a bona fide Web page.

The first step in creating a Web page is to put a few obligatory HTML tags at the beginning and end, including a title for the page. You then mark where paragraphs and lines end, and add horizontal rules and headings if you want. Table 2.1 summarizes all the tags introduced in this hour.

Table 2.1. HTML tags covered in Hour 2.

Tag	Function
`<HTML>...</HTML>`	Encloses the entire HTML document.
`<HEAD>...</HEAD>`	Encloses the head of the HTML document.
`<TITLE>...</TITLE>`	Indicates the title of the document. Used within `<HEAD>`.
`<BODY>...</BODY>`	Encloses the body of the HTML document.
`<P>...</P>`	A paragraph. The closing tag (`</P>`) is optional.
` `	A line break.
`<H1>...</H1>`	A first-level heading.
`<H2>...</H2>`	A second-level heading.
`<H3>...</H3>`	A third-level heading.
`<H4>...</H4>`	A fourth-level heading (seldom used).
`<H5>...</H5>`	A fifth-level heading (seldom used).
`<H6>...</H6>`	A sixth-level heading (seldom used).

Q&A

Q **Okay, so I've got this HTML Web page on my computer now. How do I get it on the Internet so everyone else can see it?**

A Hour 4, "Publishing Your HTML Pages," explains how to put your pages on the Internet as well as how to get them ready for publishing on a local network or CD-ROM.

Q **I've seen Web pages on the Internet that don't have `<HTML>` tags at the beginning. I've also seen pages with some other weird tags in front of the `<HTML>` tag. You said pages always have to start with `<HTML>`. What's the deal?**

A Many Web browsers will forgive you if you forget to put in the `<HTML>` tag, and display the page correctly anyway. Yet it's a very good idea to include it, because some software does need it to identify the page as valid HTML.

In fact, the official standard goes one step further and recommends that you put a tag at the beginning that looks like this: `<!DOCTYPE HTML PUBLIC "-//IETF//DTD HTML//EN//4.0">` to indicate that your document conforms to the HTML 4.0 standard. No software that I've ever heard of pays any attention to this tag, however. It is not likely to be required in the near future, because so few of the millions of Web pages in the world include it.

2

Quiz

Questions

1. What four tags are required in every HTML page?

2. Insert the appropriate line break and paragraph break tags to format the following lines with a blank line between them:

   An itsy, bitsy spider

   went up the water spout

   Down came the rain,

   And washed the spider out!

3. Write the HTML for the following to appear one after the other:

   ☐ A small heading with the words, "We are Proud to Present"

   ☐ A large heading with the one word "Orbit"

   ☐ A medium-sized heading with the words, "The Geometric Juggler"

4. Write a complete HTML Web page with the title "The Acoustic Café Home Page" and a heading at the top that reads "Live Music at the Café" followed by the words, "Come on down!" in regular type.

Answers

1. `<HTML>`, `<HEAD>`, `<TITLE>`, and `<BODY>` (along with their closing tags, `</HTML>`, `</HEAD>`, `</TITLE>`, and `</BODY>`).

2. ```
   An itsy bitsy spider<BR>

   went up the water spout.

   <P>

   Down came the rain,<BR>

   and washed the spider out.
   ```

3. ```
   <H3>We are Proud to Present</H3>

   <H1>Orbit</H1>

   <H2>The Geometric Juggler</H2>
   ```

4. ```
   <HTML><HEAD><TITLE>The Acoustic Café Home Page</TITLE></HEAD>

   <BODY><H1>Live Music at the Acoustic Café</H1>

   Come on down!

   </B></BODY></HTML>
   ```
   ```

Activities

☐ Even if your main goal in reading this book is to create Web pages for your business, you might want to make a personal Web page just for practice. Type a few paragraphs to introduce yourself to the world, and use the HTML tags you've learned in this hour to make them into a Web page.

☐ You'll be using the HTML tags covered in this hour so often that you'll want to commit them to memory. The best way to do that is to take some time now and create several Web pages before you go on. You can try creating some basic pages with serious information you want to post on the Internet, or just use your imagination and make some fun *joke* pages.

Hour 3

Linking to Other Web Pages

In the previous two hours, you learned how to create an HTML page with some text on it. However, to make it a fully functional page, you need to link it to the rest of the World Wide Web, or to your personal or corporate *web* of pages.

In this hour, you'll learn

- ☐ What makes an HTML page *hyper*
- ☐ How the <A> (anchor) tag is used to create text-based links
- ☐ Relative linking
- ☐ Absolute linking

Though the same HTML tag you'll learn in this hour is also used to make graphics images into clickable links, graphical links aren't explicitly discussed here. You'll learn to create those in Hour 9, "Putting Images on a Web Page." The more advanced technique of setting up several links from different regions of the same image is explained in Hour 15, "Image Maps." For today's lesson, the focus is on *text* linking.

What Makes HTML Hyper

Hyper means *more than* or *outside of.* If you think about this in terms of a Web page, it makes complete sense. A hyperlink takes you to another page that gives you *more than* what was on the original page. That page is *outside of* the main page, although it is connected to it (see Figures 3.1 and 3.2).

Figure 3.1.

Hypertext links typically appear in a different color, and are usually underlined, as shown in this figure. Visit Sams Publishing - Developer's Solution Center Home Page to see the color in action.

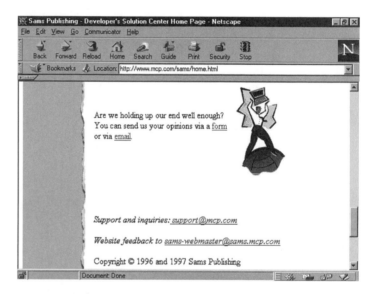

Figure 3.2.

Click on the link, and this feedback page appears!

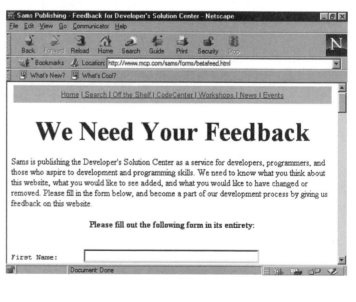

3

The Web is a series of millions of pages that create information that is made more complete by the internal—but especially external—pages that it links to.

Linking to another page with text is easy, and it is dependent upon a specific HTML tag.

The Anchor Tag

The tag to create a link is <A>, which stands for *anchor*.

The anchor tag begins with the <A> and is followed by a reference comment (HREF) and then the name of the page or the URL at which the page you want to link to resides. After closing the initial anchor commands, you type in the text you want to have highlighted as a link, and then you close the tag with the companion </A>.

Here's an example:

```
Follow  <A HREF="http://netletter.com/dicko/welcome.htm"> this link </A> to the
➥newsletter!
```

The link above would display the words this link! in blue with an underline. When someone clicks on it, they would see the Web page named welcome.htm, which is located in the dicko folder on the Web server computer whose address is netletter.com—just as if they had typed the address into the Web browser by hand.

Internet Web addresses, such as the one above, begin with http (HyperText Transfer Protocol) and are referred to as URLs (read letter by letter or pronounced *Earl*). URL stands for Uniform Resource Locator, a complicated way of saying *Web address*!

COFFEE BREAK

You can easily transfer the address of a page from your Web browser to your own HTML page using the Windows or Mac Clipboard. Just highlight the address in the Location, Address, Bookmark Properties, or Edit Favorites box in your Web browser, and select Edit | Copy (or press Ctrl+C). Then type <A HREF=" and select Edit | Paste (Ctrl+V) in your HTML editor.

At the 24-Hour HTML Café, you can explore a list of useful HTML learning resources on the Web from

http://www.mcp.com/info/1-57521/1-57521-366-4/

Before you follow the links on that page, view the document's HTML source to see a simple example of how to put hypertext links to work.

You'll need to know a site's URL if you're going to be linking from your pages to other pages on the World Wide Web.

JUST A MINUTE

As you may know, you can leave out the `http://` or `http://www.` at the front of any address when typing it into many Web browsers, including 3.0 and above editions of Internet Explorer and Netscape Navigator. You *cannot* leave that part out when you type an address into an `<A HREF>` link on a Web page, however.

One thing you *can* often leave out of an address is the actual name of the HTML page, because most computers on the Internet will automatically pull up the home page for a particular address or directory folder. For example, you can use `http://netletter.com` to refer to the page located at `http://netletter.com/welcome.htm` because my server computer knows `welcome.htm` is the page you should see first. (See Hour 4, "Publishing Your HTML Pages.")

`HREF` stands for hypertext reference and is called an attribute of the `<A>` tag. You'll learn more about attributes in Hour 5, "Text Formatting and Alignment." The hypertext reference is the point within the link that you place the filename or URL of the file you want to link to.

Methods of Linking

There are two important ways of linking pages. These are called *relative* and *absolute* linking, or *addressing*.

Relative Linking

When you create a link from one page to another page on the same computer, it isn't necessary to specify a complete Internet address. If the two pages are in the same directory folder, you can simply use the name of the HTML file, like this:

```
<A HREF="pagetwo.htm">Go to page 2.</A>
```

Using just filenames instead of complete Internet addresses saves you a lot of typing. More importantly, the links between your pages will work properly no matter where the pages are located. You can test the links while the files are still right on your computer's hard drive. Then you can move them to a computer on the Internet, or to a CD-ROM or DVD disc, and all the links will still work correctly.

There is one especially good reason to sometimes use the complete address of your own pages in links. If someone saves one of your pages on his or her own hard drive, any links to your other pages from that page won't work unless he or she includes full Internet addresses.

Using only the filename is considered *relative* linking. A good way to remember this is that the link page is nearby, or relative to, the originating page.

If you have many pages, you'll want to put them in more than one directory folder. In that case, you don't have to use the full Internet address to link between them. You can use an extended relative address, which includes the directory in question as well as the filename.

NEW TERM A relative address describes the path from one Web page to another, instead of a full (or *absolute*) Internet address.

For instance, suppose you are creating a page named zoo.htm in a directory folder named webpages on your hard drive. You want to include a link to a page named african.htm, which is in a sub-folder named elephants within webpages. The link would look like this:

```
<A HREF="elephants/african.htm">Learn about African elephants.</A>
```

Notice that the / (forward-slash) is always used to separate directory folders in HTML. Don't use the \ (backslash) normally used in Windows and DOS. You'll end up confusing yourself—and your browser!

Now you want to link from a page residing in the elephants directory back to a page that is contained in the main, or root directory.

To do this, use a double-dot before the filename:

```
<A HREF=../zoo.htm>Return to the zoo.</A>
```

The double-dot (..) is a special code that means "the folder containing the current folder." (The .. means the same thing in DOS, Windows, MacOS, and UNIX.)

You can then move these pages to another directory folder, disk drive, or Web server without changing the links, as long as you always put african.htm inside a sub-folder named elephants (see Figures 3.3 and 3.4).

Relative linking is considered the conventional linking method for any links within your own site.

3

Figure 3.3.

A relative link as seen coded within Notepad.

```
<HTML>

<HEAD>
<TITLE>A Relative Link</TITLE>

</HEAD>

<BODY>

<A HREF="../elephants.htm">All About Elephants</A>
<P>

This page is all about elephants!

</BODY>

</HTML>
```

Figure 3.4.

The link appears as underlined text on the page, indistinguishable from any other kind of link.

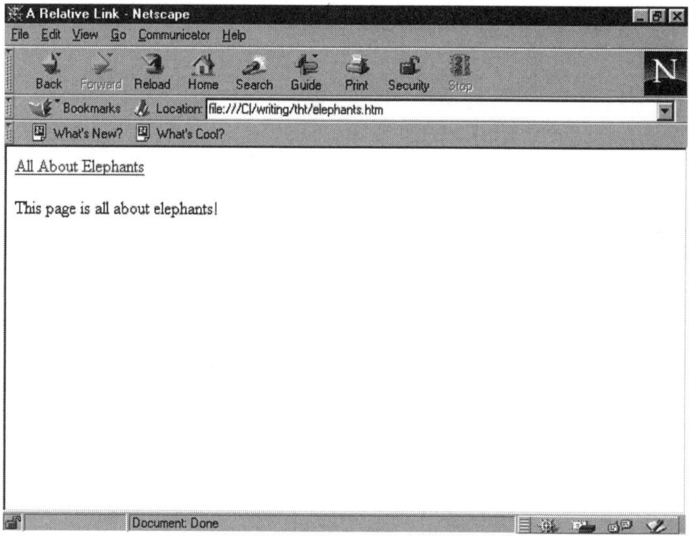

Absolute Linking

But how do you link to another site? As you glimpsed earlier in the hour, you can use entire URLs to get to any other Web page. Using the entire URL is called *absolute linking*, because it is the precise address at which the page resides.

New Term   *Absolute linking* is the use of the absolute URL. This is an exact pointer to the location, directory, and page where the information you want to link to resides.

Absolute linking is the solution for any link that will take you from a page on your site, to a page somewhere else on the Internet. An absolute link looks like this:

```
<A HREF="http://molly.com/">Molly E. Holzschlag</A>
```

3

Click on the link (See Figure 3.5) and voilá! You're at Molly's Home Page. (See Figure 3.6.)

To Do

You created a page or two of your own while working through Hour 2, "Creating a Web Page." Now is a great time to add a few more pages and link them together.

☐ Use a home page as a main entrance and central "hub" to which all your other pages are connected. If you created a page about yourself or your business in Hour 2, use that as your home page. You also might like to make a new page now for this purpose.

☐ On the home page, put a list of <A HREF> links to the other HTML files you've created (or plan to create soon). Be sure that the exact spelling of the filename, including any capitalization, is correct in every link.

☐ On every other page, include a link at the bottom (or top) leading back to your home page. That makes it simple and easy to navigate around your site.

☐ You may also want to include a list of links to sites on the Internet, either on your home page or a separate *hotlist* page. People often include a list of their friends' personal pages on their own home page. (Businesses, however, should be careful not to lead potential customers away to other sites too quickly; there's no guarantee they'll come back!)

Remember to use only filenames (or relative addressing) for links between your own pages, but full Internet addresses for links to other sites.

Figure 3.5.

The absolute link in this article on Microsoft's site is hotlinked to Molly's site.

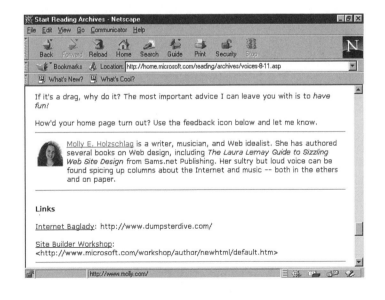

Figure 3.6.

Click on the link, and Molly's home page appears!

Summary

The <A> tag is what makes hypertext *hyper*. With it, you can create clickable links between pages, as well as links to specific anchor points on any page.

When creating links to other people's pages, include the full Internet address of each page in an <A HREF> tag. For links between your own pages, include just the filenames and enough directory information to get from one page to another.

Table 3.1 summarizes the two attributes of the <A> tag discussed in this hour.

Table 3.1. HTML tags and attributes covered in Hour 3.

Tag	Attribute	Function
<A>...</A>		With the HREF attribute, creates a link to another document or anchor; with the NAME attribute, creates an anchor that can be linked to.
	HREF="..."	The address of the document and/or anchor point to link to.
	NAME="..."	The name for this anchor point in the document.

Q&A

Q **When I make links, some of them are blue and some of them are purple. Why? And how come most of the links I see on the Internet aren't blue and purple?**

A A link will appear blue to anyone who hasn't recently visited the page it points to. Once you visit a page, any links to it will turn purple. These colors can be (and often are) changed to match any color scheme a Web page author wants, so many links you see on the Web won't be blue and purple. (Hour 13, "Backgrounds and Color Control," tells how to change the colors of text and links on your Web pages.)

Q **What happens if I link to a page on the Internet and then the person who owns that page deletes or moves it?**

A That depends on how that person has set up his server computer. Usually, people will see a message when they click on the link saying `Page not found` or something to that effect. They can still click the back button to go back to your page.

Quiz

Questions

1. Your best friend from elementary school finds you on the Internet and says he wants to trade home page links. How do you put a link to his page at `www.cheapsuits.com/~billybob/` on your page?

2. Your home page will be at `http://www.mysite.com/home.htm` when you put it on the Internet. Write the HTML code to go on that page so that when someone clicks on the words "All about me," they see the page located at `http://www.mysite.com/mylife.htm`.

3. You plan to publish a CD-ROM disc containing HTML pages. How do you create a link from a page in the `\guide` directory folder to the `\guide\maine\katahdin.htm` page?

4. How about a link from `\guide\maine\katahdin.htm` to the `\guide\arizona\superstitions.htm` page?

Answers

1. On your page, put

```
<A HREF="http://www.cheapsuits.com/~billybob/">
My Buddy Billy Bob's Page of Inexpensive Businesswear</A>
```

2. `<A HREF="mylife.htm">All about me</A>`

3. `<A HREF="maine/katahdin.htm">Mount Katahdin</A>`

4. `<A HREF="../arizona/superstitions.htm">`

   `The Superstition Range</A>`

Activities

☐ To make a formatted list of your favorite sites, select Go To Bookmarks and then select File | Save As in Netscape Navigator. You can then open that bookmark file in any HTML editor and add other text and HTML formatting as you wish, using the linking techniques you've learned here to add pages as you see fit.

Hour 4

Publishing Your HTML Pages

Here it is, the hour you've been waiting for! Your Web pages are ready for the world to see, and this hour explains how to get them to appear before the eyes of your intended audience.

This hour covers all of these options, and offers advice on designing your pages to work best with the distribution method you choose.

In this hour, you will

- ☐ Learn about Web site hosting
- ☐ Understand what a domain name is and whether you want one
- ☐ Learn how to transfer files to a Web server
- ☐ See why testing pages is so important
- ☐ Explore alternatives to Web-based publishing

The most obvious avenue for publishing Web pages is, of course, the Internet. Yet you may want to limit the distribution of your pages to a local intranet within your organization instead of making your pages available to the general public. You may also choose to distribute your Web pages on CD-ROMs, floppy disks, Zip disks, or the new DVD-ROM discs.

An *intranet* is a private network with access restricted to one organization, but which uses the same standards and protocols as the global public Internet.

Publishing HTML

To make your pages visible to as many people as possible all over the world, Internet publishing is a must. And, while it's likely to be the type of Web page publishing you're after, there are other means of publishing HTML. Depending upon your needs, it's wise to not rule out other distribution methods; you can easily adapt Internet-based pages for distribution on disks and/or local networks.

You might want to reach a specific group of people who have computers, but are not yet on the Internet. By publishing your pages on floppy disk or CD-ROM you can offer the same information customized to your specific group's needs.

If you're providing very large graphics, multimedia, or other content that would be too slow to transfer over today's modems, publishing on a CD-ROM or other portable media file is going to be a great way to distribute information. You can easily link the CD-ROM to an Internet Web site, providing expanded services you can easily update. Furthermore, you can offer the CD-ROM to people who find you through the Internet, providing them with the extended graphics and multimedia you've published on the CD.

These examples demonstrate how HTML can be used in a variety of situations off of the Web.

Setting Up an Internet Web Site

Because most of you are going to want to put your pages on the Web, I'll begin by showing you how to set up an Internet Web site. There are several steps involved in this process, including finding a server to host your site, transferring your files to that site, and testing your pages for accuracy. Finally, some people want to "brand" their sites with a *domain name.*

Web Site Hosting

To make an HTML page part of the publicly accessible World Wide Web, you need to put it on a Web server, which is a computer permanently connected to the Internet. Web servers are equipped to send out Web pages upon request. If you run your own Web server, this procedure is simply a matter of copying the file to the right directory. But most people use a Web server run by an Internet service provider (ISP) to host their pages.

Almost all service providers who offer Internet access also offer space to place your own personal Web pages for little or no additional cost. This is referred to as *Web site hosting.* However, if you plan to attract large numbers of people, you should pay a little more money to get a fully supported business site with a major Internet service provider.

4

JUST A MINUTE

> Don't think that you have to use the same local company that provides you with Internet access to host your pages. If you run a busy business Web site, you may save a lot of money and get more reliable service from a company in another city. For example, I use a company in Vermont to access the Internet, but my Web site is hosted by a different company in Boston.
>
> To comparison shop the hosting services offered by various Internet service providers, go to the list of ISPs at
>
> `http://thelist.com/`

Prices for a business site start well under $100 per month, but you will pay more depending upon the space and the amount of traffic you generate. Definitely shop around, as some ISPs charge extra for visits, although with today's high-speed, high-access technology, you should be able to find an ISP who can manage your traffic at little or even no extra cost.

Transferring Pages to a Web Server

When a Web server computer sends Web pages to people through the Internet, it uses an information exchange standard called HyperText Transfer Protocol (HTTP). To upload a page to your Web site, however, you need software that uses an older communications standard called File Transfer Protocol (FTP).

NEW TERM *File Transfer Protocol* is the standard that your file transfer software must adhere to when sending files from your local machine to a remote Web server.

Once you've FTP'd your files to a live server, the server then sends those files out to anyone who asks for them using the HyperText Transfer Protocol.

To Do

Netscape Navigator can receive files using both the HTTP and FTP standards. It can also send files using FTP, so you can use it to upload your pages to a Web server. Follow these steps:

1. Enter the address of your Web directory in Netscape Navigator's Location box, as in the following example:

   `ftp://myname:mypassword@myisp.net/home/web/wherever/`

   Put your username and password for accessing the site instead of *myname* and *mypassword*, your Internet service provider's address instead of *myisp.net*, and the top-level directory where your Web pages reside instead of */home/web/wherever/*.

2. Drag the icons for the HTML and graphics files you want to upload from any Windows 95 file management program (such as Windows Explorer) into the Netscape Navigator window.

4

3. A dialog box appears and asks you whether you want to upload the files. Click OK, and wait while the files are transferred.

4. Test your page by clicking on the HTML file you just uploaded in the FTP directory listing (in the Netscape window). You're on the Web!

Even though Netscape Navigator 2.0 or 3.0 can send files to any Web server on the Internet, specialized FTP programs such as the popular WS_FTP and CuteFTP offer much more control for managing your Web pages. For example, Navigator doesn't give you any way to delete an old Web page that you want to get rid of, or change the name of a Web page on the server computer. You'll definitely want a specialized FTP program to maintain your Web site.

Figure 4.1 shows one of the most popular FTP programs, CuteFTP for Windows. You can download a free copy of CuteFTP (see the following "To Do" section), though CuteFTP does require a modest registration fee for business users.

Figure 4.1.

CuteFTP is a powerful and user-friendly FTP program that individuals can use for free.

ybi.com (ybi.com) - CuteFTP 1.8

FTP Session Bookmarks Commands View Directory Window Help

226 Transfer completed. 880 (8) bytes transferred.
STATUS:>   Successfully received INDEX.HTML;1

C:	c:\aviation	DISK$EBONY:[YBI.WWW]		
📁..		📁 TROIKA-TEST	512	03/26/97 8:38
📁 images		📁 WELLMAN	512	04/06/96 22:39
📄 aviationpal.psd		📁 WWW	512	09/29/95 15:08
📄 bbsmain.htm		📄 BBSMAIN.HTM;1	6,144	07/16/97 20:07
📄 chatmain.htm		📄 BOOKS.HTM;3	5,632	07/11/97 8:12
📄 contents.htm		📄 CONTACT.HTM;2	1,536	08/11/97 19:26
📄 default.htm		📄 INDEX.HTML;1	1,024	04/26/97 0:24
📄 hed.psd		📄 MOLLY.HTM;1	3,072	07/27/97 8:13
📄 info.htm		📄 P-1.HTM;1	2,560	04/26/97 0:21
📄 libmain.htm		📄 P-2.HTM;1	3,072	04/26/97 0:21
📄 linksmain.htm		📄 P-3.HTM;1	2,048	04/26/97 0:21
📄 sidebar.htm		📄 P-4.HTM;1	4,096	04/26/97 0:21
📄 welcome.htm		📄 P-5.HTM;1	2,048	04/26/97 0:21
📄 whatsnew.htm		📄 POEMS.HTM;1	3,072	05/26/97 8:04
		📄 PRESS.HTM;1	3,072	05/26/97 8:05
		📄 STF-COV.GIF;1	13,824	07/11/97 8:09
		📄 WORK.HTM;1	3,584	04/26/97 0:21
		📄 WRITE.HTM;2	4,096	07/11/97 8:09

Similar programs are available for Macintosh computers (Fetch is a popular favorite), and FTP utilities come pre-installed on most UNIX computers. You can find these and other FTP programs at http://www.shareware.com.

To Do

I recommend that you download CuteFTP now and use it to send some files to your own Web site as you read on (if you have a Web site set up, that is).

1. Go to the CuteFTP home page at http://www.cuteftp.com/ and follow the Download CuteFTP links.

2. Once the download is complete, run the self-extracting .exe program, which will install the CuteFTP program.

No matter which FTP program you choose, transferring your Web pages to a Web server involves the following steps. In the following example, I've illustrated how to transfer files with CuteFTP, but other FTP programs work similarly.

To Do

1. Before you can access the Web server, you must tell your FTP program its address, as well as your account name and password. In CuteFTP, select a category for your site in the FTP Site Manager window (Personal FTP Sites in Figure 4.2), and click Add site to access the FTP Site Edit dialog box in Figure 4.3.

Figure 4.2.

CuteFTP includes an intuitive FTP Site Manager, though most Web page authors only need a single FTP site entry.

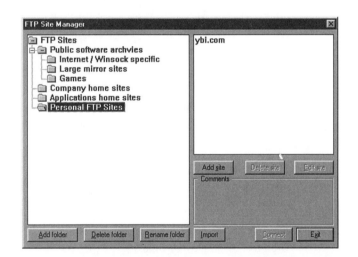

Figure 4.3.

Clicking on Add site or Edit site in Figure 4.2 brings up this dialog box.

2. Here's how to fill in each of the items in Figure 4.3.

   Site Label is the name you'll use to refer to your own site. Nobody else will see this name, so enter whatever you want.

   Host Address is the FTP address of the Web server that you need to send your Web pages to. This usually—but not always—starts with ftp. Notice that it may or may not resemble the address that other people will use to view your Web pages. The Internet service provider that runs your Web server will be able to tell you the correct address to enter here.

   User ID and Password are also issued by the company that runs the Web server. Be aware that CuteFTP and most other FTP programs will remember your password automatically, which means that anyone who has physical access to your computer may be able to modify your Web site.

   You should set the Login type to Normal unless somebody important tells you otherwise. The Anonymous setting is for downloading files from public FTP services that don't require user IDs or passwords.

   Set the Transfer type to Auto-Detect. This will automatically send HTML and other text files using a slightly different protocol than images and other non-text files, to ensure complete compatibility with all types of computers.

   For the Initial Remote Directory, fill in the name of the main directory folder on the Web server where your Web pages will be located. The people who run your Web server will tell you the name of that directory. In some cases, you don't need to enter anything here, because the Web server computer will automatically put you in the directory when you connect to it.

   For the Initial Local Directory, enter the drive and directory folder on your computer's hard drive, where you keep your Web pages.

   Normally, you won't need to change the Port, Retry, Delay, Max Safe Index Size, and Host Type settings unless you experience problems with your connection. If that happens, have your service provider help you figure out the best settings. You should also make sure that Use firewall and the other checkbox options are unchecked unless someone in the know says to check them.

   You can enter any Comments or reminders to yourself that you like. Only you will see them.

3. When you click OK, you'll go back to the window shown in Figure 4.2. Make sure you are connected to the Internet, and click Connect to establish a connection with the Web server computer.

   Most server computers issue a short message to everyone who connects to them. Many FTP programs ignore this message, but CuteFTP presents it to you as shown in Figure 4.4. It seldom says anything important, so just click OK.

4

Figure 4.4.

CuteFTP displays the boilerplate message that some server computers send whenever you connect to them.

```
Login Messages                                                        ×

220 cello.Opus1.COM MultiNet FTP Server Process V4.0[15] at Tue 19-Aug-97 8:33AM-MST
331 User name [ybi] ok. Password, please.
230 User YBI logged into DISK$EBONY:[YBI] at Tue 19-Aug-97 8:33AM-MST, job 2668e346.




                              OK
```

4. Once you're connected to the server, you'll see two lists of files, as shown earlier in Figure 4.1. The left window pane lists the files on your computer, while the right pane lists the files on the server computer.

   To transfer a Web page to the server, select the HTML file and any accompanying image files in the left window. (Remember that you can hold down the Ctrl key and click the mouse to select multiple files in any Windows program.) Then select Commands | Upload, as in Figure 4.5, or click on the Upload button on the toolbar.

4

Figure 4.5.

To send files to the server, select Commands | Upload in CuteFTP.

```
ybi.com (ybi.com) - CuteFTP 1.8                                       _ 8 ×
FTP  Session  Bookmarks  Commands  View  Directory  Window  Help

                           Download       Ctrl+PgDn
                           Upload..        Ctrl+PgUp
STATUS:>   Time: 0         View            Ctrl+V      s [3074 bytes/s]
STATUS:>   Succes          Execute         Ctrl+E

D:       d:\ybi            Get link as file            ONY:[YBI.WWW.SKY-ISLAND]
                           Manual get..
 ..
 Linus                     Change dir      Ctrl+D      .JPG;1      14,336    01/20/97 20:46
 noise                     Delete          Del         ML;1         5,120    03/29/97 15:06
 WORK                      Rename          Ctrl+N      ;1          10,240    01/20/97 20:46
 3.htm                     Change file attributes Ctrl+A .JPG;1    11,776    01/20/97 20:46
 4.htm                     Make new dir    Ctrl+M      P.JPG;1     16,384    01/20/97 20:46
 author.jpg                                            JPG;1       22,528    01/20/97 20:46
 contact.GIF               Stop            F9          HTML;1       3,072    03/29/97 15:06
 contact.htm                                           G;1         14,336    01/20/97 20:46
 CONTAC~1.HTM              Custom Commands        ▶    V-B.JPG;1   22,016    01/20/97 20:46
 ee.jpg                                               OWENV.JPG;1  17,408    01/20/97 20:47
 head.jpg                                             PHCREEK.JPG;1 19,968   01/20/97 20:46
 index.htm                                            SCHED-A.HTML;1 2,560  06/21/97 20:01
 index2.htm                                           SCHED.HTML;1  3,072   06/21/97 20:03
 molly.htm                                            SHED-S.HTML;1 5,120   03/29/97 15:06
 mollybak.gif                                         SKY-AB.GIF;1  4,608   01/20/97 20:47
 mollybak.jpg                                         SKY-HED.GIF;1 3,072   01/20/97 20:47
 more.jpg                                             SKY-HED.PSD;1 37,888  01/20/97 20:47
                                                      SKY-MENU.GIF;1 3,072  01/20/97 20:47
```

As you can see, the same menu contains commands to delete or rename files (on either your computer or the server), as well as commands to make and change directory folders.

Most Web servers have a special name for the file that should be sent if someone doesn't include a specific filename when he requests a page. For example, if you go to http://netletter.com/, my Web server will automatically give you the welcome.htm file. Other Web servers use different names for the default file, such as index.html.

Be sure to ask your service provider the default filename so you can give your home page that name.

5. That's all there is to it! In most cases, you can immediately view the page you just put on the Web server using Netscape Navigator (see Figure 4.6) or Microsoft Internet Explorer.

6. When you're done sending and modifying files on the Web server, select FTP | Disconnect to close the connection.

The next time you need to upload some Web pages, you won't need to fill in all the information in step 2. You can just click Connect, select the pages you want to send, and click on the Upload button.

Most Web servers are set up so that any documents placed onto them are immediately made available to the entire World Wide Web. However, some require that users manually change file permission settings, which controls who is allowed to access individual files. Your Internet service provider can tell you exactly how to change permission settings on their server and whether it's necessary to do so.

Testing Your Pages

Whenever you transfer Web pages to a disk, Internet site, or intranet server, you should immediately test every page thoroughly.

The following checklist will help you make sure everything on your pages behaves the way you expected.

Before you transfer the pages, follow all of these ten steps to test the pages while they're on your hard drive. After you transfer the pages to the master disk or Web server, test them again—preferably through a 28.8Kbps modem connection, if your pages are on the Internet.

Do each of the following steps with the latest version of Netscape Navigator, the latest Microsoft Internet Explorer, and if necessary, at least one older browser such as DOS Lynx or Netscape Navigator 2.0.

4

Figure 4.6.

*Most Web servers make
pages immediately
available on the Internet
seconds after you upload
them.*

☐ Make sure the computer you're testing with is set to 256-color mode. Pages look
better in higher color modes, but you want to see the "bad news" of how they'll
look to most people.

☐ Test pages using a resolution of 640×480. This is the resolution most people view
the Web at. Then, you can switch to 800×600 if your computer allows you to, and
even higher resolutions. It's a good idea to see how your site is going to look as
viewed by a variety of people.

☐ Turn off auto image loading in Netscape Navigator before you start testing, so you
can see what each page looks like without the graphics. Then hit the Load Images
button on the toolbar to load the graphics and review the page carefully again.

☐ Use Microsoft Internet Explorer's font size button (the big A on the toolbar) to
look at each page at all font sizes to ensure that your careful layout doesn't fall to
pieces.

☐ Start at the home page and systematically follow every link. (Use the Back button
to return after each link, then click the next link on the page.)

☐ Wait for each page to completely finish loading, and scroll down all the way to
make sure all your information appears where it should.

☐ If you have a complex site, it may help to make a checklist of all the pages on your
site to make sure they are all tested.

☐ Time how long it takes each page to load through a 28.8Kbps modem, preferably
when connected through a different Internet service provider than the one who

4

runs the Web server. Then multiply that time by two to find out how long 14.4Kbps modem users will need to wait to see the page. Is the information on that page valuable enough to keep them from hitting the Stop button and going elsewhere before the page finishes loading?

☐ It's to your advantage if you can test your pages on both a Macintosh and Windows machine. The reason is two-fold. First, font defaults are different in each, resulting in layouts that will appear differently on the screen. Second, the way that Macs and PCs handle colors results in pages looking darker on Macs.

If your pages pass all those tests, you can be pretty certain that they'll look great to every Internet surfer in the world. Depending upon your audience, however, you'll have more flexibility. For example, don't be too concerned if your page doesn't look great at 256 colors if the text is readable, the links linkable, and the navigation navigable; that's what's important. While these steps ensure the greatest stability in terms of cross-browser viewing, you will learn over time where you can take liberties, and where you cannot.

Domain Names

Now that you've got your pages up and running on a Web server, you'll need to make some choices as to how you're going to manage the addressing of that site. Your URL is going to default to the server's URL, with your specific directory defined. Here's an example:

`http://ybi.com/molly/`

But let's say I had a reason to want to "brand" my site. One such reason is if I'm a business. Branding my site using a *domain name* allows people to find me with ease.

JUST A MINUTE

> Try it out! Type in an address using a company's name. I did it with IBM and McDonald's and sure enough—I found the sites.

A domain name involves a few things. Cash is one of them; domain names cost $100.00 to register and $50.00 to maintain each year. Another imperative is that the name you select isn't already in use. You can check to see whether the name you want is already registered by visiting

`http://domain-registration.com/`

Once you find a name that isn't already taken, ask your Internet service provider to help you apply for that name as soon as possible. You can find more information from InterNIC (`http://internic.net/`), which is the organization that manages and regulates domain names.

4

Alternatives to Internet-Based Publishing

The procedure outlined above for sending pages to a public Internet server is fairly standard. However, as mentioned earlier in the hour, there are non-Internet alternatives you might very well want, and need, to consider.

Publishing Pages on an Intranet

The internal workings of private corporate intranets vary considerably from company to company. In some cases, you may need to use an FTP program to send files to an intranet server. In others, you may be able to transfer files using the same file management program you use on your own computer. You may also need to adjust permission settings, or make special allowances for the firewall that insulates a private intranet from the public Internet.

Because of the diverse nature of intranets, it's wise to consult with your systems administrator. He or she can help you put your Web pages on the company server in the way that best ensures their accessibility and security.

Publishing Web Pages on Disk

Unless you were hired to create documents for a company intranet, you have probably assumed that the Internet is the best way to get your pages in front of the eyes of the world. However, there are three major incentives for considering distribution on some form of disk instead:

- ☐ Almost all people with computers have disk drives, whereas not everyone has an Internet connection.
- ☐ Disks can deliver information to the computer screen much faster than people can download it from the Internet.
- ☐ You can distribute disks to a select audience whether or not they are connected to the Internet or any particular intranet.

In the not-too-distant future, as Web-enabled televisions and high-speed networks become more commonplace, these advantages may disappear. But for now, publishing on disk can be an excellent way to provide a bigger, faster, and more tightly targeted Web presentation than you could on today's Internet.

Publishing on 1.44MB floppy disks or 100MB Zip disks is simply a matter of copying files from your hard disk with any file management program. You just need to keep in mind that any links starting with http:// will only work if and when someone reading your pages is also connected to the Internet. The cost is currently about $0.50 per floppy disk, or $10 per Zip disk, plus any delivery or mailing costs.

CAUTION

> Never use drive letters (such as C:) in <A HREF> link tags on your Web
> pages or they won't work when you copy the files to a different disk. Refer
> to Hour 3, "Linking to Other Web Pages," for more details on how to
> make links that will work both on disk and on the Internet.

Publishing on CD-ROM or the new DVD-ROM (Digital Video) discs isn't much more complicated; you either need a drive (and accompanying software) capable of creating the disks, or you can send the files to a disk mastering and duplication company. Costs for CD-ROM duplication vary a lot depending on how many disks you need. For less than a hundred CD-ROMs, it may cost more than $10 per disk. But for thousands of copies, expect to pay less than $1 each plus delivery or mailing costs. DVD-ROM pricing hasn't settled down yet, but it will eventually be similar to CD-ROM pricing.

Summary

This hour gave you the basic knowledge you need to choose between the most common distribution methods for Web pages. It also guided you through the process of placing Web pages on a Web server computer using freely available file transfer software. Finally, it offered a checklist to help you thoroughly test your Web pages once they are in place.

Q&A

Q When I try to send pages to my Web site from home, it works fine, but when I try it from the computer at work, I get error messages. Any idea what the problem might be?

A The company where you work probably has a firewall, which is a layer of security protecting their local network from tampering via the Internet. You will need to set some special configuration options in your FTP program to help it get through the firewall when you send files. Your company's network administrator can help you with the details.

Q I don't know which Internet service provider to pick to host my pages—there are so many! How do I choose?

A Obviously, you should compare prices of the companies listed at `http://thelist.com` that provide hosting services, but you should also ask for the names of some customers with sites about the same size as you plan yours to be, and ask them (via e-mail) how happy they are with the company's service and support. Also, make sure that your provider has at least two major (T3 or bigger) links to the Internet, preferably provided to them by two different network companies.

Q **All the tests you recommend would take longer than creating my pages! Can't I get away with less testing?**

A If your pages aren't intended to make money or provide an important service, then it's probably not a big deal if they look funny to some people or produce errors once in a while. In that case, just test each page with a couple of different window and font sizes and call it good. However, if you need to project a professional image, there is no substitute for rigorous testing.

Q **I wanted to name my site `jockitch.com`, but another company beat me to it. Is there anything I can do?**

A Well, if your company was named Jockitch, Inc., before the other company registered the word as a trademark, you could always try suing them. Yet even if you don't have the budget to take on their lawyer army, there may be hope. Many new three-letter extensions for site names will probably soon be approved for use, so you may be able to get `jockitch.inc` or `jockitch.biz`.

Quiz

Questions

1. How do you put a few Web pages on a floppy disk?

2. Suppose your Internet service provider tells you to put your pages in the `/top/ user/~elroy` directory at `ftp.bigisp.net`, your username is `elroy`, and your password is `rastro`. You have the Web pages all ready to go in the `\webpages` folder on your C drive. Where do you put all that information in CuteFTP so you can get the files on the Internet?

3. What address would you enter in Netscape Navigator to view the Web pages you uploaded in question 2?

4. If the following Web page is named `mypage.htm`, which files would you need to transfer to the Web server to put it on the Internet?

```
<HTML><HEAD><TITLE>My Page</TITLE></HEAD>
<BODY BACKGROUND="joy.gif">
<IMG SRC="me.jpg" ALIGN="right">
<H1>My Web Page</H1> Oh happy joy I have a page on the Web!<P>
<A HREF="otherpage.htm">Click here for my other page.</A>
</BODY></HTML>
```

4

Answers

1. Just copy the HTML files and image files from your hard drive to the disk. Anyone can then insert the disk in his computer, start his Web browser, and open the pages right from the floppy.

2. Click Add site in the FTP Site Manager window, then enter the information into the appropriate fields.

3. You can't tell from the information given in question 2. A good guess would be `http://www.bigisp.net/~elroy/`, but you might choose a completely different domain name, such as `http://elroy-and-astro.com/`.

4. You would need to transfer all three of the following files into the same directory on the Web server:

   ```
   mypage.htm
   joy.jpg
   me.gif
   ```

   If you want the link on that page to work, you must also transfer `otherpage.htm` (and any image files that are referred to in that HTML file).

Activities

☐ Select the type of publishing method above that best serves your needs, and put it into action!

4

PART
II

Web Page Text

Hour

Hour **5**

Text Formatting and Alignment

As you discovered in Hour 2, "Creating a Web Page," making your Web page can be as easy as typing some text and adding a few standard HTML tags to the beginning and end. In that hour, you learned how to emphasize important text with headings, how to create a break between lines, and how to format paragraphs. In this hour, you will learn to control the appearance and arrangement of text on your pages.

In this hour, you will learn

- ☐ How to emphasize text by adding bold and italics
- ☐ Methods used to align text
- ☐ How to create a simple margin
- ☐ How to work with special characters

To do these things, you'll need a few more HTML tags. You'll also need to learn how to control optional settings (called attributes) for some of the tags you already know.

NEW TERM   An *attribute* is a command placed within a tag that further defines a feature, or an attribute, of that tag.

To Do

Before you proceed, you should get some text to work with so you can practice formatting it as you read this hour.

☐ Any text will do, but try to find (or type) some text that you want to put onto a Web page. The text from a company brochure or your personal résumé might be a good choice.

☐ If the text is from a word processor file, be sure to save it as plain text or ASCII text before you add any HTML tags. Word processor files use a variety of character formatting that will get in the way of your computer's ability to read the plain-text HTML you've created if you don't save properly.

☐ Add the `<HTML>`, `<HEAD>`, `<TITLE>`, `<BODY>`, and `<P>` tags (discussed in Hour 2) before you use the tags introduced in this hour to format the body text.

Now that you have some text, it's time to add some new tags to your work.

Emphasizing Text with Boldface and Italics

Way back in the age of the typewriter, we were content with plain text and an occasional underline for emphasis. But today, boldface and italicized text have become "de rigueur" in all paper communication. Naturally, you can add bold and italic text to your Web pages, too.

For boldface text, put the `<B>` tag at the beginning of the text and `</B>` at the end. Similarly, you can make any text italic by enclosing it between `<I>` and `</I>`. If you want bold italics, put `<B><I>` in front and `</I></B>` after the text. You can also use italics within headings, but boldface usually won't show in headings because they are already bold.

The article in Figure 5.1 uses the `<B>` and `<I>` tags extensively, and Figure 5.2 shows the resulting text as it appears in Netscape Navigator.

Figure 5.1.

Using the <B> tag for boldface text and the <I> tag for italics.

```
<HTML>
<HEAD><TITLE>Cantrell: Little Singer with a Big Song</TITLE></HEAD>
<BODY>

<H2>Cantrell</H2>

<B>TWENTY-FOUR YEARS</B> ago on that hallowed Tucson Fourth Avenue spot once
known as Choo-Choo's, later known as the <B>Night Train</B>, and more
recently known as <B>Berky's</B>, a 16 year old girl took the stage for the
first time.

<P>I wasn't there, but I'm <I>positive</I> that people looked up from their
drink and drug induced hazes to hear just where that voice--daring, belting
and full of soul--was coming from. I imagine their amazement when they
learned this truly big noise filling the bar and sneaking into their hearts
was being expressed by a petite teenage known as <B><I>Cantrell</I></B>.

<P>Since that distant night in the early '70s the music world has, in a
sense, owned Cantrell. The fates have played a large part in that, perhapse.
Her very name means <I>"little singer."</I>

<P>"I <I>never</I> planned on being a singer" she muses. "For the first
fifteen years of my career people came to me."

<P>Asked to be in band after band, Cantrell didn't say no. That first
performance with <B>Mint Julep</B> set the stage for later involvement in
groups such as the <B>Air Brothers, Swingshift, Visionary Blues Band</B>,
and <B>Regular Girls</B>. Cantrell has also worked with <B>Carlos Nakai,
Howe Gelb</B>, and <B>Mitzi Cowell</B> as well as performing solo. Despit
these unplanned relationships, she has managed to explore countless genres
and experience thousands of life lessons through music.

</BODY>
</HTML>
```

Figure 5.2.

The many <B> and <I> tags in Figure 5.1 certainly add plenty of emphasis to this Web page.

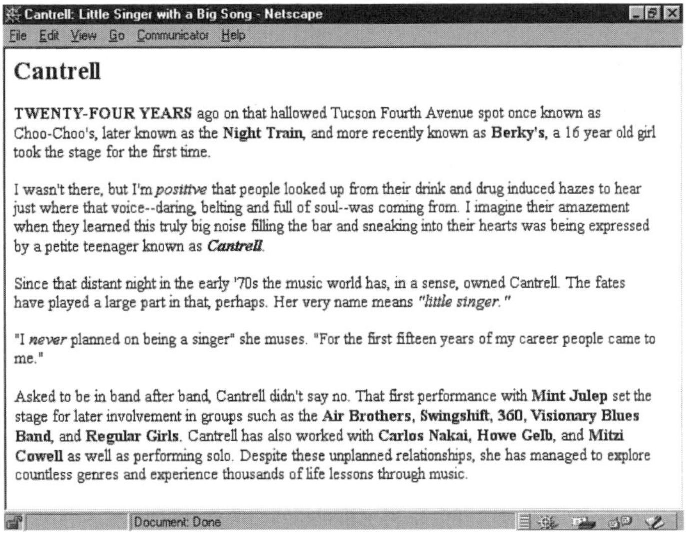

Cantrell

TWENTY-FOUR YEARS ago on that hallowed Tucson Fourth Avenue spot once known as Choo-Choo's, later known as the **Night Train**, and more recently known as **Berky's**, a 16 year old girl took the stage for the first time.

I wasn't there, but I'm *positive* that people looked up from their drink and drug induced hazes to hear just where that voice--daring, belting and full of soul--was coming from. I imagine their amazement when they learned this truly big noise filling the bar and sneaking into their hearts was being expressed by a petite teenager known as *Cantrell*.

Since that distant night in the early '70s the music world has, in a sense, owned Cantrell. The fates have played a large part in that, perhaps. Her very name means *"little singer."*

"I *never* planned on being a singer" she muses. "For the first fifteen years of my career people came to me."

Asked to be in band after band, Cantrell didn't say no. That first performance with **Mint Julep** set the stage for later involvement in groups such as the **Air Brothers, Swingshift, 360, Visionary Blues Band**, and **Regular Girls**. Cantrell has also worked with **Carlos Nakai, Howe Gelb**, and **Mitzi Cowell** as well as performing solo. Despite these unplanned relationships, she has managed to explore countless genres and experience thousands of life lessons through music.

There are two ways to make text boldface; the <B> tag and the <STRONG> tag do the same thing in most Web browsers. Likewise, all popular browsers today interpret both <I> and <EM> as italics.

Many purists prefer the <STRONG> and <EM> tags because they imply only that the text should receive special emphasis, rather than dictating exactly how that effect should be achieved. Meanwhile, the vast majority of Web authors use the shorter and easier-to-remember <B> and <I> tags. I'll use <B> and <I> throughout this book, but if you like to be philosophically pure, by all means use <STRONG> and <EM> instead.

To Do

Use headings, boldface, and italics to emphasize some of the text on your own Web page.

1. Use <H2> or <H3> to add any headings and subheadings your page may need. (End each heading with </H2> or </H3>.)
2. If any of the text on your page should be in boldface, mark the beginning of it with <B> and the end with </B>. Use <I> and </I> to mark text to be italicized.

Text Alignment

Some HTML tags allow you to specify a variety of options, or attributes, along with the basic tag itself. For example, when you begin a paragraph with the <P> tag, you can specify whether the text in that paragraph should be aligned to the left margin, right margin, or center of the page.

To align a paragraph to the right margin, you can put ALIGN="right" inside the <P> tag at the beginning of the paragraph, like this:

```
<P ALIGN="right">
```

To center a paragraph, use

```
<P ALIGN="center">
```

Similarly, the tag to align a paragraph to the left is

```
<P ALIGN="left">
```

The word ALIGN is called an attribute of the <P> tag. You can use the ALIGN attribute with just about any HTML tag that contains text, including <H1>, <H2>, the other heading tags, and some tags you will read about later. There are many other attributes besides ALIGN. You will find out how to use them as you learn more HTML tags.

Attributes are special code words used inside an HTML tag to control exactly what the tag does.

Keep in mind that sometimes the same attribute word can have different meanings when used with different tags. For instance, you will discover in Hour 9, "Putting Images on a Web Page," that ALIGN="left" does something quite different when used with the <IMG> image tag than it does with the text tags discussed in this hour.

When you want to set the alignment of more than one paragraph or heading at a time, you can use the ALIGN attribute with the <DIV>, or division, tag. By itself, <DIV> and its corresponding closing tag </DIV> actually don't do anything at all, which would seem to make it a peculiarly useless tag!

Yet if you include an ALIGN attribute, <DIV> becomes quite useful indeed. Everything you put between <DIV ALIGN="center"> and </DIV>, for example, will be centered.

This may include lines of text, paragraphs, headings, images, and all the other things that you'll learn how to put on Web pages in upcoming hours. Likewise, <DIV ALIGN="right"> will right-align everything down to the next </DIV> tag.

When you look at Web pages that other people have created, you may see <CENTER> and </CENTER> used to center text. The <CENTER> tag is officially obsolete, and it may not work with future Web browsers, so you should always use <DIV ALIGN="center"> and </DIV> instead.

Figure 5.3 demonstrates the ALIGN attribute with both the <P> and <DIV> tags. <DIV ALIGN="center"> is used to center two headings and some text at the top of the page, and all three ALIGN options are used with <P> tags to alter the alignment of the verse. The results are shown in Figure 5.4.

Figure 5.3.

The ALIGN attribute allows you to left-justify, right-justify, or center text.

```
<HTML>
<HEAD><TITLE>Tomy THumb's Pretty Song Book</TITLE></HEAD>
<BODY>

<DIV ALIGN=CENTER>
<H3>Selections From</H3>
<H2>Tommy Thumbs's Pretty Song Book</H2>
<I>Published in 1744</I>
</DIV>

<P ALIGN=LEFT>
I'll tell you a story<BR>
of Jacky Nory,<BR>
Will you have it now or anon?

<P ALIGN=CENTER>
I'll tell you another<BR>
of Jack and his Brother,

<P ALIGN=RIGHT>
And my story's done.|

</BODY>
</HTML>
```

5

Figure 5.4.

*The alignment settings in
Figure 5.3, as they
appear in a Web
browser.*

> Tomy THumb's Pretty Song Book - Netscape
>
> File Edit View Go Communicator Help
>
> Back Forward Reload Home Search Guide Print Security Stop
>
> Bookmarks Location: file:///C|/writing/tht/tommyt.htm
>
> What's New? What's Cool?
>
> **Selections from**
>
> ## Tommy Thumb's Pretty Song Book
>
> *Published in 1744*
>
> I'll tell you a story
> of Jacky Nory,
> Will you have it now or anon?
>
> I'll tell you another
> of Jack and his Brother,
>
> And my Story's done.
>
> Document: Done

Whenever you don't use an ALIGN attribute, text will be aligned to the left. Therefore, there's usually no point in wasting your time typing ALIGN="left". For example, using <P> instead of <P ALIGN="left"> for the first paragraph in Figure 5.3 would have resulted in exactly the same Web page in Figure 5.4.

One place where you would need ALIGN="left" is when you want to left-align a single heading or paragraph within a larger region that has been centered or right-justified with <DIV ALIGN="center"> or <DIV ALIGN="right">.

For example, if you changed the <H2> tag in Figure 5.3 to <H2 ALIGN="left">, Tommy Thumb's Pretty Song Book would be left-aligned while Selections from and Published in 1744 would both still be centered.

COFFEE BREAK

> To see how centering and text formatting can improve the look of a page, compare the new 24-Hour HTML Café home page to the older versions introduced in previous hours. The new page is found at
>
> http://www.mcp.com/sites/1-57521/1-57521-366-4/

Margins

There are several ways to create margins, but I'm going to focus on one easy method that you can start using right away.

5

One of the best reasons to put margins into your pages right away is because most default text will run from extreme ends of the browser, with very little side margin space. This makes long sections of text difficult to read. Your eyes get tired, you get bored, and there is no aesthetic value to the page.

The <BLOCKQUOTE> tag can put an end to this problem. Simply put the tag at the top of the page, underneath the body, and then close it at the end of your page, before the closing <BODY> tag (see Figure 5.5). This will create an attractive margin, as shown in Figure 5.6, hassle-free!

Figure 5.5.

Blockquotes added to the HTML.

```
<HTML>
<HEAD><TITLE>Cantrell: Little Singer with a Big Song</TITLE></HEAD>
<BODY>

<BLOCKQUOTE>

<H2>Cantrell</H2>

<B>TWENTY-FOUR YEARS</B> ago on that hallowed Tucson Fourth Avenue spot once
known as Choo-Choo's, later known as the <B>Night Train</B>, and more
recently known as <B>Berky's</B>, a 16 year old girl took the stage for the
first time.

<P>I wasn't there, but I'm <I>positive</I> that people looked up from their
drink and drug induced hazes to hear just where that voice--daring, belting
and full of soul--was coming from. I imagine their amazement when they
learned this truly big noise filling the bar and sneaking into their hearts
was being expressed by a petite teenage known as <B><I>Cantrell</I></B>.

<P>Since that distant night in the early '70s the music world has, in a
sense, owned Cantrell. The fates have played a large part in that, perhaps.
Her very name means <I>"little singer."</I>

</BLOCKQUOTE>

</BODY>
</HTML>
```

Figure 5.6.

The attractive results.

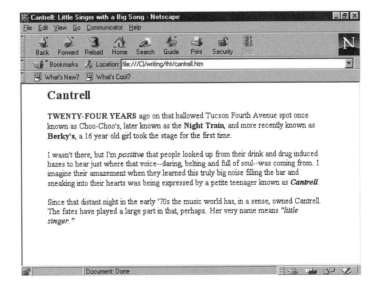

5

For more information on margins, see Hour 14, "Page Design and Layout."

Special Character Formatting

In addition to `<B>`, `<I>`, `<EM>`, and `<STRONG>` tags, there are several other HTML tags for adding special formatting to text. Table 5.1 summarizes all of them (including the boldface and italic tags).

Table 5.1. HTML tags that add special formatting to text.

Tag	Function
`<SMALL>`	Small text
`<BIG>`	Big text
`<SUPER>`	Superscript
`<SUB>`	Subscript
`<STRIKE>`	Strikethrough (draws a line through text)
`<U>`	Underline
`<TT>`	Monospaced (typewriter) font
`<PRE>`	Monospaced font, preserving spaces and line breaks
`<EM>` or `<I>`	Emphasized (italic) text
`<STRONG>` or `<B>`	Strong (boldface) text

JUST A MINUTE

> Use the `<U>` tag sparingly, if at all. People expect underlined text to be a link and may get confused if you underline text that isn't a link.

The `<TT>` tag usually changes the typeface to Courier New, a monospaced font. However, Web browsers let users change the monospaced `<TT>` font to the typeface of their choice (under Options | General Preferences | Fonts in Netscape Navigator 3.0 and View | Options | General | Font Settings in Microsoft Internet Explorer 3.0). The monospaced font may not even be monospaced for some users. However, the vast majority of people just stick with the standard fonts that their browser comes set up with, so you should design and test your pages with those default fonts, too. (The standard proportional font is usually Times New Roman, and the standard monospaced font is almost always Courier or Courier New.)

5

The <PRE> tag also causes text to appear in the monospaced font, but it does something more unique and useful. As you learned in Hour 2, multiple spaces and line breaks are normally ignored in HTML files. However, <PRE> causes exact spacing and line breaks to be preserved. For example, without <PRE> the following text

```
Qty     Description         Price       Total
 1      Rubber chicken       $7.98       $7.98
 2      Vibrating fake hand $14.97      $29.94
12      Plastic cockroaches  $0.25       $3.00
                                       - - - - - - - -
                                       $40.92
```

would look like this:

```
Qty Description Price Total 1 Rubber chicken $7.98 $7.98 2 Vibrating fake hand
$14.97 $29.94 12 Plastic cockroaches $0.25 $3.00 - - - - - - - -$40.92
```

Even if you added <BR> tags at the end of every line, the columns wouldn't line up properly. However, if you put <PRE> at the beginning of the invoice and </PRE> at the end, the columns would line up properly, and no <BR> tags would be needed.

There are fancier ways to make columns of text line up, and you'll learn all about them in Hour 16, "Advanced Layout with Tables." The <PRE> tag gives you a quick and easy way to preserve the alignment of any monospaced text files that you might want to transfer to a Web page with a minimum of effort.

You can use the <PRE> tag as a quick way to insert vertical space between paragraphs or graphics without having to use a "spacer" image—a clear graphic that forces space between visual sections. For example, to put several blank lines between the words Up and Down, you could type

```
Up<PRE>
```

5

```
</PRE>Down
```

Summary

This hour shows you how to make text appear as boldface, italic, or with other special formatting, such as superscripts, subscripts, or strikethrough text. You saw how to make everything line up properly in preformatted passages of monospaced text.

Finally, you learned that attributes are used to specify options and special behavior of many HTML tags. You also learned to use the ALIGN attribute to center or right-justify text.

Table 5.2 summarizes the tags and attributes discussed in this hour.

Table 5.2. HTML tags and attributes.

Tag	Attribute	Function
<EM>...</EM>		Emphasis (usually italic).
<STRONG>...</STRONG>		Stronger emphasis (usually bold).
<B>...</B>		Boldface text.
<I>...</I>		Italic text.
<TT>...</TT>		Typewriter (monospaced) font.
<PRE>...</PRE>		Preformatted text (exact line endings and spacing will be preserved; usually rendered in a monospaced font).
<BIG>...</BIG>		Text is slightly larger than normal.
<SMALL>...</SMALL>		Text is slightly smaller than normal.
_{...}		Subscript.
^{...}		Superscript.
<STRIKE>...</STRIKE>		Puts a strikethrough line in text.
<DIV>...</DIV>		A region of text to be formatted.
	ALIGN="..."	Align text to CENTER, LEFT, or RIGHT. (May also be used with <P>, <H1>, <H2>, <H3>, and so on.)
<BLOCKQUOTE> ... </BLOCKQUOTE>		Block sections of text by creating margins to the left and right of the text.

Q&A

Q Other books talk about some text formatting tags that you didn't cover in this hour, such as <CODE> and <ADDRESS>. Shouldn't I know about them?

A A number of tags in HTML indicate what kind of information is contained in text. The <ADDRESS> tag, for example, was supposed to be put around addresses. The only visible effect of <ADDRESS> in most browsers, however, is that the text is made

5

italic. So Web page authors today usually just use the `<I>` tag instead. Similarly, `<CODE>` and `<KBD>` do essentially the same thing as `<TT>`. You may also read about `<VAR>`, `<SAMP>`, or `<DFN>` in some older HTML references, but nobody uses them in ordinary Web pages.

Q **Some HTML pages I've seen use `ALIGN=CENTER` or `ALIGN=center` instead of `ALIGN="center"`. Which is correct?**

A As with tags, it generally makes no difference whether attributes are in lowercase or uppercase. It also usually doesn't matter if you include the quotes around attribute values such as `center`. The only time you really do need the quotes is when the value contains a blank space or a character that has special meaning in HTML. In this book, I always include the quotes so that you don't have to worry about when they're needed and when they're not.

Q **You mentioned that `<DIV ALIGN="center">` is a new tag that replaces the old `<CENTER>` tag. Won't my pages be incompatible with older Web browsers if I use the new tag?**

A Yes, but in practice the only incompatibility will be that some text appears left-aligned instead of centered. If this deeply concerns you, you can use both the old and new tags, like this:

```
<DIV ALIGN="center">
<CENTER>
This text will be centered in both old and new browsers.
</CENTER>
</DIV>
```

Quiz

Questions

1. Write the HTML to produce the following:

   Come for ~~cheap~~ free H_2O on May 7th at 9:00PM

2. What's the difference between the following two lines of HTML?

   ```
   Deep <TT>S p a a c e</TT> Quest
   ```

   ```
   Deep <PRE>S p a a c e</PRE> Quest
   ```

3. What's the easiest way to center a single paragraph or heading?

4. How would you center everything on an entire page?

5

Answers

1. Come for `<STRIKE>cheap</STRIKE>` free H`<SUB>`2`</SUB>`O on May
   7`<SUPER><U>`th`</U></SUPER>` at 9:00`<SMALL>`PM`</SMALL>`

2. The line using `<TT>` will look like this:

   Deep S p a a c e Quest

   The line using `<PRE>` will produce the following lines of text on the Web page
   (`<PRE>` always skips a line before and after the preformatted text):

   Deep

   S p a a c e

   Quest

3. Start it with `<P ALIGN="center">` (or `<H1 ALIGN="center">`, and so on).

4. Put `<DIV ALIGN="center">` immediately after the `<BODY>` tag at the top of the page
   and `</DIV>` just before the `</BODY>` tag at the end of the page.

Activities

☐ Professional typesetters use small capitals for the AM and PM in clock times. They
also use superscripts for dates like the 7th or 1st. Use the `<SMALL>` and `<SUPER>` tags
to typeset important dates and times correctly on your Web pages.

Hour 6

Font Control and Special Characters

Controlling fonts is a challenging aspect of HTML. Originally, HTML only allowed for whatever font your computer, or you, defined as a default. Nowadays, HTML authors can override defaults with special tags, giving power over different aspects of fonts.

In this hour, you will learn

☐ How to size fonts

☐ All about font color

☐ How to select font faces

☐ Coding for special characters, such as common symbols and foreign marks

Working with fonts falls under the study of *typography*. Designers have spent entire careers working with the way type appears! It's a fine art and technology, and recent additions to HTML are providing you with more and more power over type.

This doesn't mean you should immediately run out and apply every technique you'll learn in this hour to a Web page. In fact, a light touch with these techniques is preferred for pages that you're going to publish on the Internet or for your company, at least until you get the hang of Web typography. This doesn't mean you can't go wild and have some fun on your own. In fact, I hope you will!

Font Size

To set the size of any text on a Web page, use the <FONT> tag:

```
<FONT SIZE=5>This text will be big.</FONT>
```

The SIZE attribute can take any value from 1 (tiny) to 7 (fairly big), with 3 being the normal default size.

JUST A MINUTE

The <BIG> and <SMALL> tags discussed in Hour 5, "Text Formatting and Alignment," produce effects that you can also achieve with <FONT SIZE>. <FONT SIZE> gives you more precise control over the size, but <BIG> and <SMALL> may work with some older browsers that don't support the <FONT> tag.

The actual size of fonts will depend on each reader's screen resolution and preference settings, but you can be assured that SIZE=6 will be a lot bigger than SIZE=2.

A good rule of thumb when working with font size is to make everything proportional. In other words, you don't want a huge title followed by tiny text (see Figure 6.1). Use text size to draw attention to headers and other important text. You should usually leave long sections of body text at the default 3 size. Less-emphasized information, such as copyrights and notes, can be set at smaller sizes (see Figure 6.2).

Figure 6.1.

A huge header followed by tiny text doesn't work! Use common sense when coding for font size.

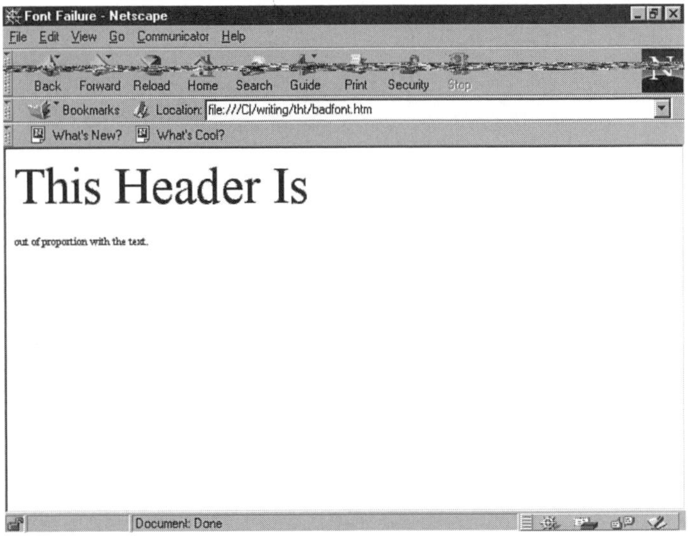

Figure 6.2.

Here's a better look! Everything is proportional, even though I've used three different font sizes: 5 for the header, 3 (default) for the body text, and 1 for the copyright and URL.

6

Font Color

Adding color to fonts can add zest to a page. Again, the caution is to use a light hand with colors, unless the context of your page calls for something a bit more wild. If you are making a page for your company, sedate colors are probably going to be in order, but if you're advertising a party, you have more flexibility.

Color is added to fonts using the `color` attribute, just as you would use the `size` attribute:

```
<FONT SIZE="4" color="purple">This text is a size 4 and is purple.</FONT>
```

Note that I've used the literal name `"purple"` to indicate color. The color attribute accepts the following standard color names: black, white, red, green, blue, yellow, aqua, fuchsia, gray, lime, maroon, purple, navy, olive, silver, or teal. Newer Web browsers, such as Internet Explorer 4.0 and Netscape Navigator 4.0, include more options. Those of you very new to Web authoring will enjoy this quick way to add color to your pages, however, if you are interested in having more colors available to you, I recommend learning about hexadecimal color attributes.

You've probably noticed hexadecimal attributes, which are usually a combination of letters and numbers used in `body`, `font`, and other HTML tags to indicate a range of colors. A font color attribute using a hexadecimal rather than literal color name looks like this:

```
<FONT SIZE="4" color="#0033FF">This text is size 4 and is also purple.</FONT>
```

For more information on how to work with these numeric color codes, I recommend visiting the HTML Station's Hexadecimal Color Codes page:

```
http://www.december.com/html/spec/color.html
```

JUST A MINUTE

You'll learn more about controlling the color of the text on your pages in Hour 13, "Backgrounds and Color Control." That hour also shows you how to create your own custom colors and control the color of text links.

Font Face

With the 3.0 versions of both Navigator and Internet Explorer, Netscape and Microsoft added another extremely powerful form of font control: the `<FONT FACE>` attribute. This allows you to specify the actual typeface that should be used to display text. This has been a source of much rejoicing among Webmasters who have felt very limited by the lack of available font controls.

By defining the face of a font, you can control the appearance of that font. This gives you the ability to add visual texture to a page without ever touching a graphic. Typography is as much a part of a page's design as is a graphic, and with this added control, Web design has moved forward in leaps and bounds. The following example shows this control in action:

```
<FONT FACE="arial" size="4" color="#0033FF">

This text is size 4 and is also purple.</FONT>
```

But just because you have this control doesn't mean there aren't restrictions—there are. The ability to read a font depends upon whether or not the computer used to view the page *has that font!* If it does not, the font you've so carefully argued for will default back to the computer and browser's default, available font.

This means that in order to be safe, you need to choose fonts that you expect most people to have on their computers. Macs and PCs have slightly different main fonts, with different names. Fortunately, the <FONT FACE> tag and attribute allow you to "stack" face names, so you can cover your bases:

```
FONT FACE="arial,helvetica" size="4" color="#0033FF">

This text is size 4 and is also purple.</FONT>
```

In the preceding example, I've called for the Arial font, which is popular on PCs. I've *also* argued for the Helvetica font, which is a font similar to Arial found on Macs. This way, I've pretty much ensured that people will see the font face I have argued for.

Figure 6.3 shows the code for a page with a header in a Times face (common to PCs) or a Garamond face (common to Macs), with the body text in Arial or Helvetica. See Figure 6.4 for the results.

Figure 6.3.

The HTML code showing a different header and body font. Note that I've coded for two similar font faces— anticipating Macintosh and PC page visitors.

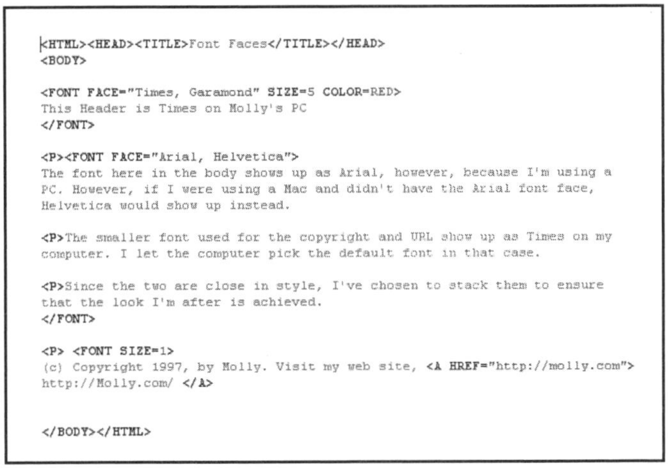

```
<HTML><HEAD><TITLE>Font Faces</TITLE></HEAD>
<BODY>

<FONT FACE="Times, Garamond" SIZE=5 COLOR=RED>
This Header is Times on Molly's PC
</FONT>

<P><FONT FACE="Arial, Helvetica">
The font here in the body shows up as Arial, however, because I'm using a
PC. However, if I were using a Mac and didn't have the Arial font face,
Helvetica would show up instead.

<P>The smaller font used for the copyright and URL show up as Times on my
computer. I let the computer pick the default font in that case.

<P>Since the two are close in style, I've chosen to stack them to ensure
that the look I'm after is achieved.
</FONT>

<P> <FONT SIZE=1>
(c) Copyright 1997, by Molly. Visit my web site, <A HREF="http://molly.com">
http://Molly.com/ </A>


</BODY></HTML>
```

6

Figure 6.4.

Here are the attractive results, as seen on Molly's PC.

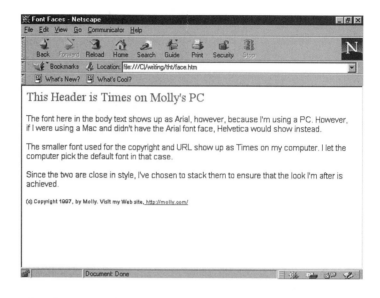

Another consideration is that the exact spelling of the font names is important, and many common fonts go by several slightly different names. Extensions to HTML will soon support a new, highly compact font format that can be automatically downloaded along with your pages to solve these problems.

For now, it's best to choose the most common fonts and make sure your pages still look acceptable in Times New Roman.

Figure 6.4 shows many common TrueType fonts, most of which are also available in PostScript format.

JUST A MINUTE

Microsoft offers a number of these fonts that both Macintosh and PC owners will appreciate, available for free download from this site:

`http://www.microsoft.com/truetype/`

TIME SAVER

The base font tag, `<BASEFONT>`, is a time-saving tag for setting the overall size of all text in a document. The size of all headings will also be relative to the `<BASEFONT SIZE>`. This tag can't take any attributes other than `SIZE`, and doesn't require a closing `</BASEFONT>` tag.

To Do

To Do

All the Web pages associated with a single "site" should usually use the same fonts and text color scheme. You don't need to be a professional typographer to make good font choices if you follow the guidelines below.

If you *are* a professional typographer, you know how to break these rules and still make a page look great. If you try to deviate from them without much experience, however, your pages are likely to stand out as unprofessional looking, even to people who can't articulate exactly why:

- ☐ Choose a typeface with serifs (those little beveled points on the edges of the letters) for the main body of your text. The serif typefaces that a significant number of people are likely to have installed are Times New Roman, Georgia, Book Antiqua, and Calisto MT.

- ☐ For headings, choose a heavy typeface without serifs, such as Arial Black, Impact, or Verdana. For captions and other short passages of text, either use your body text font or a "light" version of your heading font, such as Arial Light.

  Medium-weight fonts without serifs are suitable for both headings and short passages of text. These include Arial, Trebuchet MS, Verdana, Lucida Sans, Lucida Sans Unicode, and News Gothic MT.

- ☐ Use one color for all body text, and either the same color or a "stronger" complementary color for all headings and captions. Unless you are an experienced graphics designer, stay with a dark color such as black, blue, maroon, olive, or purple for body text, and put it on a contrasting, light background. If you want a wilder color, headings (and graphics images) are the best place for it.

- ☐ Use ornamental fonts such as Comic Sans MS, Lucida Handwriting, and OCR A Extended very sparingly and for main headings or highly stylistic pages only. Better yet, reserve these fonts for use in graphics images where you can also accent them with textures, shadows, or other effects.

- ☐ If your company has a standard set of TrueType or PostScript fonts for all communications, specify those fonts as the first choice in your <FONT FACE> tags. However, you should always include one or two second choice fonts from Figure 6.4 as well.

6

Special Characters

Most fonts now include special characters for European languages, such as the accented e in Café. There are also a few mathematical symbols and special punctuation marks, such as the circular bullet.

You can insert these special characters at any point in an HTML document by looking up the appropriate codes in Table 6.1. (This table includes only the most commonly used codes for English-language usage. You'll find a complete table of all special characters for European language fonts in Appendix A, "HTML Quick Reference.")

For example, the word Café would look like this:

`Caf&#233;`

Each symbol also has a mnemonic name that might be easier to remember than the number. Another way to write Café, for instance, is

`Caf&eacute;`

Notice that there are also codes for the angle brackets (< >), quote symbol ("), and ampersand (&) in Table 6.1. You need to use the codes if you want these symbols to appear on your pages, because the Web browser will otherwise interpret them as HTML commands.

TIME SAVER

> Looking for the copyright (©) or registered trademark (®) symbols? The codes you need are `&copy;` and `&reg;` respectively.
>
> To create an unregistered trademark (™) symbol, use `<SUPER>TM</SUPER>` or `<SMALL><SUPER>TM</SUPER></SMALL>` for a smaller version.

Table 6.1 lists some of the special characters you might need to use on your Web page.

Table 6.1. Important special characters.

Character	Numeric Code	Code Name	Description
"	`&#34;`	`&quot;`	Quotation mark
&	`&#38;`	`&amp;`	Ampersand
<	`&#60;`	`&lt;`	Less than
>	`&#62;`	`&gt;`	Greater than
¢	`&#162;`	`&cent;`	Cent sign
£	`&#163;`	`&pound;`	Pound sterling
¦	`&#166;`	`&brvbar; or brkbar;`	Broken vertical bar
§	`&#167;`	`&sect;`	Section sign
©	`&#169;`	`&copy;`	Copyright
®	`&#174;`	`&reg;`	Registered trademark
°	`&#176;`	`&deg;`	Degree sign
±	`&#177;`	`&plusmn;`	Plus or minus
^{2}	`&#178;`	`&sup2;`	Superscript two
^{3}	`&#179;`	`&sup3;`	Superscript three

6

Character	Numeric Code	Code Name	Description
·	&#183;	&middot;	Middle dot
^{1}	&#185;	&sup1;	Superscript one
$^1/_4$	&#188;	&frac14;	Fraction one-fourth
$^1/_2$	&#189;	&frac12;	Fraction one-half
$^3/_4$	&#190;	&frac34;	Fraction three-fourths
Æ	&#198;	&AElig;	Capital AE ligature
æ	&#230;	&aelig;	Small ae ligature
É	&#201;	&Eacute;	Accented capital E
é	&#233;	&eacute;	Accented small e
×	&#215;		Multiply sign
÷	&#247;		Division sign

JUST A MINUTE

Some older Web browsers will not display many of the special characters in Table 6.1. Some fonts may also not include all of these characters. See Table A.1 in Appendix A for a complete list of special symbols and European language characters.

The Future of Web Fonts

There are two major advances in the works which promise to revolutionize Web page typography.

Cascading style sheets (CSS) work very differently from normal HTML. With style sheets, you can create special tags and arguments containing only information about the fonts and formatting to be used on a Web page.

More information on cascading style sheets can be found in Hour 17, "Using Style Sheets."

The other revolutionary advance in typography that's afoot is *font embedding*. This will allow you to retrieve the actual typeface along with a Web page, so even people who don't have the correct font preinstalled on their computer will see it on the page.

There has been a standard for embedding TrueType fonts in documents for a while, but it doesn't yet include some features that are necessary for it to work with Web pages. The most important feature to be added is font compression, which minimizes the file size of fonts so

6

they can be transferred over the Internet quickly. Transferring only the letterforms actually used in a document and allowing font publishers to control how the font can be reused are also key features to make font embedding a reality.

The upcoming OpenType font standard will also combine both TrueType and PostScript (the two competing font formats) into a single standard.

Support for font embedding should appear in Netscape Navigator and Microsoft Internet Explorer at the same time as style sheet support. These two technologies together will dramatically expand your ability to control the appearance of your Web pages.

COFFEE BREAK

> At the 24-Hour HTML Café, I chose Georgia as the main font for body text. Because I wanted to use fonts that most people don't have installed for headings, I used Paint Shop Pro to render all headings as graphics. When embedded fonts become a reality, I may choose to replace some of the graphics at the Café with regular headings that use the Parisian and Present Script fonts. In the meantime, check it out at:
>
> http://www.mcp.com/sites/1-57521/1-57521-366-4
>
> You'll also notice that I used one of the codes discussed under the "Special Characters" section to finally spell Café with the accent-acute it deserves!
>
> If you go to the address above and still see most of the text as Times New Roman, you don't have Georgia installed on your computer yet. I highly recommend that you download it from Microsoft by going to http://www.microsoft.com/truetype/ and following the free Web fonts link. Georgia will be included with future versions of Microsoft Internet Explorer, and is likely to become a popular font on the Web due to its excellent readability and stylish appearance at low resolutions.
>
> While you're at Microsoft, pick up Verdana, Trebuchet, and whatever new free fonts they have, too. Then go back to the 24-Hour HTML Café for links to some sample pages that use them.

Summary

This hour has shown you how to control the size, color, and typeface of any section of text on a Web page. This hour also provided an overview of some exciting advances in font control that are just around the bend, including HTML style sheets and font embedding.

Table 6.2 summarizes all the tags and attributes covered in this hour. (See Table A.1 in Appendix B for special character codes.)

Table 6.2. Summary of tags and attributes covered in Hour 6.

Tag	Attribute	Function
`<FONT>...</FONT>`		Controls the appearance of the enclosed text.
	`SIZE="..."`	The size of the font, from 1 to 7. Default is 3. Can also be specified as a value relative to the current size; for example, +2.
	`COLOR="..."`	Changes the color of the text.
	`FACE="..."`	Name of font to use if it can be found on the user's system. Multiple font names can be separated by commas, and the first font on the list that can be found will be used.
`<BASEFONT>`		Sets the default size of the font for the current page.
	`SIZE="..."`	The default size of the font, from 1 to 7.

Q&A

Q How do I find out the exact name for a font that I have on my computer?

A On a Windows or Macintosh computer, open the Control Panel and click on the Fonts folder. The TrueType fonts on your system will be listed. Use the exact spelling of font names when specifying them in the `<FONT FACE>` tag. Windows 95 users can view all the characters in any font with the Character Map utility, usually located in the Accessories folder.

To find the name of PostScript fonts in Windows if you use Adobe Type Manager, run the ATM Control Panel.

Q How do I put Kanji, Arabic, Chinese, and other non-European characters on my pages?

A First of all, everyone who you want to be able to read these characters on your pages must have the appropriate language fonts installed. They must also have selected that language character set and font under Options | General Preferences | Fonts in Netscape Navigator or View | Options | General | Fonts in Microsoft Internet Explorer. You can use the Character Map accessory in Windows 95 (or a similar program in other operating systems) to get the numerical codes for each character in any language font. If the character you want has a code of 214, use Ö to place it on a Web page.

6

The best way to include a short message in an Asian language (such as `We speak Tamil—Call us!`) is to include it as a graphics image. That way everyone will see it, even if they use English as their primary language for Web browsing.

Quiz

Questions

1. How would you say, "We're having our annual Nixon Impeachment Day SALE today!" in normal-sized blue text, but with the word "SALE" at the largest possible size in bright red?

2. How would you make all text on a page green and a little larger than normal, but make all headings yellow?

3. How do you say "1997, My Page, Inc." on a Web page?

Answers

1. ```
<FONT COLOR="blue">We're having our annual Nixon Impeachment Day
<FONT COLOR="red" SIZE=7>SALE</FONT> today!</FONT>
```

2. Put the following at the beginning of the Web page:

   ```
<BODY TEXT="green"><BASEFONT SIZE=4>
```

   Then make each heading look like this:

   ```
<H1><FONT COLOR="yellow">Heading goes here</FONT></H1>
```

3. ```
© 1997, My Page, Inc.
```

   The following would also produce the same result:

   ```
&#169; 1997, My Page,Inc.
```

Activities

☐ Go through all the Web pages you've created so far, and ask yourself whether they would look significantly better if you used a different typeface or font color. Use the `<FONT>` tag to enhance the pages that would benefit from it most, and leave the rest alone.

Hour 7

Arranging Text in Lists

When you present information you often need to include lists of numbered steps or *bullet points*. You also need to create many indented lists to organize information such as terms and their definitions, or an outline. Because lists are so common, HTML provides tags that automatically indent text and add numbers or bullets in front of each listed item.

In this hour, you'll find out about

☐ Ordered (numbered) lists

☐ Unordered (bulleted) lists

☐ Definition lists

These lists will enable you to organize information on your pages in a clean and logical fashion.

Ordered (Numbered) Lists

An *ordered list* is just that, a simple list that begins with a number, and each subsequent listing has another number. HTML provides an easy way to do this.

An ordered list begins with the `<OL>` tag and ends with a closing `</OL>` tag. Numbers and line breaks appear automatically at each `<LI>` tag, and the entire list is indented, as seen in Figure 7.1.

Figure 7.2 shows the results.

Figure 7.1.

The HTML code for an ordered list.

```
<HTML>
<HEAD><TITLE>Ordered Lists</TITLE></HEAD>
<BODY>

Here is an example of an ordered list.

<P>
What Band would you like to listen to? Within reach I have:

<P>
<OL>
        <LI>The Cranberries
        <LI>Faith No More
        <LI>Todd Rundgren
        <LI>Live
        <LI>K.D. Lang
</OL>

</BODY>
</HTML>
```

Figure 7.2.

The ordered list as it appears in Netscape Navigator.

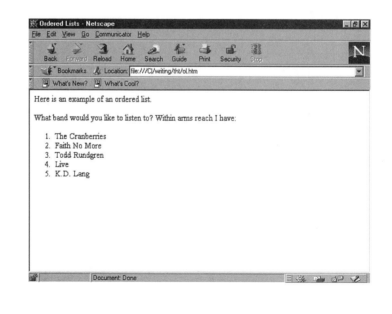

7

JUST A MINUTE

The <LI> tag can be optionally closed with </LI> but this usage is rarely seen.

Unordered (Bulleted) Lists

A *bulleted list* is called an *unordered list* for the obvious reason that the information in the list is not purposely ordered. Typically, these lists are used to pull specific points out of a larger body of text for the sake of emphasis.

Bulleted lists are created using the <UL> tag and companion closing tag, </UL>. It looks just like an ordered list (see Figure 7.3), except that special bullet symbols appear at each <LI> tag instead of numbers, as shown in Figure 7.4.

Figure 7.3.

An unordered list uses the <UL> *and companion* </UL> *to format the information.*

```
<HTML>
<HEAD><TITLE>Unordered Lists</TITLE></HEAD>
<BODY>

Here is an example of an unordered list.

<P>
I like all kinds of music

<P>
<UL>
        <LI>Rock and Roll
        <LI>World Beat
        <LI>Jazz
        <LI>Folk
        <LI>Classical
</UL>

</BODY>
</HTML>
```

Figure 7.4.

An unordered list uses bullet symbols rather than numbers to emphasize each list selection.

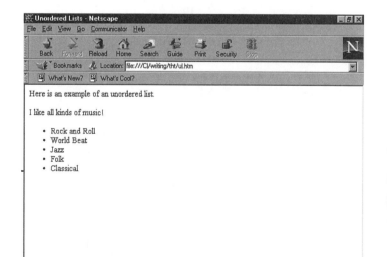

7

JUST A MINUTE

In Netscape Navigator and several other browsers, different bullet symbols can be specified with the TYPE= attribute, as explained more fully later in the "More Lists Within Lists" section.

As shown in Figure 7.3, the <UL> tag can be optionally closed with the </UL> tag.

Definition Lists

Definition lists were originally designed to code for terms and their related meanings. They can be used for a number of other purposes too, such as blocking off sections of text. While it's good to be familiar with the <DL> tag and its related tags, it's also important to bear in mind that use of these tags is becoming less common as HTML becomes more sophisticated in terms of layout.

A definition list starts with the <DL> tag and ends with </DL>. The <DT> tag goes in front of each term to be defined, with a <DD> tag in front of each definition. Line breaks and indentation appear automatically.

JUST A MINUTE

The <DT> and <DD> tags can be optionally closed with corresponding </DT> and </DD> tags, but this is usually not done.

Using Definition Lists in Other Ways

Although definition lists are officially supposed to be used for defining terms, Web page authors use them anywhere they'd like to see some indentation. In practice, you can indent any text simply by putting <DL><DD> at the beginning of it and </DL> at the end.

You can indent items further by nesting one list inside another, like this:

```
<DL><DD>This item will be indented
<DL><DD>This will be indented further
<DL><DL><DD>And this will be indented very far indeed
</DL></DL></DL></DL>
```

Just make sure you always have the same number of closing </DL> tags as opening <DL> tags. As mentioned, other techniques—particularly the use of alignment and page layout with tables (see Hour 16, "Advanced Layout with Tables")—have become more popular and should be considered before using the definition list.

To recap:

- ☐ Ordered (`<OL>`...`</OL>`) lists are indented lists that have numbers or letters in front of each item.
- ☐ Unordered (`<UL>`...`</UL>`) lists are indented lists with a special bullet symbol in front of each item.
- ☐ Definition lists (`<DL>`...`</DL>`) are indented lists without any number or symbol in front of each item.

JUST A MINUTE

Remember that different Web browsers can display Web pages quite differently. The HTML standard doesn't specify exactly how Web browsers should format lists, so people using older Web browsers may not see the same indentation that you see.

Software of the future may also format HTML lists differently, though all current Web browsers now display lists in almost exactly the same way.

More Lists Within Lists

Ordered and unordered lists can also be nested inside one another, down to as many levels as you wish. In Figure 7.5, a complex indented outline is constructed from several unordered lists. You'll notice in Figure 7.6 that Netscape Navigator automatically uses a different type of bullet for each of the first three levels of indentation, making the list very easy to read.

As shown in Figure 7.6, Netscape Navigator will normally use a solid disc for the first-level bullet, a hollow circle for the second-level bullet, and a solid square for all deeper levels. However, you can explicitly choose which type of bullet to use for any level by using `<UL TYPE="disc">`, `<UL TYPE="circle">`, or `<UL TYPE="square">` instead of using the default symbol.

7

Figure 7.5.

You can build elaborate outlines by placing lists within lists.

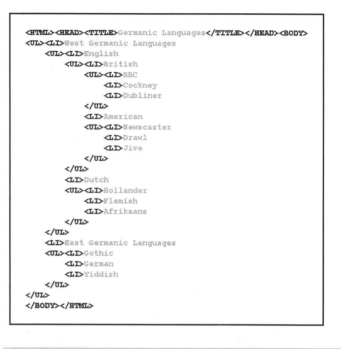

```
<HTML><HEAD><TITLE>Germanic Languages</TITLE></HEAD><BODY>
<UL><LI>West Germanic Languages
    <UL><LI>English
        <UL><LI>British
            <UL><LI>BBC
                <LI>Cockney
                <LI>Dubliner
            </UL>
            <LI>American
            <UL><LI>Newscaster
                <LI>Drawl
                <LI>Jive
            </UL>
        </UL>
        <LI>Dutch
        <UL><LI>Hollander
            <LI>Flemish
            <LI>Afrikaans
        </UL>
    </UL>
    <LI>East Germanic Languages
    <UL><LI>Gothic
        <LI>German
        <LI>Yiddish
    </UL>
</UL>
</BODY></HTML>
```

Figure 7.6.

Multi-level unordered lists are neatly indented and bulleted for readability.

Netscape - [Germanic Languages]

File Edit View Go Bookmarks Options Directory Window Help

- West Germanic Languages
  - English
    - British
      - BBC
      - Cockney
      - Dubliner
    - American
      - Newscaster
      - Drawl
      - Jive
  - Dutch
    - Hollander
    - Flemish
    - Afrikaans
- East Germanic Languages
  - Gothic
  - German
  - Yiddish

Document Done

You can even change the bullet for any single point in an unordered list by using the TYPE attribute in the <LI> tag. For example, the following would display a hollow circle in front of the words "Extra" and "Super," but a solid square in front of the word "Special."

```
<UL TYPE="circle">
<LI>Extra
<LI>Super
<LI TYPE="square">Special
</UL>
```

JUST A MINUTE

Netscape Navigator is currently the only Web browser that lets you control the appearance of list bullets, but this is changing with the release of new HTML standards. All bullets will appear as solid discs in Microsoft Internet Explorer 3.0, but by the time you read this, Microsoft IE 4.0 will add support for this and other enhancements.

The TYPE attribute also works with ordered lists, but instead of choosing a type of bullet you choose the type of numbers or letters to place in front of each item. Figure 7.7 shows how to use roman numerals (TYPE="I"), capital letters (TYPE="A"), and lowercase letters (TYPE="a"), along with ordinary numbers in a multi-level list. In Figure 7.8, you can see the resulting nicely formatted outline.

Figure 7.7.

The TYPE attribute lets you make multi-tiered lists with both numbered and lettered points.

```
<HTML><HEAD><TITLE>Sure-Fire Business Plan</TITLE></HEAD>
<BODY>
<OL TYPE="I"><LI>Invent Something
    <OL><LI>Find Some Geniuses
        <OL TYPE="A"><LI>Look for Nerdy Names in:
            <OL TYPE="a"><LI>Cambridge, MA Phone Book
                <LI>IBM Research Labs Lay-Off Roster
                <LI>"Nanotechnology Today" Subscriber List
            </OL>
            <LI>Send Friends to Look in:
            <OL TYPE="a"><LI>Some Big Libraries
                <LI>CalTech Dorms
                <LI>Restrooms at a Science Convention
            </OL>
        </OL>
        <LI>Hire Them to Design and Build It
        <OL TYPE="A"><LI>Take Out a Loan
            <LI>Wave Cash Under Their Noses
            <LI>Rent a Big House with a Lab in the Back
        </OL>
    </OL>
    <LI>Market It Big Time
    <OL><LI>Run Lots of TV Ads
        <LI>Open a Web Site
        <LI>Rake In the Green
    </OL>
</OL>
</BODY></HTML>
```

7

Figure 7.8.

A well-formatted outline can make almost any plan look plausible.

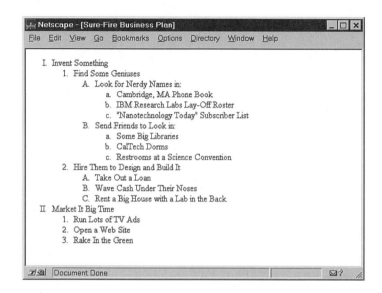

Though Figure 7.7 uses only the TYPE attribute with the <OL> tag, you can also use it for specific <LI> tags within a list (though it's hard to imagine a situation where you would want to). You can also explicitly specify ordinary numbering with TYPE="1", and you can make lowercase roman numerals with TYPE="i".

Here's one more seldom-used but handy-when-you-need-it trick: You can start an ordered list with any number (or letter) with the START attribute. <OL START="3">, for example, starts a numbered list at 3 instead of 1. Individual points can be renumbered with the VALUE attribute (<LI VALUE="12">, for example).

Note that you must always use numbers with the START and VALUE attributes. To make a list that starts with the letter C, for example, you need to type <OL TYPE="A" START="3">.

JUST A MINUTE

By combining ordered, unordered, and definition lists within one another, you can organize the most complex information in a readable and attractive way. To get your creative juices flowing, I've created a "list of lists" for you to browse through before you begin organizing your own HTML lists.

To check it out, go to the 24-Hour HTML Café List-O-Mania page at

`http://www.mcp.com/sites/1-57521/1-57521-366-4/`

Have some fun while you're there by trying to figure out what the real titles of the sample lists might be, based on the information they contain. Answers are given—as a nested HTML list, of course—at the end of the page.

You can also see how a list was used to enhance the 24-Hour HTML Café welcome page during the early stages of its development, at

`http://www.mcp.com/sites/1-57521/1-57521-366-4/`

To Do

Make a list or two of your own, and try to find the best way to present the information so that it can be easily understood.

☐ Which type of list or combination of list types best suits your list? Use ordered lists only for lists that have a natural order to them. Try to avoid more than seven bullet points in a row in any unordered list, or the list will be hard to read. Use definition lists whenever indenting is sufficient to convey the structure of your information.

☐ Start each list (or new level within a multi-tiered list) with an <OL> or <DL>. Start each point within the list with <LI>. Use the TYPE attribute if you want non-standard bullets or letters instead of numbers.

☐ If you want a blank line between list items, put a <P> tag next to each <LI> tag.

☐ Be very careful to close every <OL> list with </OL>, and to make sure that each <UL> or <DL> has a corresponding </UL> or </DL>. Unclosed lists can make pages look very strange, and can even cause some Web browsers not to display the list at all.

Summary

In this hour, you learned to create and combine three basic types of HTML lists: ordered lists, unordered lists, and definition lists. Lists can be placed within other lists to create outlines and other complex arrangements of text.

Table 7.1 lists all the tags and attributes covered in this hour.

Table 7.1. HTML tags and attributes covered in Hour 7.

Tag	Attribute	Function
<OL>...</OL>		An ordered (numbered) list.
	TYPE="..."	The type of numerals used to label the list. Possible values are A, a, I, i, 1.
	START="..."	The value with which to start this list.
<UL>...</UL>		An unordered (bulleted) list.
	TYPE="..."	The bullet dingbat used to mark list items. Possible values are DISC, CIRCLE, and SQUARE.

continues

Table 7.1. continued

Tag	Attribute	Function
<LI>		A list item for use with <OL> or <UL>.
	TYPE="..."	The type of bullet or number used to label this item. Possible values are DISC, CIRCLE, SQUARE, A, a, I, i, 1.
	VALUE="..."	The numeric value this list item should have (affects this item and all below it in <OL> lists).
<DL>...</DL>		A definition list.
<DT>		A definition term, as part of a definition list.
<DD>		The corresponding definition to a definition term, as part of a definition list.

Q&A

Q I used <UL TYPE="square">, but the bullets still came out round, not square.

A Are you using Netscape Navigator version 2.0 or higher? Alternate bullet types don't show up in any other Web browser yet, but they probably will in future versions.

Q I've seen pages on the Internet that use three-dimensional looking little balls or other special graphics for bullets. How do they do that?

A That trick is a little bit beyond what this hour covers. You'll find out how to do it yourself in Hour 9, "Putting Images on a Web Page."

Quiz

Questions

1. Write the HTML to create the following ordered list:

    X. Xylophone

    Y. Yak

    Z. Zebra

2. How would you indent a single word and put a square bullet in front of it?

3. Use a definition list to show that the word glunch means a look of disdain, anger, or displeasure, and the word glumpy means sullen, morose, or sulky.

4. Write the HTML to create the following indentation effect:

Apple pie,

        pudding,

                and pancake,

All begin with an A.

Answers

1. `<OL TYPE="A" START="24">`

    `<LI>Xylophone`

    `<LI>Yak`

    `<LI>Zebra`

    `</OL>`

    The following alternative will also do the same thing:

    `<OL TYPE="A"><LI VALUE="24">Xylophone<LI>Yak<LI>Zebra</OL>`

2. `<UL TYPE="square"><LI>Supercalifragilisticexpealidocious</UL>`

    (Putting the `TYPE="square"` in the `<LI>` tag would give the same result, because there's only one item in this list.)

3. `<DL>`

    `<DT>glunch<DD>a look of disdain, anger, or displeasure`

    `<DT>glumpy<DD>sullen, morose, or sulky`

    `</DL>`

4. `<DL><DT>Apple pie,<DD>pudding,<DL><DD>and pancake,</DL>`
    `All begin with an A.</DL>`

    Note that blank lines will appear above and below and `pancake,` in Microsoft Internet Explorer, but not in Netscape Navigator.

Activities

☐ Try producing an ordered list outlining the information you'd like to put on your Web pages. This will give you practice formatting HTML lists, and also give you a head start on thinking about the issues covered in Part VI, "Dynamic Web Pages."

Hour 8

Intra-Page and E-mail Links

In Hour 3, "Linking to Other Web Pages," you learned to use the anchor <A> tag to create links between HTML pages. In this hour you will learn how to use the same tag to allow visitors to jump between different parts of a single page.

This gives you a convenient way to put a table of contents at the top of a long document, or at the bottom of a page you can put a link that returns you to the top. You'll also learn how to link to a specific point within a separate page, too.

Another lesson in this hour shows you how to embed a live link to your e-mail address in a Web page. This way, readers can instantly compose and send a message to you from within most Web browsers.

In this hour, you'll learn about

☐ Named anchors

   Moving within the page

   Moving to a particular place on another page

☐ Linking to an e-mail address

Named Anchors

By taking a standard anchor <A> tag and adding a name, you add several powerful features to your linking, including the ability to link to that anchor's location from anywhere else on the Web or within your HTML project. Naming an anchor creates a target.

NEW TERM A *target* is a named anchor. Once an anchor is named, it can be used as a target from any reference on the Web or inside an individual project.

A named anchor looks like this:

```
<A NAME="top">Top of Page</A>
```

Using Named Anchors to Move Within a Page

Once you've named an anchor, you can point to it from within the page using a *referenced link.* This link uses the anchor name rather than a relative or absolute link to identify the target point within the HTML code:

```
<A HREF="#top">Return to top of document.</A>
```

The pound (#) symbol means that the word "top" refers to a named anchor point within the current document, rather than a separate page. So when a reader clicks on Return to top of document., the Web browser will display the part of the page starting with the <A NAME="top"> tag.

Here's an easy way to remember the difference between these two different types of <A> tags: <A HREF> is what you click on, and <A NAME> is where you go when you click there.

Similarly, each of the <A HREF> links in Figure 8.1 makes a highlighted link leading to a corresponding <A NAME> anchor. Clicking on Schedule, for instance, takes you to the part of the page shown in Figure 8.2.

Figure 8.1.

Anchors and targets within an HTML page.

```
<UL>
      <LI><A HREF="#features">Inn Features</A>
      <LI><A HREF="#amenities">Amenities</A>
      <LI><A HREF="#direct">Directions</A>
</UL>

<P>
<A NAME="features">
<IMG SRC="innf.gif" ALT="Ramada Inn Features" WIDTH=200 HEIGHT=42 BORDER=0>
</A>

<P>
```

8

Figure 8.2.

Notice the links and the related headers. When you click on one of the links in the list, you'll snap to the related section of the page.

To Do

Now that you have several pages of your own linked together, you might want to add an index at the top of your home page so people can easily get an overview of what your pages have to offer.

1. Place <A NAME> tags in front of each major topic on your home page, or any long page you make.

2. Copy each of the major topic headings to a list at the top of the page, and enclose each heading in an <A HREF> linking to the corresponding <A NAME> tag.

Moving to a Particular Place on Another Page

You can link to a named anchor on another page by including the address or name of that page followed by # and the anchor name.

Figure 8.3 shows several examples.

Figure 8.3.

To link to a specific part of another page, put both the page address and anchor name in the `<A HREF>` *tag.*

```
<HTML><HEAD><TITLE>U.S. Constitution</TITLE></HEAD>
<BODY>
<H3>THE CONSTITUTION OF THE UNITED STATES OF AMERICA</H3>
We the people of the United States, in order to form a
more perfect union, establish justice, insure domestic
tranquility, provide for the common defense, promote the
general welfare, and secure the blessings of liberty to
ourselves and our posterity, do ordain and establish this
Constitution for the United States of America.<P>
<A HREF="articles.htm#one">I. The Congress</A><BR>
<A HREF="articles.htm#two">II. The President</A><BR>
<A HREF="articles.htm#three">III. The Courts</A><BR>
<A HREF="articles.htm#four">IV. The States</A><BR>
<A HREF="articles.htm#five">V. Amendment</A><BR>
<A HREF="articles.htm#six">VI. Application</A><BR>
<A HREF="articles.htm#seven">VII. Ratification</A><P>
<A HREF="rights.htm">The Bill of Rights (1791)
</A><BR><A HREF="amends.htm">
Other Amendments (1798-1971)</A>
</BODY></HTML>
```

Clicking on "II. The President" in Figure 8.4 will bring up the page named `articles.htm` and go directly to the point where `<A NAME="two">` occurs on that page.

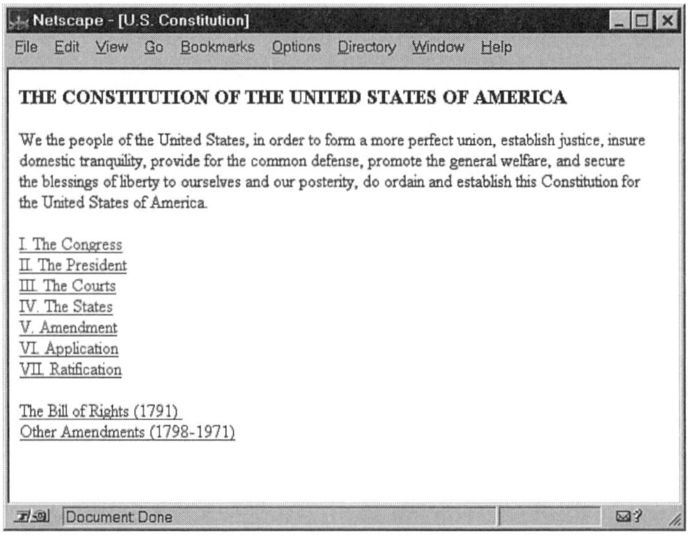

Figure 8.4.

The first seven links of this page all go to different parts of a page named `articles.htm`.

```
Netscape - [U.S. Constitution]                           _ □ ×
File  Edit  View  Go  Bookmarks  Options  Directory  Window  Help

THE CONSTITUTION OF THE UNITED STATES OF AMERICA

We the people of the United States, in order to form a more perfect union, establish justice, insure
domestic tranquility, provide for the common defense, promote the general welfare, and secure
the blessings of liberty to ourselves and our posterity, do ordain and establish this Constitution for
the United States of America.

I. The Congress
II. The President
III. The Courts
IV. The States
V. Amendment
VI. Application
VII. Ratification

The Bill of Rights (1791)
Other Amendments (1798-1971)


         Document Done
```

Coffee Break

Be sure to only include the # symbol in <A HREF> link tags. Don't put a # symbol in the <A NAME> tag, or links to that name won't work.

One of the most common uses for the <A NAME> tag is creating an alphabetical index. The bad news for anyone with an alphabetical list that they want to index is that typing out 26 links to 26 anchors is a rather tedious endeavor. The good news is that I've already done it for you and dropped off the indexed page at the 24-Hour HTML Café:

```
http://www.mcp.com/info/1-57521/1-57521-366-4/
```

You can just save this document to your hard drive, and then cut-and-paste your own alphabetical information after each letter.

While you're at the Café, stop by

```
http://www.mcp.com/info/1-57521/1-57521-366-4/
```

to see how the progress on the "construction site" is going. This page uses <A HREF> tags to link all the sample pages discussed so far in the book and <A NAME> tags to provide an index at the top.

Linking to an E-mail Address

In addition to linking between pages and between parts of a single page, the <A> tag allows you to link to your e-mail address. This is the simplest way to enable readers of your Web pages to "talk back" to you.

An HTML link to my e-mail address would look like this:

```
<A HREF="mailto:dicko@netletter.com">Send me an e-mail message.</A>
```

The words Send me an e-mail message. will appear just like any other <A> link, highlighted according to the color you set for links in the LINK or VLINK attributes of the <BODY> tag. In most Web browsers, when someone clicks on the link they get a window where they can type in a message, which will be immediately sent to you.

If you want people to see your actual e-mail address (so they can make note of it or send a message using a different e-mail program), type it both in the HREF attribute and as part of the message between the <A> and </A> tags.

For example, the HTML in Figure 8.5 is an e-mail directory page for my little mom-and-pop software shop, Cedar Software. The resulting page in Figure 8.6 shows the principal officers with a clickable e-mail link for each.

Figure 8.5.

Links to e-mail addresses use the same <A> tag as links to Web pages.

```
<HTML>
<HEAD><TITLE>Cedar Software E-Mail Directory</TITLE></HEAD>
<BODY>
<H1>Cedar Software E-Mail Directory</H1>
<UL>
<LI><A HREF="mailto:dick@netletter.com">
    <I>Dick Oliver, President</I><BR>
        dick@netletter.com</A><P>
<LI><A HREF="mailto:jan@netletter.com">
    <I>Jan Oliver, Chief Advisor</I><BR>
        jan@netletter.com</A><P>
<LI><A HREF="mailto:erica@netletter.com">
    <I>Erica Oliver, Senior VP of Toddling</I><BR>
        erica@netletter.com</A><P>
<LI><A HREF="mailto:ona@netletter.com">
    <I>Ona Oliver, Junior VP of Toddling</I><BR>
        ona@netletter.com</A><P>
<LI><A HREF="mailto:molly@netletter.com">
    <I>Molly Stubbs, Toddler Supervisor</I><BR>
        molly@netletter.com</A><P>
<LI><A HREF="mailto:pippin@netletter.com">
    <I>Pippin, Office Dustmop</I><BR>
        pippin@netletter.com</A><P>
<LI><A HREF="mailto:lucy@netletter.com">
    <I>Lucy, Dustmop Assistant</I><BR>
        lucy@netletter.com</A><P>
<LI><A HREF="mailto:dandyo@netletter.com">
    <I>Dandy, Company Horse</I><BR>
        dandy@netletter.com</A><P>
</UL>
</BODY></HTML>
```

Figure 8.6.

The `"mailto:"` *links in Figure 8.6 look just like any other anchor links on the page.*

8

When someone clicks on the top link in Figure 8.6, the program associated with e-mail on his or her computer will open with spaces for him or her to enter a subject line and e-mail message. The e-mail address from the link will be automatically entered and he or she can simply click on the mail button to send the message.

JUST A MINUTE

> It is handy to put an e-mail link to the Web page author at the bottom of every Web page. Not only does this make it easy for customers or others to contact you, it also gives them a way to tell you about any problems with the page that your testing may have missed.

Summary

This hour has shown you three uses for the <A> tag not covered in Hour 3. You now understand how to create named anchor points within a page and how to create links to a specific anchor. You also know how to link to your e-mail address so readers can easily send you messages.

Table 8.1 summarizes the two attributes of the <A> tag discussed in this hour.

Tag	Attribute	Function
<A>...</A>		With the HREF attribute, creates a link to another document or anchor; with the NAME attribute, creates an anchor that can be linked to.
	HREF="..."	The address of the document and/or anchor point to link to.
	NAME="..."	The name for this anchor point in the document.

Q&A

Q Can I put both HREF and NAME in the same <A> tag? Would I want to for any reason?

A You can, and it might save you some typing if you have a named anchor point and a link right next to each other. But it's generally better to use <A HREF> and <A NAME> separately to avoid confusion, because they play very different roles in an HTML document.

Q What happens if I accidentally spell the name of an anchor wrong, or forget to put the # in front of it?

A If you link to an anchor name that doesn't exist within a page (or you misspell the anchor name), the link just goes to the top of that page.

Q What if I use a different company to handle my e-mail than my Web pages? Will my e-mail links still work?

A Yes. You can put any e-mail address on the Internet into a link, and it will work fine. The only situation where e-mail links won't work is when the person who clicks on the link hasn't set up the e-mail part of his Web browser properly, or is using an older version that isn't capable of sending e-mail. For this reason, it's a good idea to include a plain-text listing of your e-mail address in or near the link, so that the widest number of people can e-mail you conveniently.

Quiz

Questions

1. Write the HTML to make it possible for someone clicking on the words "About the Authors" at the top of the page to skip down to a list of credits at the bottom of the page.

2. Suppose your company has three employees and you want to create a company directory page listing some information about each of them. Write the HTML for that page, and the HTML to link to one of the employees from another page.

3. If your e-mail address is bon@soir.com, how would you make the text "goodnight greeting" into a link that people can click on to compose and send you an e-mail message?

Answers

1. At the top of the page, put

   ```
   <A HREF="#credits">About the Authors</A>
   ```

   And at the beginning of the credits section, put

   ```
   <A NAME="credits"></A>
   ```

2. The company directory page would look like this:

```
<HTML><HEAD><TITLE>Company Directory</TITLE></HEAD>
<BODY><H1>Company Directory</H1>
<A NAME="jones"><H2>Jane Jones</H2>
Ms. Jones is our accountant... etc.
<A NAME="smith"><H2>Sam Smith</H2>
Mr. Smith is our salesman.. etc.
<A NAME="bharwahniji"><H2>R.K. Satjiv Bharwahniji</H2>
Mr. Bharwahniji is our president... etc.
</BODY></HTML>
```

A link to one employee's information from another page would look like this (if the above file was named directory.htm):

```
<A HREF="directory.htm#bharwahniji">About our president</A>
```

3. Type the following on your Web page:

```
Send me a <A HREF="mailto:bon@soir.com">goodnight greeting</A>!
```

Activities

☐ When you link back to your home page from other pages, you might want to skip some of the introductory information at the top of the home page. Using a link to a named anchor just below that introductory information will avoid presenting it to people who have already read it, making your pages seem less repetitive. Also, if any pages on your site are longer than two screens of information when displayed in a Web browser, consider putting a link at the bottom of the page back up to the top.

☐ Look through your Web pages and consider whether there are any places in the text where you'd like to make it easy for people to respond to what you're saying. Include a link right there to your e-mail address. If you're running a business, you can never provide too many opportunities for people to contact you and tell you what they need or think about your products.

PART III

Web Page Graphics

Hour

Hour **9**

Putting Images on a Web Page

In the first eight hours, you learned to create Web pages containing text. However, you'd be hard-pressed to find many Web pages these days that don't also include graphics images. This hour shows you how easy it is to put graphics on your pages with HTML.

Hour 10, "Creating Web Page Images," will help you come up with some good graphics of your own, and Hour 11, "Making Pages Display Quickly," will show you how to make your graphical pages appear onscreen as fast as possible.

In this hour, you'll learn about

☐ Using the HTML Café
☐ The `<IMG>` tag
☐ The `ALT` attribute
☐ Image alignment
   Vertical
   Horizontal
   Floating Images
☐ Linking an image

Using the HTML Café

To Do

There are some supplies you'll need in order to put images on your pages. If you already have JPEG or GIF images of your own, you may use those. If not, please visit the HTML Café. You'll want to do this in order to follow along with some of the exercises in this hour. This is how you would do it:

1. Enter the following address into your Web browser:

    `http://www.mcp.com/sites/1-57521/1-57521-366-4`

    You should see a page with four images of hats and stars at the bottom.

2. Save the images to your computer's hard drive by clicking on each image with the right mouse button (or holding down the mouse button if you use a Macintosh computer), then selecting Save Image As from the pop-up menu.

    Put them on your hard drive in whichever folder you use for creating Web pages.

    If you aren't using Netscape Navigator or Microsoft Internet Explorer, you may need to call up each of the images individually at the following addresses, and select File | Save As to save each one:

    `http://www.mcp.com/sites/1-57521/1-57521-366-4`

    `http://www.mcp.com/sites/1-57521/1-57521-366-4`

    `http://www.mcp.com/sites/1-57521/1-57521-366-4`

    `http://www.mcp.com/sites/1-57521/1-57521-366-4`

3. As you read this hour, use the hat and star image files to practice putting images on your pages. (You'll find out how to locate or create the perfect images for your Web pages in the next hour.)

COFFEE BREAK

At the 24-Hour HTML Café, you'll find live links to many graphics and multimedia hotlists and hot sites where you can find ready-to-use graphics. To access these links, go to

`http://www.mcp.com/sites/157521/1-57521-366-4`

The familiar Web search engines and directories such as Yahoo! (`http://www.yahoo.com/`), Excite (`http://www.excite.com`), and InfoSeek (`http://www.infoseek.com/`) can help you find a gold mine of graphics images, just by leading you to sites related to your own theme. They can also help you discover the oodles of sites specifically dedicated to providing free and cheap access to reusable media collections.

9

The `<IMG>` Tag

There is one primary tag to use for images: the `<IMG>` tag. There are many attributes that can be used with this tag, and you'll be introduced to a number of them throughout this book. To get started, you'll need to know the following:

☐ `<IMG>`. This is the image tag. It alerts the Web browser that an image needs to be loaded. Note that it has no companion closing tag—it's one of those HTML exceptions!

☐ `SRC`. This attribute stands for *source* or *image source*; it names the graphic file you want to place on the tag.

JUST A MINUTE

In a sense, the SRC attribute is much like the HREF attribute in that they both call for another piece of the Web puzzle. The HREF attribute calls for a page or a part of a page, whereas the SRC attribute calls for various media—in this case, a graphic image.

To put an image on a Web page, first move the image file into the same directory folder as the HTML text file. Then insert the following HTML tag at the point in the text where you want the image to appear. Of course, you'll need to use the name of your image file instead of `myimage.gif`):

```
<IMG SRC="myimage.gif">
```

Figure 9.1, for example, inserts the image named `seattle.jpg` between the first and second paragraphs of text. Whenever a Web browser displays the HTML file, as shown in Figure 9.1, it will automatically retrieve and display the image file shown in Figure 9.2.

Figure 9.1.

Use the `<IMG>` tag to place an image on a Web page.

```
<H2>Seattle</H2>

I go to Seattle for business frequently, and I always come back feeling
invigorated.

<P>
<IMG SRC="seattle.jpg" ALT="Seattle Skyline">

<P>
Sure, it's rainy and dark most of the time, but there's a lot to love about
this city. Music, for one thing, and great coffee! Who knows? Maybe i'll move
there some day.

<P>
```

Figure 9.2.
*When a Web browser
displays the HTML page
as shown in Figure 9.1,
it will load the text and
graphic.*

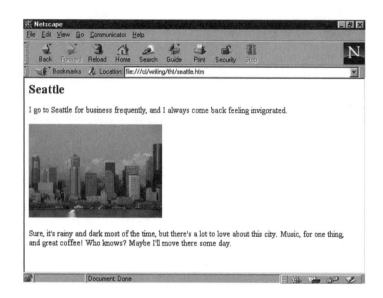

Just as with the <A HREF> tag (covered in Hour 3, "Linking to Other Web Pages"), you can
specify any complete Internet address as the <IMG SRC> or you can specify just the filename
if an image will be located in the same directory folder as the HTML file. You may also use
relative addresses such as photos/birdy.jpg or ../smiley.gif.

JUST A MINUTE

Theoretically, you can include an image from any Internet Web page
within your own pages. For example, you could include the hat image
from my "Sample Images" page by putting the following on your Web
page:

<IMG SRC="http://www.mcp.com/sites/1-57521/1-57521-366-4

The image would be retrieved from my server computer whenever your
page was displayed.

However, even though you could do this, you shouldn't! Not only is it bad
manners, it can also make your pages display more slowly. If someone
gives you permission to use an image from one of their pages, you can
transfer a copy of that image to your computer, and use a local file
reference such as <IMG SRC="hat.gif">.

The ALT **Attribute**

The ALT attribute means *alternate text.* The text message you define within this attribute will appear in place of the image in older Web browsers that don't display graphics.

The message you put in the ALT attribute will be seen by people who are using the latest Web browser software, too. As the page loads, the comments within the ALT attribute will appear before the images. Also, some people—especially those with slow modems—prefer to turn off images so they can see the text on Web pages without waiting for images to download.

When automatic image loading is off, the ALT message appears instead of an image. Clicking on that message causes the image to be downloaded and displayed, and clicking on the Image Download button causes all images on the page to appear. Figure 9.3 shows the same page as in Figure 9.2, but with Auto Load Images turned off.

Figure 9.3.

Anyone who turns off images in their browser will see the ALT message instead of the image.

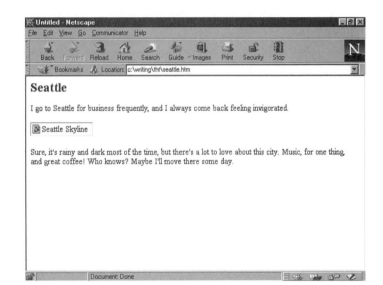

You should generally include a suitable ALT attribute in every <IMG> tag on your Web pages, keeping in mind the variety of situations where people might see that message. A very brief description of the image is usually best, but Web page authors sometimes put short advertising messages or subtle humor in their ALT messages. For very small images, it's fine to omit the ALT message altogether.

Image Alignment

Aligning images helps add visual interest to your pages and gives you added control about where the image will appear. There are a variety of alignment options from within the <IMG> tag, using the ALIGN attribute.

Vertical Alignment

Sometimes, you may want to insert a small image right in the middle of a line of text, or perhaps you would like to put a single line of text next to an image as a caption. In either case, it would be handy to have some control over how the text and images line up vertically. Should the bottom of the image line up with the bottom of the letters? Or should the text and images all be arranged so their middles line up? You can choose between these and several other options:

☐ To align the top of an image with the top of the tallest image or letter on the same line, use <IMG ALIGN="top">.

☐ To align the bottom of an image with the bottom of the text, use <IMG ALIGN="bottom">.

☐ To align the bottom of an image with the bottom of the lowest image or letter on the same line, use <IMG ALIGN="absbottom">. (If there are some larger images on the same line, ALIGN="absbottom" might place an image lower than ALIGN="bottom".)

☐ To align the middle of an image with the middle of the text, use <IMG ALIGN="middle">.

☐ To align the middle of an image with the overall vertical center of everything on the line, use <IMG ALIGN="absmiddle">. This might be higher or lower than ALIGN="middle", depending on the size and alignment of other images on the same line.

All these options are shown in Figure 9.4. You can see how they affect two different lines of images and text in Figure 9.5. Notice that the large hat image in the top line radically changes where the small stars with ALIGN="top" and ALIGN="absbottom" are placed. The second line doesn't have a big image in it, so the effect of ALIGN="top" and ALIGN="absbottom" are much less dramatic.

Figure 9.4.

You can control vertical alignment of images with the ALIGN attribute.

```
<HTML>
<HEAD><TITLE>Image Alignment Magick Tricks</TITLE></HEAD>
<BODY>
<H1 ALIGN="center">
IMAGE ALIGNMENT<P>
<IMG SRC="magic.gif" ALIGN="middle">
<IMG SRC="star.gif" ALIGN="bottom">M
<IMG SRC="star.gif" ALIGN="top">A
<IMG SRC="star.gif" ALIGN="absmiddle">G
<IMG SRC="star.gif" ALIGN="absbottom">I
<IMG SRC="star.gif" ALIGN="absmiddle">C
<IMG SRC="star.gif" ALIGN="top">K
<IMG SRC="star.gif" ALIGN="bottom">
<P>
<IMG SRC="star.gif" ALIGN="bottom">T
<IMG SRC="star.gif" ALIGN="top">R
<IMG SRC="star.gif" ALIGN="absmiddle">I
<IMG SRC="star.gif" ALIGN="absbottom">C
<IMG SRC="star.gif" ALIGN="absmiddle">K
<IMG SRC="star.gif" ALIGN="top">S
<IMG SRC="star.gif" ALIGN="bottom">
</H1>
</BODY></HTML>
```

Figure 9.5.

The top, middle, and bottom of each line depend on the size of the text and images on that line.

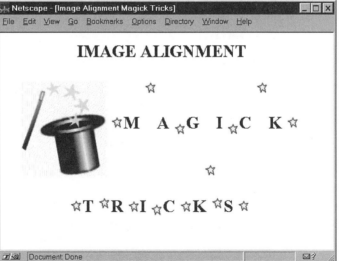

JUST A MINUTE

If you don't include any ALIGN attributes in an <IMG> tag, the image will line up with the bottom of any text next to it. That means you never actually have to type in ALIGN="bottom" because it does the same thing.

In fact, you probably won't use any of the vertical alignment settings much. So don't worry about memorizing all the options listed previously—you can always refer to this book if you ever do need them!

Horizontal Alignment

In order to control where an image appears on a page, you'll use the ALIGN attribute and choose from either a left or right argument, depending upon which side of the page you'd like the image to appear.

A left-aligned image is coded as follows:

```
<IMG SRC="seattle.jpg" ALT="seattle skyline" ALIGN=left>
```

Figure 9.6 shows the results.

To align an image to the right, use the following HTML:

```
<IMG SRC="seattle.jpg" ALT="seattle skyline" ALIGN=right>
```

You'll note that, in Figure 9.7, the image is to the right of the text.

Figure 9.6.

The image in this example is aligned to the left of the page and text.

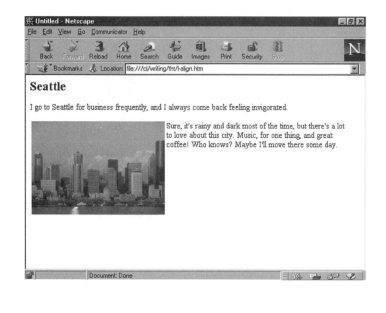

Figure 9.7.

Here you see right alignment in action.

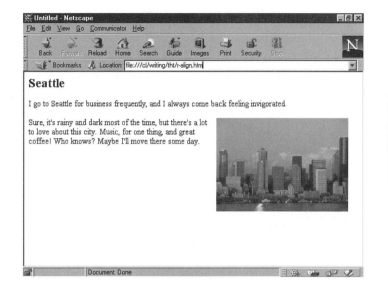

Floating Images

A floating image is one that seems to float within the text. You've seen this technique used often in magazines and newspapers. It looks great on an HTML page, too!

To make an image float, be sure to remove any breaking characters such as a <BR> or <P> between the text and image. This way, the text will naturally wrap around the image. I've done that in my paragraph in Figure 9.8. When you look at the way the page displays within the browser, you see that the image floats.

JUST A MINUTE

You can align images using other techniques, including the <DIV ALIGN=X> technique, where X equals the type of alignment you're after. This is especially helpful if you'd like to center an image, because the ALIGN attribute doesn't support centering. Remember that when you use this tag, anything within the start tag and its companion </DIV> tag will be aligned as well. For more information on other alignment techniques, see Hour 14, "Page Design and Layout."

Figure 9.8.

This image appears to float above the page.

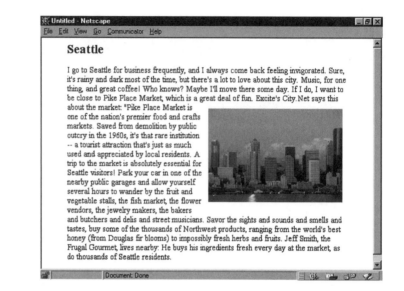

To Do

Try adding some images to your Web pages now, and experiment with all the different values of ALIGN. To get you started, here's a quick review of how to add the magic hat image to any Web page:

1. Copy the magic.gif image file to the same directory folder as the HTML file.

2. With a text editor, add <IMG SRC="magic.gif"> where you want the image to appear in the text.

3. If you want the image to be centered, type <DIV ALIGN="center"> before the <IMG> tag and </DIV> after it. To wrap text around the image instead, add ALIGN="right" or ALIGN="left" to the <IMG> tag.

If you have time for a little more experimentation, try combining multiple images of various sizes (such as the star and the magic hats) with various vertical alignment settings for <IMG ALIGN>.

Linking an Image

With the same <A HREF> tag used to make text links, you can make any image into a clickable link to another page. Figures 9.9 and 9.10 show a sample page. Clicking on the Seattle image retrieves the Seattle page located on Excite's CityNet.

Figure 9.9.

Any images (and/or text) between <A HREF> and </A> tags become clickable links. You'll see a thin border appear around the image indicating that the image is "hot." In color, this appears purple.

Figure 9.10.

Click on the hotlinked image, and it takes you to the Web site it's coded for, in this case Excite's City.Net Seattle page.

Normally, Web browsers draw a colored rectangle around the edge of each image link. Like text links, the rectangle will usually appear blue to people who haven't visited the link recently (usually within a month, unless otherwise defined by the user in the browser software), and purple to people who have visited it.

Hour 13, "Backgrounds and Color Control," explains how to change the link colors, and Hour 14 explains how to eliminate or change the size of the rectangle drawn around image links.

All the same rules and possibilities discussed in Hour 3 and Hour 8, "Intra-Page and E-mail Links," apply to image links exactly as they do for text links. (You can link to another part of the same page with `<A HREF="#name">` and `<A NAME="name">`, for example.)

COFFEE BREAK

> The addition of images can make an enormous difference in the impact a page has on the people who visit it. I added a few graphics to our developing 24-Hour HTML Café site at
>
> `http://www.mcp.com/sites/1-57521/1-57521-366-4`
>
> To appreciate the improvement, compare this to the site with the same text content at
>
> `http://www.mcp.com/sites/1-57521/1-57521-366-4`
>
> In the next hour, you'll find out how to build (or borrow) your own great graphics like these.

Summary

This hour has shown you how to use the `<IMG>` tag to place graphics images on your Web pages. You learned to include a short text message to appear in place of the image as it loads. Those who choose not to download graphics automatically will also value the ALT tag message. You also learned to control the horizontal and vertical alignment of each image, and how to make text wrap around, or float, above the image.

Finally, you learned how to hotlink to other pages using the same `<A>` tag introduced in Hour 3.

Table 9.1 summarizes the attributes of the `<IMG>` tag covered in this hour.

Table 9.1. HTML attributes.

Attribute	Function
`SRC="..."`	The address or filename of the image.
`ALT="..."`	A text message that may be displayed in place of the image.
`ALIGN="..."`	Determines the alignment of the given image. If LEFT or RIGHT, the image is aligned to the left or right column, and all following text flows beside that image. All other values, such as TOP, MIDDLE, BOTTOM, ABSMIDDLE, or ABSBOTTOM, determine the vertical alignment of this image with other items in the same line.

9

Q&A

Q **I found a nice image on a Web page on the Internet. Can I just use Save Image As to save a copy and then put the image on my Web pages?**

A It's easy to do that, but unfortunately it's also illegal in most countries. You should get written permission from the original creator of the image first. Most Web pages include the e-mail addresses of their authors, which makes it a simple matter to ask for permission—a lot simpler than going to court, anyway!

Q **How long of a message can I put after `ALT=` in an `<IMG>` tag?**

A Theoretically, as long as you want. But practically, you should keep the message short enough so that it will fit in less space than the image itself. For big images, ten words may be fine. For small images, a single word is better.

Q **How do I control both the horizontal and vertical alignment of an image at once?**

A The short answer is that you can't. For example, if you type `<IMG ALIGN="right" ALIGN="middle" SRC="myimage.gif">`, the `ALIGN="middle"` will be ignored.

There are ways around this limitation, however. Hour 14 will explain how to position text and images exactly where you want them in both the horizontal and vertical directions.

Quiz

Questions

1. How would you insert an image file named `elephant.jpg` at the very top of a Web page?

2. How would you make the word *Elephant* appear whenever the actual `elephant.jpg` image couldn't be displayed by a Web browser?

3. Write the HTML to make the `elephant.jpg` image appear on the right side of the page, with a big headline reading "Elephants of the World Unite!" on the left side of the page next to it.

4. Write the HTML to make a tiny image of a mouse (named `mouse.jpg`) appear between the words "Wee sleekit, cow'rin," and the words "tim'rous beastie."

5. Suppose you have a large picture of a standing elephant named `elephant.jpg`. Now make a small image named `fly.jpg` appear to the left of the elephant's head, and `mouse.jpg` appear next to the elephant's right foot.

Answers

1. Copy the image file into the same directory folder as the HTML text file, and type `<IMG SRC="elephant.jpg">` immediately after the `<BODY>` tag in the HTML text file.

2. Use the following HTML: `<IMG SRC="elephant.jpg" ALT="Elephant">`

3. `<IMG SRC="elephant.jpg" ALIGN="right">`
   `<H1>Elephants of the World Unite!</H1>`

4. `Wee sleekit, cow'rin,<IMG SRC="mouse.jpg">tim'rous beastie`

5. `<IMG SRC="fly.jpg" ALIGN="top">`
   `<IMG SRC="elephant.jpg">`
   `<IMG SRC="mouse.jpg">`

Activities

☐ Try using any small image as a bullet to make lists with more flair. If you also want the list to be indented, use the `<DL>` definition list and `<DD>` for each item (instead of `<UL>` and `<LI>`, which would give the standard boring bullets). Here's a quick example, using the star.gif file from my sample images page:

```
<DL><DD><IMG SRC="star.gif">A murder of crows
<DD><IMG SRC="star.gif">A rafter of turkeys
<DD><IMG SRC="star.gif">A muster of peacocks</DL>
```

Hour 10

Creating Web Page Images

You don't have to be an artist to put high-impact graphics and creative type on your Web pages. You don't need to spend hundreds or thousands of dollars on software, either. This hour tells you how to create the images you need to make visually exciting Web pages. It also explains how to make those images appear as quickly as possible, even for people using slow modems to access them. You can see Hour 11, "Making Pages Display Quickly," to learn more techniques for speeding up the display of your graphics.

In this hour, you'll learn about

- ☐ Graphics tools
- ☐ Image resources
- ☐ Scanning images
- ☐ Sizing images
- ☐ Image file types: GIF and JPEG
- ☐ Optimizing images for speed
- ☐ Other imaging techniques, such as progressive rendering and transparency
- ☐ Creating banners and buttons

Graphics Tools

You can use almost any computer graphics program to create graphics images for your Web pages, from the simple Paintbrush program that comes free with Microsoft Windows to the more expensive but highly recommended professional program, Adobe Photoshop. If you have a digital camera or scanner attached to your computer, it probably came with some graphics software capable of creating Web page graphics.

If you already have some software that you think might be good for creating Web graphics, try using it to do everything described in this hour. If it can't do some of the tasks covered here, it probably won't be a good tool for Web graphics. In the rest of this hour, you'll learn exactly how to create graphics with big visual impact and small file sizes. The techniques you'll use to accomplish this depend on the contents and purpose of each image. There are as many uses for Web page graphics as there are Web pages, but four types of graphics are by far the most common:

- ☐ Photos of people, products, or places
- ☐ Graphical banners and logos for the tops of pages
- ☐ Snazzy-looking buttons or icons to link between pages
- ☐ Background textures or paper to go behind pages

The last of these is covered in Hour 13, "Backgrounds and Color Control," but you can learn to create the other three kinds of graphics right here in Hour 10.

To Do

One excellent and inexpensive program that does provide everything you'll need for this hour is Paint Shop Pro from JASC, Inc. If you are using a Windows computer, I highly recommend that you download a free, fully functional evaluation copy of this product before reading the rest of this hour. Bear in mind that Paint Shop Pro is a good starting place for you to test your wings, but for those serious-minded about creating Web graphics, purchasing Adobe Photoshop is a must. For demonstration purposes, I've used Paint Shop Pro for the examples because it is so widely available.

Note that Macintosh users should download BME, a graphics program that you can use with the lessons in this hour, at http://www.softlogik.com instead, because Paint Shop Pro is currently available for Windows only.

1. Start your Web browser, and go to `http://www.jasc.com/pspdl.html`.
2. Follow the directions to transfer the latest version of Paint Shop Pro onto your hard drive. (As of this writing, the file you need is called `psp41.zip`.)

10

3. You will need a program capable of handling Zip archives in order to install Paint Shop Pro. If you don't have such a program, go to `http://www.winzip.com` and follow the instructions there to download and install WinZip.

4. Use WinZip (or an equivalent program) to remove the Paint Shop Pro installation programs from the Zip file and put them in a directory folder of their own.

5. Run the `pspsetup.exe` program to install Paint Shop Pro.

The Paint Shop Pro software you can get online is a fully functional shareware evaluation copy. If you continue to use this product for working with Web page images, please be prompt about sending the registration fee to the program's creators at JASC Software.

Graphics Resources

One of the best ways to save time creating the graphics and media files is, of course, to avoid creating them altogether. Any graphic or media clip you see on any site is instantly reusable as soon as the copyright holder grants (or sells) you the right to copy it.

Grabbing a graphic from any Web page is as simple as clicking on it with the right mouse button and picking Save Image As in Netscape Navigator or Save Picture As in Microsoft Explorer. Extracting a background image from a page is just as easy: Right-click on the background and choose Save Background As.

JUST A MINUTE

Many sites on the Web make "free" graphics available for anyone to use without payment, although there can be conditions attached. In many cases, the catch is only to include a link somewhere on your pages telling people where you found your image, which is a courtesy even if it's not a condition.

Be cautious about "borrowing" graphics without permission, however. Many people (and companies) are quite possessive of their hard work and won't take it kindly if you use their image without either paying for it or obtaining their permission first.

Here are some good starting points for finding graphics on the Web:

☐ Amber's Free Art: `http://www.solarflare.com/freeart/`.

☐ A+ Art: `http://aplusart.simplenet.com/aplusart/index.html`.

☐ Molly's personal favorite, The Internet Baglady: `http://www.dumpsterdive.com/`. She's got the goods on free and cheap stuff on the Web, without your having to dig through piles of junk to get to it.

☐ Gini Schmitz' Cool Graphics: `http://www.geocities.com/SiliconValley/Heights/1272/index.html`.

☐ HTML Writers Guild Icon Library: `http://www.hwg.org/archives/graphics/graphics.html`.

☐ HTML Writers Guild Graphics Libraries: `http://www.hwg.org/resources/design/graphics.html`.

Scanning Images

To put photos on your Web pages, you'll need some kind of scanner or digital camera. You'll often need to use the custom software that comes with your scanner or camera to save pictures on your hard drive. Note, however, that you can control any scanner that is compatible with the TWAIN interface standard directly from Paint Shop Pro and most other graphics programs. Refer to your software documentation for details.

JUST A MINUTE

If you don't have a scanner or digital camera, any Kodak film-developing store can transfer photos from 35mm film to a CD-ROM for a modest fee. You can then use Paint Shop Pro to open and modify the Kodak PhotoCD files.

Once you have the pictures, you can use Paint Shop Pro or Photoshop to get them ready for the Web.

Sizing Images

You want Web page graphics to be as compact as possible, so you'll usually need to crop or reduce the size of scanned images. Follow these steps to crop an image in Paint Shop Pro:

1. Click on the rectangular selection tool on the tools palette. (The tools palette is shown on the left in Figure 10.1. You can drag it wherever you want it, so it might be in a different place on your screen.)

Figure 10.1.

Use the rectangular selection tool to crop images as tightly as possible.

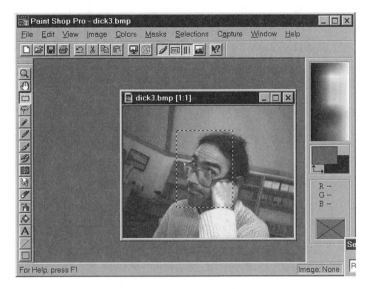

2. Click on the top-left corner of the part of the image you want to keep, and hold down the mouse button while you drag down to the lower-right corner (see Figure 10.1).

3. Select Image | Crop.

Even after cropping, your image may be larger than it needs to be for a Web page. Generally, a complex photograph should be no more than 300×300 pixels, and a simpler photo can look fine at 100×50 or so.

JUST A MINUTE

Notice that in Paint Shop Pro the resolution of the current image is shown at the bottom-right corner of the window. The image may look larger or smaller than it really is, because Paint Shop Pro automatically adjusts the image to fit in the window while you're working on it. To see the image at the size it will appear on a Web page, select View | Normal Viewing (1:1).

Most graphics programs offer two different ways to change the resolution of an image, and one technique gives much nicer-looking results than the other. The names of these techniques vary from program to program, but in Paint Shop Pro you should always use the Image | Resample command (instead of Image | Resize). You'll get the Resample dialog box, which is shown in Figure 10.2.

Figure 10.2.

*To change the size
of a photographic
image, always use
Image | Resample.*

You'll almost always want Custom Size and Maintain Aspect Ratio selected. When you enter the width (in pixels) that you'd like the image to be, the height will be calculated automatically to keep the image from squishing out of shape.

Many photographs will require some color correction to look their best on a computer screen. Like most photo-editing programs, Paint Shop Pro offers many options for adjusting the brightness, contrast, and color balance of an image.

Most of these options are pretty intuitive to use, but the most important and powerful one may be unfamiliar if you're not an old graphics pro. Whenever an image appears too dark or too light, select Colors | Adjust | Gamma Correction. For most images, this works better than Colors | Adjust | Brightness and Contrast, because it doesn't "wash out" bright or dark areas.

As shown in Figure 10.3, you can click on the small arrow buttons in the Gamma Correction dialog box to adjust the correction factor until the image looks about right. (Numbers above 1 make the image lighter; numbers between 1 and 0 make the image darker.)

Most of the other image-editing tools in Paint Shop Pro offer small preview windows such as the one in Figure 10.3, so a little playful experimentation is the best way to find out what each of them does.

Figure 10.3.

Gamma Correction is the best way to fix images that are too dark or too light.

About Image File Types

There are two main types of image formats you'll commonly see and use on the Web: `.gif` and `.jpg` (or `.jpeg`), usually called GIFs ("giffs" or "jiffs") and JPGs (or JPEGs).

GIF

Line art files, images that you create from scratch or simple drawings that you can scan in, usually look best and load faster as GIFs (CompuServe Graphic Interchange Format). GIFs use 8-bit color (256 colors) to make simple pictures as small as possible. They are great for images with a limited number of colors but are not as good for photographs or images with lots of colors or gradations of color.

JPEG

Photographic images usually look best when saved in the JPEG (Joint Photographic Experts Group) file format, which uses 24-bit color (millions of colors) to make pictures look as realistic as possible. When you're finished adjusting the size and appearance of your photo, select File | Save As and choose the JPG-JPEG-JFIF Compliant file type with Standard Encoding, as shown in the bottom half of Figure 10.4.

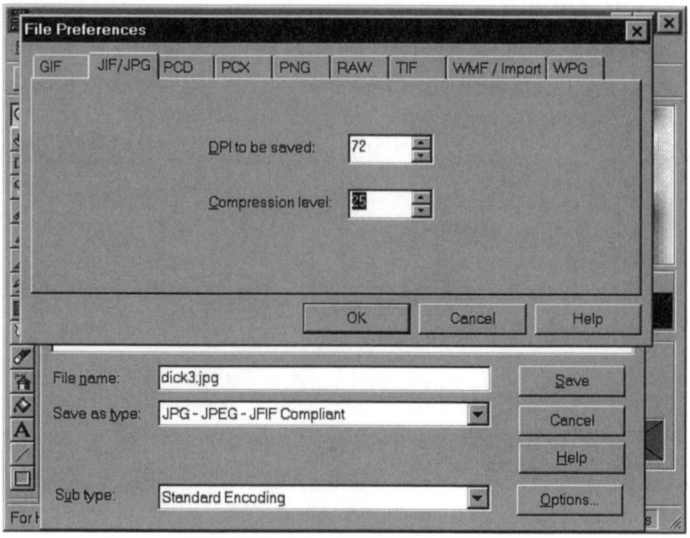

Figure 10.4.
Paint Shop Pro allows
you to trade reduced file
size for image quality
when saving JPEG
images.

Optimizing Images for Speed

Two forces are always at odds when you post graphics and multimedia on the Net. Your eyes and ears want everything to be as detailed and accurate as possible, but your clock and wallet want files to be as small as possible. Intricate, colorful graphics can mean big file sizes that can take a long time to transfer, even over a fast connection.

So how do you maximize the quality of your presentation while minimizing file size? To make these choices, you need to understand how color and resolution work together to create a subjective sense of quality.

The *resolution* of an image is the height and width measured in pixels (the individual dots that make up a digital image). Large, high-resolution images take longer to transfer and display than small, low-resolution images. Resolution is usually written as the width times the height; a 300×200 image, for example, is 300 dots wide and 200 dots high.

The standard DPI (dots per inch) of Web graphics is 72, the lowest available resolution for graphics! Be sure you process all your Web graphics at this resolution.

You might be surprised to find that resolution isn't the most significant factor determining the storage size (and transfer time) of an image file. This is because images used on Web pages are always stored and transferred in compressed form. The mathematics of image compression is complex, but the basic idea is that repeating patterns or large areas of the same color can be squeezed out when the image is stored on a disk. This makes the image file much smaller, and allows it to be transferred faster over the Internet. The original appearance of the image can then be restored by the Web browser program when the image is displayed.

NEW TERM   *Image compression* is the mathematical manipulation that images are put through to squeeze out repetitive patterns. It makes them load and display much faster.

JPEG Compression Ratios

JPEGs use a special compression algorithm that allows you to trade image quality for file size. This technique is sometimes called *lossy* compression.

Figure 10.4 also shows the File Preferences dialog box you'll see when you click the Options button. You can control the compression ratio for saving JPEG files by adjusting the compression level setting between 1% (high quality, large file size) and 99% (low quality, small file size).

In Hour 11 you'll see how various JPEG compression levels affect the quality of typical images.

Reducing the Number of Colors in GIFs

One of the most effective ways to reduce the download time for a GIF image is to reduce the number of colors. This can drastically reduce the visual quality of photographic images, but works great for most banners, buttons, and other icons.

GIFs use a *lossless* compression method, which means that every pixel is put back on the screen exactly where it was created, but adjacent sections having the same color are squeezed into a smaller size. (That this works means the less shading there is the better, as far as image size goes.) A GIF image can also use fewer colors than the standard 256 colors, which "squeezes" the total file size even more. Reducing the number of colors accomplishes both of these goals at once.

In Paint Shop Pro, you can do this by selecting Colors | Reduce Color Depth. (Most other graphics programs have a similar option.) The software will automatically find the best palette of 16 or 256 colors for approximating the full range of colors in the image.

JUST A MINUTE

Even if you use only two or three colors in an image, you should still select Colors | Reduce Color Depth | 16 Colors before you save it. If you don't, the image file will waste some space by leaving room for lots of colors even though very few are actually in use.

When you reduce the number of colors in an image, you will see a dialog box with several choices (see Figure 10.5). For Web page images, you will almost always want to choose the Optimized Palette, and Nearest color instead of Error diffusion or any form of dithering.

10

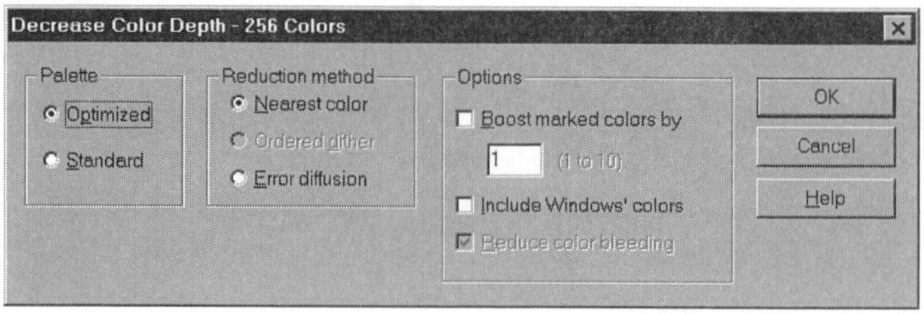

Figure 10.5.

Reducing the number of colors in an image can dramatically decrease file size without changing the appearance of the image much.

| NEW TERM | *Dithering* (called *error diffusion* in Paint Shop Pro) means using random dots or patterns to intermix palette colors. |

Dithering can make images look better in some cases, but usually should be avoided for Web page graphics. Why? Because it substantially increases the information complexity of an image, and that almost always results in much larger file sizes and slower downloads. The ideal is to not select dithering.

To save a GIF image in Paint Shop Pro, select File | Save As and choose GIF-CompuServe as the image type.

Other Imaging Techniques

There are a number of other imaging techniques that you will want to know about in order to make your graphics the best they can be. Such techniques include methods of making the information progressively visible on the screen, or transparent so as to mesh professionally with a background design.

Progressive Rendering

Both the GIF and JPEG image file formats offer a nifty feature to make images appear faster than they possibly could otherwise. An image can be stored in such a way that a rough draft of the image appears quickly, and then the details are filled in as the download finishes. This has a profound psychological effect, because it gives people something "complete" to look at instead of making them sit and drum their fingers while waiting for a large image to pour slowly onto the screen.

A file stored with this feature is called an *interlaced GIF* or a *progressive JPEG*. Despite the two different names, the visual results are similar.

An interlaced GIF file is an image that will appear blocky at first, and then more and more detailed as it finishes downloading. Similarly, a progressive JPEG file appears blurry at first, and then gradually comes into focus.

Most graphics programs that can handle GIF files allow you to choose whether to save them interlaced or noninterlaced. In Paint Shop Pro, for example, you can choose the Version 89a-Interlaced Sub type in the Save As dialog box just before you save a GIF file (see Figure 10.6).

Figure 10.6.

Paint Shop Pro lets you save interlaced GIF images, which appear to display faster when loading.

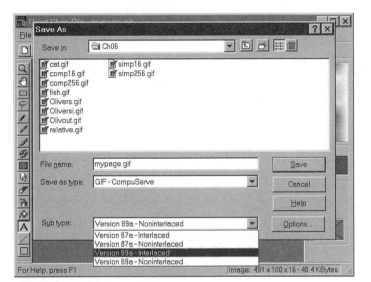

To save a progressive JPEG file, choose the JPG-JPEG-JFIF Compliant image type and the Progressive Encoding Sub type.

The progressive JPEG standard is quite new and is supported only by Netscape Navigator version 2.0 or later and Microsoft Internet Explorer version 3.0 or later.

JUST A MINUTE

> Browsers that don't support progressive JPEG will *not* display the file as if it were just a regular JPEG—they will display nothing at all or a message saying the file isn't recognizable. Interlaced GIFs, on the other hand, will appear correctly even in older browsers that don't support two-stage display.

Figure 10.7 shows a Web page with a title banner saved in the interlaced GIF format being downloaded from the Internet. Notice that the banner appears blocky. If this weren't an interlaced GIF, only the top half of the image would be showing at this point in the download.

Figure 10.7.

The banner at the top of this page looks blocky because the interlaced GIF file isn't done loading yet.

Figure 10.8 shows the same page a few seconds later, when the download is complete.

Figure 10.8.

The same page as in Figure 10.7, after all images are done loading.

10

JUST A MINUTE

Image files smaller than about 3KB will usually load so fast that no one will ever see the interlacing or progressive display anyway. In fact, very small images may actually load *more slowly* when interlaced, so save these tricks for larger images only.

Transparency

Sometimes, you want to place an irregular image on a texture or background image and don't want to have a white square surrounding it. Luckily, the GIF format allows you to define one color as transparent so that the background will show through.

To make part of an image transparent, the image must have 256 or fewer colors, and you must save it in the GIF file format. (JPEG images can't be transparent.) Most graphics programs that support the GIF format allow you to specify one color to be transparent.

To Do

To save a transparent GIF in Paint Shop Pro, follow these steps:

1. Select Colors | Decrease Color Depth | 256 Colors or Colors | Decrease Color Depth | 16 Colors, and check the Optimized and Nearest color boxes.
2. Choose the eyedropper tool.
3. Right-click the color you want to make transparent.
4. Select File | Save As....
5. Choose the GIF-CompuServe image format and Version 89a-Noninterlaced or Version 89a-Interlaced Sub type. (Refer to the preceding section about interlaced versus noninterlaced images.)
6. Click the Options button.
7. Set the transparency value to the background color.
8. Enter a name for the file; then click OK to save it.

For a masked preview of which part of the image will be transparent, click Preview. This will temporarily replace the transparent color with the current foreground color.

To emphasize the transparent color permanently, you could select Colors | Edit Palette and change the transparent palette color to some outrageous fluorescent green or another highly visible hue. If some areas aren't transparent that should be, use the color replacer tool to change their color. Be aware, though, that some browsers don't show transparency correctly. A safer and more portable choice is to use a neutral gray or white—whichever fits best against the background of the page and avoids colors that already exist in the image.

Creating Banners and Buttons

Graphics that you create from scratch, such as banners and buttons, involve different considerations than photographs.

The first decision you need to make when you produce a banner or button is how big it should be. Almost everyone accessing the Web now (or in the foreseeable future) has a computer with one of three screen sizes. The most common resolution for notebook computers and televisions is 640×480 pixels. The resolution of most desktop computers today is 800×600 pixels, and 1024×768 pixels is the preferred resolution of most new computers and future laptops. You should generally plan your graphics so that they will always fit in the smallest of these screens, with room to spare for scrollbars and margins.

This means that full-sized banners and title graphics should be no more than 600 pixels wide. Photos and large artwork should be from 100 to 300 pixels in each dimension, and smaller buttons or icons should be 20 to 100 pixels tall and wide.

You should always begin with 16.7 Million Colors (24 Bit) as the Image Type. You can always change the size of the image later with Image | Crop or Image | Enlarge Canvas, so don't worry if you aren't sure exactly how big it needs to be.

For the Background Color, choose White to match the background that most Web browsers ordinarily use for Web pages. (You'll see how to change the background color of a page in Hour 13.) When you know you'll be making a page with a non-white background, you can choose a different background color here, too.

When you enter the width and height of the image in pixels and click OK, you are faced with a blank canvas—an intimidating sight if you're as art-phobic as most of us! Fortunately, computer graphics programs such as Paint Shop Pro make it amazingly easy to produce professional-looking graphics for most Web page applications.

To Do

If you've started working on graphics along with me, great! If not, go ahead and begin trying some of the techniques I've mentioned. Here are a few pointers to help you along:

- ☐ Stick with a few thematic colors on each page and throughout all your pages. Beginning "Web artists" tend to get carried away with the millions of colors their computer can produce.

- ☐ To save time, make a simple, unlabeled button or icon and use it as a starting point for all your links. This will also give your pages a consistent look.

- ☐ Use one font in all titles and buttons. (Okay, two fonts, tops.)

- ☐ Keep your first graphics direct and to the point. Remember, you'll learn much more about backgrounds, colors, fonts, and layout tricks in the hours to come!

10

Adding graphics to your pages opens up vast horizons of artistic possibility, and it can often be challenging to come up with an attractive, practical design for your Web page graphics.

COFFEE BREAK

To help your creative juices start flowing (and perhaps keep them from flowing too wildly), I've provided a number of sample pages with thematic images almost anyone could produce in Paint Shop Pro or an equivalent graphics program. To browse through these pages, go to

`http://www.mcp.com/sites/1-57521/1-57521-366-4`

and click on the Great Graphics Ideas link.

Summary

In this hour, you learned the basics of preparing graphics for use on Web pages. You saw how to download and use the popular graphics program Paint Shop Pro to work with photos, banners, buttons, and other Web page images. You also found out how to decide among the various graphics file formats used for Web page graphics, and how to make images that appear in stages for the illusion of speed.

Don't miss Hour 11 for more tricks for speeding up your graphics.

Q&A

Q I've heard that I need Photoshop to do Web graphics well. Is it true?

A Adobe Photoshop is the most popular commercial graphics program for creating Web page graphics, and it is arguably the most powerful as well. But unless you're an experienced graphics professional (in which case you already own Photoshop), you might find it much easier—and a bit less expensive—to learn and use Paint Shop Pro. Note that Paint Shop Pro does support all Photoshop-compatible plug-ins and add-on programs, too.

On the other hand, Photoshop occasionally comes bundled with high-end scanners, and Adobe often has good discount programs for students, so you might be able to obtain Photoshop for relatively little outlay, depending on your circumstances. Also, the time-saving features of Photoshop, combined with the power of multiple layers and available companion programs such as DeBabelizer, make it the choice of almost all professional Web designers. It has the considerable advantage that it runs on both Macs and PC machines, so you can trade files with professional graphics, print, and design houses that still use Macs almost exclusively. Before

10

purchasing any graphics product, it might make sense to consider what your plans are. If you want your Web page printed for a brochure, for example, you might regret having strayed from the standard.

Q Shouldn't I just hire a graphics artist to design my pages for me instead of learning all this stuff?

A If you have plenty of money and need a visually impressive site—or if you think that ugly building with chartreuse trim that people are always complaining about actually looks pretty nice—hiring some professional help might not be a bad idea.

Q I've produced graphics for printing on paper. Is making Web page graphics much different?

A Yes. In fact, many of the rules for print graphics are reversed on the Web. Web page graphics have to be low resolution, while print graphics should be as high a resolution as possible. White washes out black on computer screens, while black bleeds into white on paper. Also, someone may stop a Web page when only half the graphics are done, which wouldn't happen on paper. For these reasons, try to avoid falling into old habits if you've done a lot of print graphics design.

Quiz

Questions

1. Suppose you have a scanned picture of a horse that you need to put on a Web page. How big should you make it, and in what file format should you save it?

2. Your company logo is a black letter Z with a red circle behind it. What size should you draw (or scan) it, and what file format should you save it in for use on your Web page?

3. Should you save a 100×50 pixel button graphic as an interlaced GIF file?

Answers

1. Depending on how important the image is to your page, as small as 100×40 pixels or as large as 300×120 pixels. The JPEG format, with about 50% compression, would be best.

2. About 100×100 pixels is generally good for a logo, but a simple graphic like this will compress very well, so you can make it up to 300×300 pixels if you want. Save it as a 16-color GIF file.

3. No. A small file like that will load just as fast (or faster) without interlacing.

Activities

- [ ] If you have an archive of company (or personal) photos, look through it to find a few that might enhance your Web site. Scan them (or send them out to be scanned) so that you'll have a library of graphics all ready to draw from as you produce more pages in the future.

- [ ] Before you start designing graphics for an important business site, try spicing up your own personal home page. This will give you a chance to learn Paint Shop Pro (or your other graphics software) so you'll look like you know what you're doing when you tackle it at work.

10

Hour 11

Making Pages Display Quickly

This hour teaches you how to ensure that your Web pages will appear as quickly as possible when people try to read them. This is essential for making a good impression with your pages, especially with people who will be accessing them through modem connections to the Internet.

In this hour, you'll learn about

- ☐ Browser-based color techniques
- ☐ Selecting images
- ☐ Specifying image width and height
- ☐ Providing preview images

Browser-Based Color Techniques

One of the most powerful ways you can have fast-loading pages that are colorful and interesting is to exploit browser-based color. What this means is that wherever possible, you rely on the Web browser to provide color.

Graphical Web browsers, such as Netscape Navigator and Internet Explorer, come equipped with a predefined palette of colors. This means that the browser pulls up the color, rather than having to rely on the mechanics of the Internet and your computer to get information from outside the browser into the visual space of the browser.

More about browser-based techniques will be discussed in Hour 13, "Backgrounds and Color Control." Browser-based color is primarily found in background and text options, and how you choose to define those within HTML.

The point of introducing the concept now rather than later is to prepare you for a broader understanding of how pages work, and how you can exploit that technology to make fast-loading pages that are bright—and interesting, too!

Selecting the Best Image

In Hour 10, "Creating Web Page Images," you learned how to set the compression level for JPEG images and select the number of colors for GIF images. With both types of graphics files, you need to try to find a balance between acceptable image quality and maximum speed.

Figure 11.1 compares the results of saving two graphics files at various GIF- and JPEG-quality settings. Keep in mind that the differences are more obvious when seen in full color. The numbers in parentheses are the file sizes. For example, the top-left image in Figure 11.1 is 15KB, and the top-right image is 3KB.

If you examine these images closely (you can look at them in color at http://www.mcp.com/ sites/1-57521/1-57521-366-4/), you'll probably decide that 50% JPEG compression provides a good compromise of quality and size for the COMPLEXITY image. The SIMPLICITY image would both look and compress best as a 16-color GIF.

To estimate how long it will typically take for your images to download, you can assume that a standard 28.8Kbps modem with a good connection to a Net site can pull about 2KB per second on average. If you were surfing the Net, would you rather wait nearly half a minute to see this image in its full glory, or watch it pop onto your screen at 75% quality in less than six seconds?

Remember that some people are still accessing the Net through 14.4Kbps or slower modems. As a general rule, any Web page that includes more than 65KB worth of graphics is ready for a diet!

Figure 11.1.

Simple images usually look best and load fastest as 16-color GIF files, while 50% JPEG compression is good for most complex graphics.

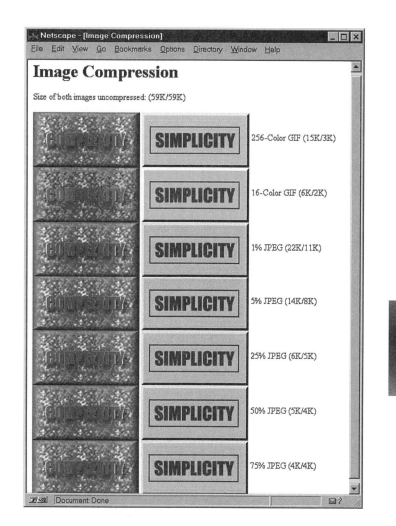

Specifying Image Width and Height

Because text moves over the Internet much faster than graphics, most Web browsers will display the text on a page before the images. This gives people something to read while they're waiting to see the pictures, which makes the whole page seem to come up much faster.

You can make sure that everything on your page appears as quickly as possible and in the right places by explicitly stating the width and height of each image. That way, a Web browser can leave the right amount of space for that image as it lays out the page and can come back to get the actual image file later.

For each image on your page, use Paint Shop Pro or another graphics program to find out the exact width and height in pixels. In Paint Shop Pro, this information appears at the bottom-right corner of the main window when you move the mouse over any part of an image. Then include those dimensions in the <IMG> tag like this:

```
<IMG SRC="myimage.gif" WIDTH=200 HEIGHT=100>
```

JUST A MINUTE

The width and height you specify for an image don't have to match the actual width and height of the image. The Web browser program will try to squish or stretch the image to whatever size you specify.

This usually makes photographic or drawn images look ugly, but there are two excellent uses for doing this: You can save a very small, totally transparent image and use it as any size "spacer" by specifying the width and height of the blank region you want to create on your page. It's also useful for creating a one pixel image that can be expanded into a "block" of color in a table or as a graphic element on the page.

Providing a Preview Image

You can also speed things up by providing a small image file to be displayed while someone is waiting for a full-sized image file to download.

Put the name of the smaller file after the word LOWSRC in the same image tag as the full-sized SRC image:

```
<IMG SRC="bigfile.gif" LOWSRC="tinyfile.jpg">
```

What happens here is that the Web browser makes its first pass through your document, and when it sees your LOWSRC tag, it loads that (presumably smaller) image first. Then it makes a second pass through your document and loads the main image.

JUST A MINUTE

Although this attribute was originally designed with the intention that the LOWSRC image would be a low-resolution or highly compressed version of the SRC image, you can also use two entirely different images to get a two-frame animation effect. This is rarely used, although you can see it on the Net from time to time.

11

Figure 11.2 is an HTML page that uses the WIDTH, HEIGHT, and LOWSRC attributes in an <IMG> tag. Figure 11.3 shows the LOWSRC and SRC images. The LOWSRC image has only two colors and contains less detail, so its GIF file is only 3KB and will load in less than two seconds through a 28.8Kbps modem. The SRC image file, with 256 colors and lots of detail, is 35KB, which takes about 10 times as long to download.

Figure 11.2.

Always include the width and height of all images. Use LOWSRC to include a small image to display while a large image loads.

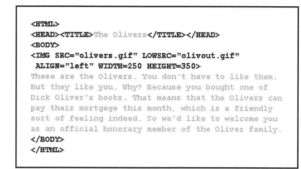

```
<HTML>
<HEAD><TITLE>The Olivers</TITLE></HEAD>
<BODY>
<IMG SRC="olivers.gif" LOWSRC="olivout.gif"
 ALIGN="left" WIDTH=250 HEIGHT=350>
These are the Olivers. You don't have to like them.
But they like you. Why? Because you bought one of
Dick Oliver's books. That means that the Olivers can
pay their mortgage this month, which is a friendly
sort of feeling indeed. So we'd like to welcome you
as an official honorary member of the Oliver family.
</BODY>
</HTML>
```

Figure 11.3.

Although these two images are the same width and height, the left image compresses into a much smaller GIF file.

11

Figures 11.4 through 11.7 show the page from Figure 11.2 as it will look to someone viewing it on the Internet. It appears in four stages:

1. 0–2 seconds: The text appears with a small icon and rectangle as a placeholder for the image. (See Figure 11.4.) If I hadn't included WIDTH and HEIGHT attributes in the <IMG> tag, the text would be in the wrong place at first and would then jump over suddenly, making it hard to read.

Figure 11.4.

When WIDTH *and* HEIGHT *attributes are included in an* <IMG> *tag, the browser draws a rectangular placeholder for an image before loading it.*

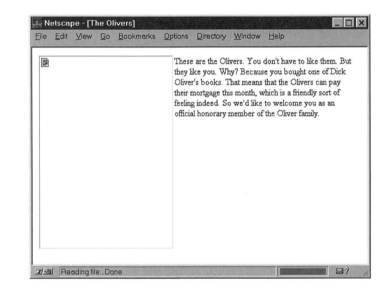

2. 2–4 seconds: The LOWSRC image appears. (See Figure 1.5.) Because I saved it as an interlaced GIF image (see Hour 10), it fades in gradually over the course of a couple seconds.

3. 4–20 seconds: The SRC image replaces the LOWSRC image. (See Figure 11.6.) I didn't save the SRC image as an interlaced GIF because I wanted it to "wipe out" the LOWSRC image in a single pass.

11

Figure 11.5.

Next, the LOWSRC *image is displayed (if one was specified).*

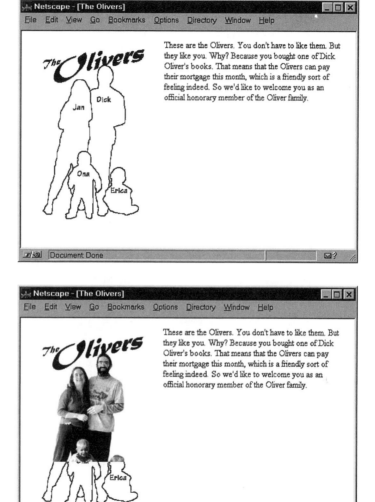

Figure 11.6.

The SRC *image gradually replaces the* LOWSRC *image as it downloads.*

4. About 20 seconds: The page is complete. Because most people will have just finished reading the text at this time, they won't feel like they had to wait at all! (See Figure 11.7.)

Figure 11.7.

If the page is loaded again by the same person a little while later, they won't see the LOWSRC *image at all.*

These are the Olivers. You don't have to like them. But they like you. Why? Because you bought one of Dick Oliver's books. That means that the Olivers can pay their mortgage this month, which is a friendly sort of feeling indeed. So we'd like to welcome you as an official honorary member of the Oliver family.

If someone comes back to a page more than once in the same day, the Web browser will usually only show the LOWSRC image the first time. After that, it will be able to quickly pull the SRC image out of its memory.

COFFEE BREAK

When you have multiple graphics elements without WIDTH and HEIGHT attributes on a page, watching the browser reshuffle elements while loading can be particularly disconcerting. To see the difference, compare the following two versions of this page at the 24-Hour HTML Café:

http://www.mcp.com/sites/1-57521/1-57521-366-4/

The latter page on this site also uses LOWSRC images for an interesting effect while loading.

11

Summary

This hour helped you choose the number of colors and compression level of images so they load fast and still look good. You also learned how to make sure that people always have text or a preview image to look at while waiting for the larger images on your page.

Table 11.1 summarizes the tags and attributes discussed in this hour.

Table 11.1. HTML tags and attributes.

Tag	Attribute	Function
`<IMG>`		Inserts an inline image into the document.
	`SRC="..."`	The address of the image.
	`WIDTH="..."`	The width, in pixels, of the image. If `WIDTH` is not the actual width, the image is scaled to fit.
	`HEIGHT="..."`	The height, in pixels, of the image. If `HEIGHT` is not the actual height, the image is scaled to fit.
	`LOWSRC="..."`	The path or URL of an image that will be loaded first, before the image specified in `SRC`. The value of `LOWSRC` is usually a smaller or lower resolution version of the actual image.

Q&A

Q This may be a dumb question, but how do I tell if my image is complex (suitable for JPEG compression) or simple (suitable for GIF compression)?

A Try reducing the number of colors to 16. If the image still looks fine, it's probably best to use GIF compression. If it looks terrible with so few colors, try saving it both as a 50% JPEG and a 256-color GIF. Then compare the file sizes to see which one is smaller.

Q How do I make a smaller file size image for use with the `LOWSRC` tag?

A There are three easy ways. One is to save the image as a JPEG file with very high compression. Another is to reduce the number of colors to 16 (or even 2), and save the file as a GIF. The third way is to resize the image to a lower resolution (say, 50×20 instead of 200×80). The Web browser will stretch the small `LOWSRC` image to fit in the same space as the big `SRC` image, as long as you include `WIDTH=200` `HEIGHT=80` in the `<IMG>` tag.

Refer to Hour 10 for detailed instructions on how to do all three of these things in Paint Shop Pro.

Quiz

Questions

1. What compression level setting is generally best for most JPEG images?
2. How could you display a picture of a wolf briefly, then replace it with a picture of a man (without using GIF animation)?
3. What four attributes should you always include in every `<IMG>` tag as a matter of habit?

Answers

1. 50% compression.
2. `<IMG SRC="man.jpg" LOWSRC="wolf.jpg">`
3. `SRC`, `ALT`, `WIDTH`, and `HEIGHT`. For example:

   `<IMG SRC="fred.jpg" ALT="Fat Fred" WIDTH=300 HEIGHT=100>`

Activities

☐ For large images (any graphics file over 15KB), it's worth a little experimentation to find the exact compression ratio or number of colors that give you the minimum acceptable quality. Save it at all the settings shown in Figure 11.1, and compare them in Netscape Navigator or Microsoft Internet Explorer.

☐ Black-and-white images make the smallest files, so many sites use a two-color version of a color graphic as the `LOWSRC` image. If simply reducing the colors of an image doesn't yield a good `LOWSRC` image, try using Paint Shop Pro's or Photoshop's Emboss or Trace Contour effects first.

Hour **12**

Creating Animated Graphics

There are several ways to add some movement to a Web page, and most of them are covered in the most advanced hour in this book—Hour 22, "Applets, ActiveX, and Objects." But you can actually add animation to standard GIF images, and it's so easy to do that the technique doesn't even qualify as "advanced."

In this hour, you'll learn about

- ☐ Animation tools
- ☐ Creating a GIF animation: selecting the source, timing the images, and looping
- ☐ Other animation methods

GIF animations are a great way to make simple, animated icons and add a little motion to spice up any Web page. In this hour, you'll learn how to create GIF animations and how to optimize them for the fastest possible display.

Animation Tools

Alchemy Mindworks's GIF Construction Set is a nifty little utility designed especially for assembling GIF animations. Other GIF animation programs are also available, including both freeware and advanced commercial software packages. Visit Royal Frazier's GIF Animation on the Web for all kinds of GIF-building tools and advice: http://members.aol.com/royalef/.

For Macintosh users, I recommend GIFBuilder, which is available free at http://www.shareware.com/. You can download a free evaluation copy of GIF Construction Set from the Internet. I recommend that you do so now so you can try your hand at building an animation or two as you read this hour.

Creating a GIF Animation

There are several important steps to creating a good GIF animation. The following sections explain the process.

Selecting the Source

The first step in creating a GIF animation is to create or select a series of images to be displayed one after the other. You can use any graphics software you like to make the images, and you don't really need to be an artist. You don't even need to use software that supports GIFs to make the images; GIF Construction Set can import BMP, JPEG, PCX, TIFF, and almost any other graphics file format you throw at it, and you can make simple animated effects using a series of similarly sized images from any graphics source.

Timing the Images

Each browser handles animations differently. Some will pause on each frame for a set time and some will run them as fast as possible, so it's important to include explicit timing information in the control block for each frame. You'll have to decide how fast you want the animation to run based on what looks best. For an animated slide show, you would want to pause long enough between frames to allow the user to see the individual pictures. For a rabbit hopping down a road, you would want the frames to go by fast enough so the action seems continuous but not so fast that it looks silly. You'll have to experiment to discover what speed works for your application.

GIF Animation software allows you to control timing, as shown in Figure 12.1.

12

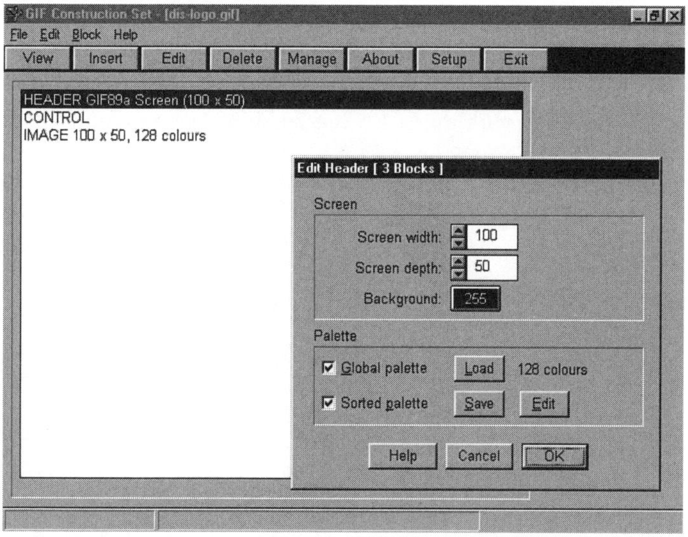

Figure 12.1.
The GIF Animation software is a small package with big punch. Here you see the window allowing you to control timing, among other options.

Looping

When you are done choosing images to include in your animation, you will have to decide whether you want the animation to run more or less continuously, a small number of times, or just once. There are situations in which all these options make sense. Some people find continuously looping animations distracting; some animated images are used to create a single effect and then stop at the last image. Only you can decide.

NEW TERM   *Iteration* is the word for a single cycle of an animation. If your animation cycles only once through each of the individual graphic pieces, that's one iteration; cycling it three times is three iterations; and so on.

A Step-by-Step Example

The fastest way to create a simple GIF animation with GIF Construction Set is to select File | Animation Wizard. This will start an "interview" that leads you through all the steps in the next exercise.

You also can create scrolling text and a number of transition effects automatically with the Edit | Banner and Edit | Transition menu options. These commands provide an easy way to add some quick animation effects to still images.

In this hour, however, I show you how to create animations "by hand," without using the wizard or automatic effects. This will give you a head start when you want to use the advanced animation tricks discussed toward the end of this hour.

12

Before you assemble an animation with GIF Construction Set, you might want to open the images you'd like to include from another graphics program so you can refer to them as you put the animation together. Figure 12.2 shows the four images for this example open in Paint Shop Pro, with the GIF Construction Set program in the foreground.

Figure 12.2.

Use Paint Shop Pro or any other graphics program to produce the individual frames of your animation.

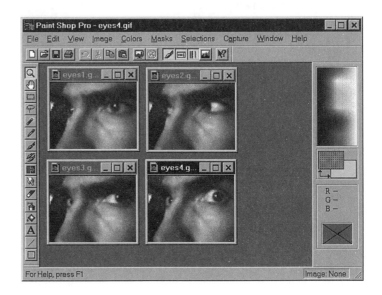

You might want to create a few frames for your own animation and use them to follow along with the numbered steps in this exercise.

JUST A MINUTE

You'll find it easier to build and modify animations if you give the images for each animation similar names. You might name the images for a dog animation dog1.gif, dog2.gif, dog3.gif, and so on.

To Do

The following is how to make a simple GIF animation:

1. To start a new animation, start GIF Construction Set and select File | New. At the top of the white area, HEADER GIF89a Screen (640×480) should appear. This is the first block in the GIF file, to which you will be adding additional image blocks and control blocks that will be listed below it.

2. Click the Edit button, and the dialog box in Figure 12.3 appears. Enter the screen width and depth (height) of the largest image you want to use in the animation and click OK. If you're not sure how big your images are, Paint Shop Pro displays the width and depth of the current image in the lower-left corner of the screen; you can come back to this step after you've loaded the first image to check it.

12

Figure 12.3.

GIF Construction Set runs in a fairly small window, allowing you to see other applications at the same time.

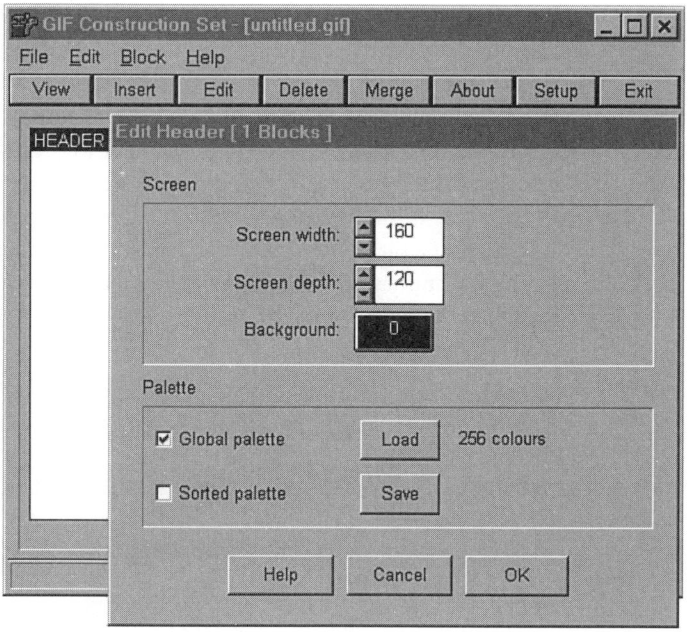

3. If you want the animation to loop continuously when viewed in Netscape Navigator, click the Insert button from the program menu, and then click Loop. This inserts a special control block that tells Navigator to immediately restart the animation when it finishes. If you highlight the loop option and select Edit, or double-click on the element itself, you can choose any number of iterations between 0 and 32,760. If you want to create an animation that plays only once and then stops (leaving the last image on display), skip this step. You can always come back and perform it at any time because the program will automatically create the loop block in the proper location.

4. Click Insert and then Image, and then choose the first image in the animation. This is also the image that will be displayed by most browsers that don't support GIF animation.

5. A dialog box will appear, with the message "The palette of the image you have imported does not match the global palette for this file." To make your animated GIF file as small as possible, select Use This Image as the Global Palette for the first image you insert. If you see this dialog box when inserting subsequent images, select Remap to Global Palette. If you have to perform the Remap step, you can click in the Use this Selection for Subsequent Images checkbox to save time. You may also want to double-click on the image, or click in the Edit box with the image highlighted, to make sure that the image options are set properly. Most animations shouldn't use interlacing, for example.

6. Press the up-arrow key once, then press Insert, and then press Ctrl, in that order. This inserts a control block in front of the image you just loaded. New elements are always inserted after the highlighted element, so you have to have the line above the image you want to control highlighted before you insert the control element. Choose Edit or double-click on the element to get the Edit Control Block dialog box shown in Figure 12.4. You can enter a time delay to wait between this image and the next in hundredths of a second. This controls the speed of the animation and should be set so that a smooth, realistic movement effect is created with traditional animation, or a slower, "slide show" effect is produced if you're animating images that do not depict movement.

Figure 12.4.

Control blocks enable you to make images transparent and to insert a time delay between images.

GIF Construction Set - [untitled.gif]

File   Edit   Block   Help

| View | Insert | Edit | Delete | Merge | About | Setup | Exit |

HEADER GIF89a Screen (160 x 120)
LOOP
CONTROL
IMAGE eyes1.gif 160 x 120, 256 colours

Edit Control Block

Flags

☐ Transparent colour   0

☐ Wait for user input

Delay: 100   1/100ths of a second

Remove by: Nothing

| Help | View | Cancel | OK |

7. Repeat steps 4 through 6 for every image in the animation. Remember that the control block for an image has to appear just above the image block in the list, but you need to insert the image first and then go back to edit the control block to add transparency or you won't be able to pick the transparency color.

JUST A MINUTE

A little confusing? Don't worry, you'll be an old pro at it by the end of this hour. In the meantime, if you make a mistake, you can highlight any block and choose Delete to get rid of it.

12

8. When all the images and control blocks are inserted in the right order (as in Figure 12.5), select File|Save As to save the animation. Be sure to give it a name ending in .gif! Some browsers that don't properly support animated GIFs will display the last image instead of the first, so it might be a good idea to save a duplicate of the first image as the last if this matters.

Figure 12.5.

The images will be listed in order, with a small preview of the current frame to the right.

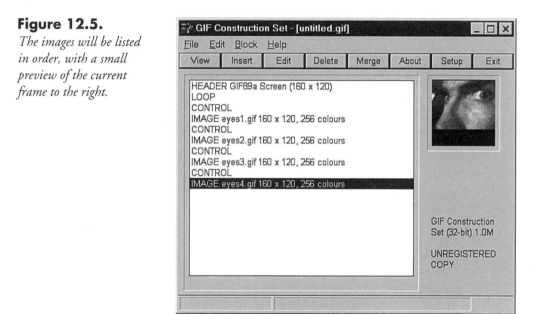

9. Using your favorite Web page editor, make an HTML document with an <IMG> tag referring to your GIF (for example, <IMG SRC="lookani.gif">). Load the document in Netscape Navigator or Microsoft Internet Explorer to see the results.

TIME SAVER

You can also preview the animation within GIF Construction Set by selecting View at any time during the construction process.

Obviously, I can't illustrate the animated effect of flipping back and forth between two images with a printed figure in a book. You can, however, load the document at http://www.mcp.com/sites/1-57521/1-57521-366-4/ to see this and another simple GIF animation.

COFFEE BREAK

Once you get started with Web page animation, it's hard not to get carried away. I couldn't resist adding a flashing neon sign for the 24-Hour HTML Café, which you can see at

`http://www.mcp.com/sites/1-57521/1-57521-366-4/`

You'll also find links to a number of other animation-enhanced pages.

Where to Look for Animated Examples

Take a look at the page at `http://www.mcp.com/sites/1-57521/1-57521-366-4/`. If you view it with Netscape Navigator version 2.0 or later, or with Microsoft Internet Explorer 3.0 or later, you'll notice that all the icons are animated: A vision appears in the crystal ball, the scepter flashes, the cauldron bubbles, and the book pages turn. These icons are actually four separate, multi-image GIFs, and the HTML code for this snazzy, action-filled page looks just like an ordinary static Web page.

Other Animation Options

GIF Construction Set and other GIF animation programs are capable of much more than the simple animations described here. Among the tasks that can be performed automatically are creating a marquee-style scrolling text display, wide-palette GIFs (up to 2295 colors), and special transition effects for animating a single image; inserting comments into the GIF; inserting plain text into the GIF that may display in some future browser; and other image-editing and display options.

But GIF animations aren't the only approach to animating Web pages. If animation interests you, I recommend you look at Macromedia's popular Flash program, which allows you to create a variety of animations with all kinds of interactive features, including sound and mouse-over changes. Macromedia has another program, Shockwave, that allows you to create animations as well. This program is recommended for the very serious student of Web design and multimedia.

For information on both Flash and Shockwave, visit Macromedia's Web site at `http://www.macromedia.com/`.

Summary

This hour introduces you to animated GIF images, which are the easiest and quickest way to add some action to your Web pages. You now know where to get GIF Construction Set, an excellent shareware program for putting together GIF animations. You also understand how to control the timing of each frame in an animation.

12

GIF animations can be placed on Web pages using the same `<IMG>` tag as ordinary, unmoving images. All the `<IMG>` attributes and options discussed in Hour 9, "Putting Images on a Web Page," also work with animated images.

Q&A

Q I've seen quite a few animations on the Web that show a three-dimensional object rotating. Can I make those with GIF Construction Set?

A Yes, but you'll also need some kind of 3D modeling and rendering software to create the individual frames.

You also might have seen interactive, three-dimensional virtual reality scenes and objects embedded in Web pages. Those are something completely different from GIF animations and are made with a special language called the *Virtual Reality Modeling Language*, or VRML. For more information on VRML, refer to *Web Page Wizardry: Wiring Your Site for Sound and Action*, from Sams.net Publishing.

Q My GIF animation looks great in Microsoft Internet Explorer but runs way too fast in Netscape Navigator. What's up?

A When you don't include a time interval between frames, some Web browsers (such as Explorer 3.0 and Navigator 2.0) leave a short pause between frames anyway, which is usually what you want. Navigator 3.0, however, will run the animation as fast as it can, which usually makes it look psychotic.

The solution is to always include a time interval in the control block before every image in the animation.

Q I've seen moving, marquee-type signs on Web pages. Are those GIF animations?

A Sometimes they are and sometimes they aren't. There are several ways to make text move across an area on a Web page. One of the easiest ways is to use GIF Construction Set, which can make several types of fancy marquees from a simple string of text that you type in. See the GIF Construction Set online help for details.

Note that GIF animations are only one way to make marquees. Java applets or ActiveX controls are often used to make marquees as well (see Hour 20, "Organizing and Managing a Web Site"). Some versions of Microsoft Internet Explorer even support a special `<MARQUEE>` tag, but it is likely to become obsolete soon.

Q I have a Windows AVI video clip. Can I turn it into a GIF animation?

A Yes. The Microsoft Web site (`http://www.microsoft.com/`) has a little program you can download called Microsoft GIF Animator that will do the trick. A more advanced video-editing program that supports AVI and GIF files is VideoCraft from Andover Advanced Technologies (`http://www.andatech.com/`).

You can also embed AVI files directly into Web pages, as discussed in Hour 20.

12

Quiz

Questions

1. If you wanted your logo to bounce up and down on your Web page, how would you do it?
2. How would you make a quarter-of-a-second pause between each frame of the animation?

Answers

1. Use Paint Shop Pro or another graphics program to make a few images of the logo at various heights (perhaps squishing when it reaches a line at the bottom). Then assemble those images using GIF Construction Set, and save them as a multi-image GIF animation file named `bounce.gif`. You can then place that animation on a Web page using the `<IMG SRC="bounce.gif">` tag, just as with any GIF image.
2. When you build the animation in GIF Construction Set, insert a control block before each image and click the Edit button to edit each control block. Enter `25` as the time delay (in hundredths of a second).

Activities

☐ GIF Construction Set can make slide shows of one image by automatically generating transition effects between successive copies of the image. This could, with some effort, be used to construct a slide show with special effects by splitting out the individual frames as GIFs and then re-importing them into a combined slide-show GIF. It would be a lot of work, but it might be worth it for certain effects. If you take a little time to explore the advanced features of this program, I'm sure you'll find it time well spent.

☐ Don't forget that GIF Construction Set is shareware, and that the free copy you downloaded is for evaluation purposes. If you like it, be sure to send Alchemy Mindworks its well-earned $20 registration fee at the address you see when you exit the program.

PART

IV

Web Page Design

Hour

Hour 13

Backgrounds and Color Control

Nearly every sample Web page in the first 12 hours had a white background and black text. In this hour, you'll learn how to make pages with the background and text colors of your choice. You'll also discover how to make your own custom-background graphics.

In this hour, you will cover

☐ Background colors
☐ Text and link colors
☐ Background graphics, including creating your own backgrounds
☐ Background resources

The black-and-white figures printed in this book obviously don't convey colors accurately, so you may want to view the sample pages online at

http://www.mcp.com/sites/1-57521/1-57521-366-4/

You can also try the colors on your own Web pages as you read about how to make them.

Background Colors

To specify the background color for a page, put BGCOLOR="blue" inside the <BODY> tag. Of course, you can use many other colors other than blue. You can take the quick road and choose from the 16 standard Windows colors: black, white, red, green, blue, yellow, magenta, cyan, purple, gray, lime, maroon, navy, olive, silver, and teal. Also, don't forget our earlier discussion of hexadecimal colors in Hour 6, "Font Control and Special Characters." If you're really interested in doing it right, you'll learn to work with hexadecimal color values.

Text and Link Colors

You can also specify colors for text and links in the <BODY> tag. For example, in Figure 13.1 you'll notice the following <BODY> tag:

<BODY BGCOLOR="red" TEXT="yellow" LINK="white" VLINK="gray" ALINK="green">

Figure 13.1.

You can specify colors for the background, text, and links in the <BODY> tag of any Web page.

```
<HTML><HEAD><TITLE>Buy Stuff Here</TITLE></HEAD>
<BODY BGCOLOR="red"
 TEXT="yellow" LINK="white" VLINK="grey" ALINK="green">
<IMG SRC="buystuff.gif"><P>
Got some dough you'd love to blow?
Well, well, well baby have you come to the right place!<P>
If you're talking big <IMG SRC="money.gif" ALIGN="middle">
in a big way, you're talking our language.
We've got it all, and we'll take it all.
Right here, right now. So
<A HREF="link.htm"> click here now </A>
or call us on our dime:<P>
<IMG SRC="buyhere.gif" ALIGN="right">
</BODY></HTML>
```

As you probably guessed, TEXT="yellow" makes the text yellow. There are three separate attributes for link colors:

- ☐ LINK="white" makes links that haven't been visited recently white.

- ☐ VLINK="gray" makes recently visited links gray.

- ☐ ALINK="green" makes links briefly blink green when someone clicks on them.

13

Because I used pure red as the background color in the graphics images, they blend right into the background of the Web page.

Figures 13.2 illustrates how color can be used in combination with links. Figure 13.3 shows an example of the hexadecimal technique in action.

Figure 13.2.

On a color screen, this page has a red background, yellow body text, and white link text, as specified in Figure 13.1.

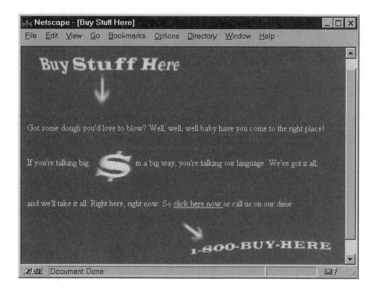

Figure 13.3.

For exact control of colors, you can use hexadecimal color codes instead of English color names.

```
<HTML><HEAD><TITLE>Hi-Ku</TITLE></HEAD>
<BODY BGCOLOR="#400040"
 TEXT="#8080FF" LINK="#FF00FF" VLINK="#FFFFFF">
<H2><I>modern moments</I></H2>
<H3><I>hi-tech haiku</I></H3>
<DIV ALIGN="center"><I>
pick up and you know<BR>
from the pause before the voice<BR>
telemarketer
<P>
CDs never change<BR>
but every time I play one<BR>
it's not quite the same
<P>
traffic jam? no prob<BR>
I've got a cel modem and<BR>
lots of batt life left<P>
</DIV><P ALIGN="right">
<A HREF="http://netletter.com/dicko/hiku.htm">more</A>
</BODY></HTML>
```

To see another handy chart showing the hexadecimal color codes, along with the colors they create, go to

```
http://www.phoenix.net/~jacobson/rgb.html
```

As another example, the custom colors specified in the code for Figure 13.4 appear as a deep indigo background with steel blue text and a fuschia link that turns white after it has been visited.

Figure 13.4.

On a color screen, the background on this page is indigo, with silvery blue as the text color.

Although the colors you specify in the <BODY> tag apply to all text on the page, you can also change the color of a particular word or section of text using the <FONT> tag. This is discussed in Hour 6.

TIME SAVER

You can set the color of an individual link to a different color than the rest by putting a <FONT> tag with a COLOR attribute after the <A HREF>. (Also include a </FONT> tag before the </A> tag.)

Background Graphics

Background graphics are a nice way to add sophistication and color to your sites. However, they should be used sparingly by the newcomer to HTML, because using backgrounds requires design skills that you'll need to gain some experience with first.

It's a good idea to learn how the technique is done, and you should attempt to use background images, even if you use them only sparingly until your confidence and skills increase.

Background images let you specify an image file to be used as the wallpaper tile behind all text and images in a document. You put the image filename after BACKGROUND= in the <BODY> tag like this:

13

```
<BODY BACKGROUND="image.gif">
```

For example, the `tile.gif` file, referred to by the <BODY> tag in Figure 13.5, is an image of one small tile. As you can see in Figure 13.6, most Web browsers will repeat the image like a floor tile, behind any text and images on the page.

Figure 13.5.

You can specify a background image to tile behind a page in the BACKGROUND *attribute of the* <BODY> *tag.*

```
<HTML><HEAD><TITLE>The Tile Room</TITLE></HEAD>
<BODY BACKGROUND="tile.gif" TEXT="red">
<IMG SRC="stall.gif" ALIGN="right">
<H1>Background tiles, text colors,
and transparent graphics
help you set that certain special
<I>ambiance</I> to make each page
like "a room of your own."</H1>
</BODY></HTML>
```

Figure 13.6.

The `tile.gif` *file (specified in Figure 13.5) is automatically repeated to cover the entire page.*

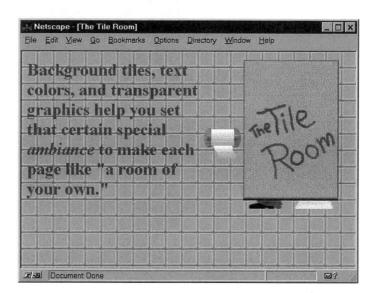

Once again, tiled background images should be implemented with great care in order to avoid distracting from the main content of the page itself. The text in Figure 13.6, for example, would be difficult to read if I hadn't made it all a big <H1> heading—which really isn't as esthetically pleasing a page as I could have created without the background. Many pages on the Web are almost impossible to read due to overdone backgrounds.

So, before you include your company logo or baby pictures as wallpaper behind your Web pages, stop and think. If you had an important message to send someone on a piece of paper, would you write it over the top of the letterhead logo or on the blank part of the page? Backgrounds should be like fine papers: attractive, yet unobtrusive.

13

The astute observer of Figure 13.6 will notice that the background tiles show through portions of the rectangular image. You'll often want to use transparent images to make nonrectangular graphics look good over any background color or background image tile. You might want to refer to Hour 10, "Creating Web Page Images," where you learned how to create transparent images using Paint Shop Pro.

Figure 13.7 shows the image from Figure 13.6, as it looked in Paint Shop Pro when I created it. (Figure 13.7 also shows the single tile used for the background in Figure 13.6.)

Figure 13.7.

When I saved this image in Paint Shop Pro, I made the background color transparent.

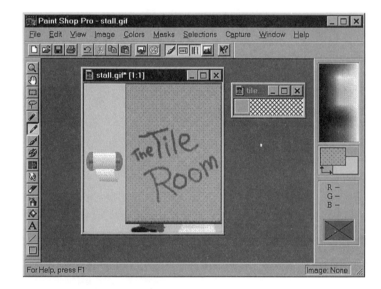

Creating Your Own Backgrounds

Any GIF or JPEG image can be used as a background tile, but pages look best when the top edge of a background tile seamlessly matches the bottom edge and the left edge matches up with the right.

If you're clever and have some time to spend on it, you can make any image into a seamless tile by meticulously touching up the graphic's edges.

Paint Shop Pro provides a much easier way to automatically make any texture into a seamless tile: You simply use the rectangular selection tool to choose the area you want to make into a tile, and then select Image | Special Effects | Create Seamless Pattern. Paint Shop Pro crops the image and uses a sophisticated automatic procedure to overlay and blur together opposite sides of the image.

In Figure 13.8, I did this with part of an image of the palm of my hand, taken with an inexpensive digital camera. The resulting tile, shown as the background of a Web page in Figure 13.9, tiles seamlessly but has the flesh tone and texture of human skin.

Figure 13.8.

Paint Shop Pro can automatically take any region of an image and make it into a background pattern that can be easily made into tiles.

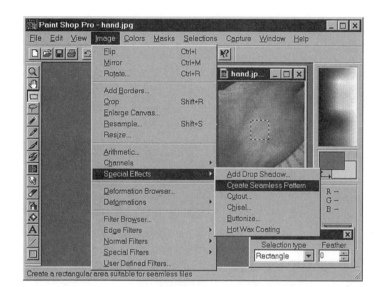

Figure 13.9.

The results of Figure 13.8 used as a background image for a Web page.

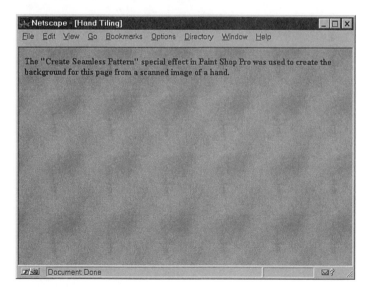

You'll find similar features in other graphics programs, including Photoshop (use Filter | Other | Offset with Wrap turned on), Kai's Power Tools, and the Macintosh programs Mordant and Tilery.

To Do

Here are some tips for making your own background tiles with Paint Shop Pro:

- ☐ If you have a scanner or digital camera, try using some textures from around the house or office, such as the top of a wooden desk, leaves of houseplants, or clothing.

- ☐ When you select an area to make into a tile, try to choose a part of the image that is fairly uniform in brightness from side to side. Otherwise, the tile may not look seamless even after you use the Create Seamless Pattern option.

- ☐ You must also use a big enough image so that you can leave at least the width and height of the tile on either side of your selection. If you don't, when you select Create Seamless Pattern, you'll get a message saying Your selection is too close to the edge to complete this operation.

- ☐ You can also make some almost-automatic textures with the paper texture feature in the Paintbrush Style palette in Paint Shop Pro. Selecting Image | Special Filters | Add Noise followed by Image | Normal Filters | Blur and Colors | Colorize can make great paper textures, too.

Background Resources

If you just cannot seem to get the pattern you want, there are hundreds of sites on the Internet that offer public-domain background images that are free to use, or inexpensive professionally designed backgrounds.

A good starting place is Textureland at

`http://www.meat.com/textures/`

If you happen to see a background image on someone else's page that you wish you could use on your page, it is a simple matter to click on the background with the right-mouse button and select Save Background As to save a copy of it. Be careful, though, to ask the person who created the image if you can use it, because the image could very well be copyrighted or legally protected in some other way.

COFFEE BREAK

You'll see an unconventional use of background tiling at the newly wallpapered 24-Hour HTML Café:

`http://www.mcp.com/sites/1-57521/1-57521-366-4/`

13

You'll also find a selection of snazzy backgrounds you can use for your own pages at the Background Underground lounge:

`http://www.mcp.com/sites/1-57521/1-57521-366-4/`

While you're checking out the backgrounds, you'll get an animated appetizer hot from Hour 12, "Creating Animated Graphics."

Summary

In this hour, you learned how to set the background and text colors for a Web page. You also found out how to make a tiled background image appear behind a Web page, how to make foreground images partially transparent so the background shows through, and how to create seamless image tiles for use as backgrounds.

Table 13.1 summarizes the attributes of the `<BODY>` tag discussed in this hour.

Table 13.1. Attributes of the `<BODY>` tag.

Tag	Attribute	Function
`<BODY>...</BODY>`		Encloses the body (text and tags) of the HTML document.
	`BACKGROUND="..."`	The name or address of the image to tile on the page background.
	`BGCOLOR="..."`	The color of the page's background.
	`TEXT="..."`	The color of the page's text.
	`LINK="..."`	The color of links that have not been followed.
	`ALINK="..."`	The color of activated links.
	`VLINK="..."`	The color of followed links.

Q&A

Q Doesn't Netscape Navigator let people choose their own background and text color preferences?

A Yes, and so does Microsoft Internet Explorer. Both programs allow users to override the colors you (as a Web page author) specify. So some may see your white-on-blue page as green-on-white, or their own favorite colors, instead. But very few people turn on the overriding document option, Always use my colors, so the colors specified in the <BODY> tag will usually be seen.

Q Can older versions of Web browsers see my custom colors and background tiles?

A Some won't. Users of Mosaic will see only gray backgrounds. Early versions of Netscape Navigator (before 2.0) will display hexadecimal-coded colors, but won't recognize color names. However, everything will look right in Netscape Navigator 2.0 or higher and in Microsoft Internet Explorer version 2.0 or higher.

Quiz

Questions

1. How would you give a Web page a black background and make all text, including links, bright green?

2. How would you make an image file named texture.jpg appear as a background tile? Would the image appear on a Web page with white text and red links that turn blue after being followed?

3. If elephant.jpg is a JPEG image of an elephant standing in front of a solid white backdrop, how do you make the backdrop transparent so only the elephant shows on a Web page?

4. Which menu choice in Paint Shop Pro automatically creates a background tile from part of any image?

Answers

1. Put the following at the beginning of the Web page:

   ```
   <BODY BGCOLOR="black"
   TEXT="lime" LINK="lime" VLINK="lime" ALINK="black">
   ```

   The following would do the same thing:

   ```
   <BODY BGCOLOR="#000000"
   TEXT="#00FF00" LINK="#00FF00" VLINK="#00FF00" ALINK="#000000">
   ```

2. ```
   <BODY BACKGROUND="texture.jpg"
   TEXT="white" LINK="red" VLINK="blue" ALINK="black">
   ```

3. Open the image in Paint Shop Pro, then use Colors | Decrease Color Depth | 256 Colors to pick the best 256 colors for the image. Right-click on the white area, and use File | Save As to save it in the GIF 89a format. Click the Options button to make the background color transparent before you save.
   ```

4. Click Image | Special Effects | Create Seamless Pattern. See the Paint Shop Pro documentation if you need a little more help using it than this hour provided.

Activities

☐ Begin adding the full <BODY> tag arguments to your pages, including colors for background, text, and link options.

☐ Try getting creative with some background tiles that don't use Create Seamless Pattern. I bet you can figure out some interesting ones on your own right now. (Hint: What if you made a background tile 2,000 pixels wide and 10 pixels tall?)

13

Hour 14

Page Design and Layout

You've learned in earlier hours how to create Web pages with text and images on them. This hour goes a step further by showing you some HTML tricks to control the spaces between your text and images.

In this hour, you'll learn about

- ☐ Little tricks for Web page design
- ☐ Image spacing and borders
- ☐ Using background images as design elements
- ☐ Using horizontal rules

The tricks presented in this section are essential for making your pages attractive and easy to read. This hour also provides practical advice to help you design attractive and highly readable pages even if you're not a professional graphics designer.

Bear in mind that Web page design is much more detailed than I can write about in a single hour. This hour simply provides some clever guidelines to help improve the look and feel of your pages.

If Web page design interests you, check out *Laura Lemay's Guide to Sizzling Web Site Design* by Molly E. Holzschlag, published by Sams.net. This book offers hot tips and plenty of inspiration for those drawn to design.

To Do

To Do

The techniques covered in this hour are intended to help you make pages you've already created better and faster. So select some of the most important or impressive pages that you've made to date, and try to see whether you can make them look even better.

Before you begin, consider the following:

☐ Choose pages with some graphics on them, because almost all the tricks in this hour involve images.

☐ If you have a page that you think might especially benefit from a creative layout or unique background, start with that one.

☐ You might have some text and images that you haven't gotten around to putting on a Web page yet. If so, this hour can help those new pages become your best yet.

To begin, copy the pages you select into their own directory folder, and play with new design possibilities for them as you read through this hour.

Web Page Design Tips

So far, this book has focused mostly on the exact mechanics of Web page creation. But before getting into the nitty-gritty of spacing and layout tricks, you should take a moment now to step back and think about the overall visual design of your Web pages. Now that you know basic HTML, you need to learn how to apply it wisely.

Every aspect of a Web page should reflect the goals that led you to create the page in the first place. Not only should the text and graphics themselves communicate your message, but the way you fit those elements together can itself make an enormous impact on readers' perceptions of you or your company.

Table 14.1 is a checklist to help you think about the key design elements of a Web page. You should aim for most of your pages to meet the recommendations in this table, although some individual pages will undoubtedly need to break the rules.

Table 14.1. Key elements of Web page design.

Things to Consider	Suggested Guidelines
Text Content	From 100–500 words per page.
Text Breaks	A headline, rule, or image every 40–100 words (except in long articles or stories).
Page Length	Two to four screens (at 640×480 resolution).
File Size	No more than 65KB per page, including images. Some designers can and do get away with more, but you should aim for less—about 45KB per page.
Speed	Have the first screen of text and key images appear in about 10 seconds over a 14.4Kbps modem.
Colors	Have two to four thematic colors be dominant.
Fonts	Have no more than three fonts in graphics and text total.
White Space	The background should show on at least 75% of the page.
Contrast	No color in the background should be close to text color, and background graphics should be used minimally, if at all.
Tone and Style	All text and graphics should be consistent in mood and theme.
Overall Impact	The page as a whole should appear balanced and attractive.

Most of the tips in this table are common to any page design, on paper or electronic. But some of them are particularly tricky to control on Web pages.

The next section of this hour presents some HTML commands for handling the white space (which can actually be any color) and overall visual impact of your pages. The hour wraps up with some techniques for meeting the speed requirements of today's Web, even when you use relatively large images.

Image Spacing and Borders

Figures 14.1 through 14.3 show the HTML text, images, and final appearance of a well-designed Web page. This page meets all the criteria outlined in Table 14.1.

14

Figure 14.1.

This page uses several techniques for adding space between images and text, including block quotes and image alignment.

```
<DIV ALIGN=CENTER>
<IMG SRC="wellhead.gif" ALT="Wellman Header Graphic">
</DIV>

<BLOCKQUOTE>
Mark Wellman has inspired millions across the country and throughout the
world. His courage and dtermination have been acclaimed on national
television, congressional commendation, and meetings with two presidents of
the United States.

<P>
<IMG SRC="bush.jpg" ALT="With President Bush" WIDTH=180 HEIGHT=129 HSPACE=10
BORDER=0 ALIGN=RIGHT>

<BR CLEAR="LEFT">

As author of the book, <B>Climbing Back</B>, and the first paraplegic to climb
El Capitan, Mark is a pioneering force in the disabled freedom movement. But
his message is not just for the phisically challenged, it's for everyone with
difficult problems in their everyday lives.
</BLOCKQUOTE>
```

Figure 14.2.

The image files for the page. Notice the margins and white space the HTML creates.

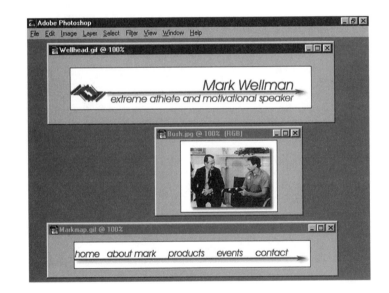

Notice the generous amount of space between images and paragraphs in Figure 14.3. Web browsers tend to crowd everything together, but you can easily add space in three different ways:

☐ When you wrap text around an image using `<IMG ALIGN="right">` or `<IMG ALIGN="left">`, you can skip down past the bottom of that image at any time with `<BR CLEAR="right">` or `<BR CLEAR="left">`. If you have images on both the right and left, you can type `<BR CLEAR"all">` to go past both of them.

☐ You can add extra space on the left and right sides of any image with `<IMG HSPACE>`. To add space on the top and bottom sides, use `<IMG VSPACE>`. For example, each image in Figure 14.3 has 20 pixels of blank space to the left and right of it. This is because each `<IMG>` tag in Figure 14.1 includes the attribute `HSPACE=10`.

14

Figure 14.3.

Thanks to generous spacing and a carefully premeditated layout, the HTML in Figure 14.1 looks great as a Web page.

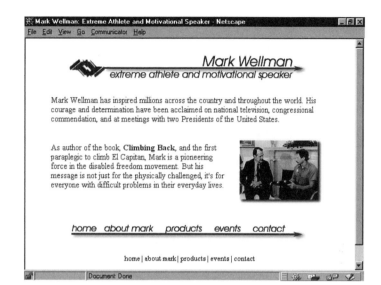

☐ Use the `<blockquote>` tag to gain margins. This ensures that your content doesn't run from end to end.

The `<IMG>` tags in Figure 14.1 also include a `BORDER=0` attribute, which eliminates the rectangular border around the images. The border is normally 1 pixel thick for any image inside an `<A>` link, but `BORDER=0` removes the border altogether. This creates a smooth relationship between the graphics and the text, taking out the visual constraints of a border. This is especially handy with transparent images, which often look funny with a rectangle around them.

Using Background Images as Design Elements

I'm sure you've seen designs where background graphics have been used cleverly to design the page. Figure 14.4 is an example of this. The site uses a left-margin background created by the background and combined with table layout to achieve the overall design. I touch on tables in Hour 16, "Advanced Layout with Tables," but overall this is a sophisticated technique. I wanted to introduce it here so you would know what it is you're seeing when encountering these designs.

14

Figure 14.4.

This page's design uses a background to achieve the left margin and tables to control the layout.

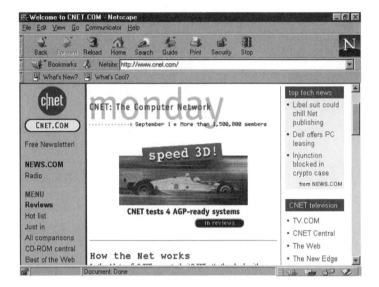

The same background techniques can be used to create bleeds off the edge of the page. By making a large image that is mostly white or another neutral background color and making that image run off the edge of the graphic (and thereby, the edge of the page) you can achieve very interesting effects similar to the typography you see in popular magazines. Top left is the easiest place to put a bleed, because it's very hard to control the actual pixel width and height of the page across browsers. The top left is the most stable point of a page.

Customizing Horizontal Rules

Horizontal rules are terribly overused, but they can be used well with a light touch. Figure 14.5 shows a nice use of horizontal rules, whereas Figure 14.6 overuses them.

There are several kinds of horizontal rules. *Architectural rules* are those that are created with HTML, and *graphic rules* are those that use a graphic to achieve the rule.

14

Figure 14.5.

Note the effective use of a horizontal rule at the bottom of this Web page.

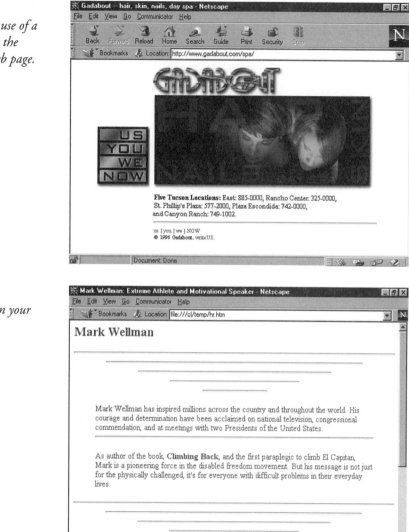

Figure 14.6.

Avoid this effect on your page!

Architectural Rules

The following <HR> tag uses some special attributes to control exactly how a horizontal rule looks:

```
<HR SIZE=10 WIDTH=70% COLOR="green">
```

The vertical size of the rule is set with the SIZE attribute. The number value in this attribute should be equal to the height in pixels that you want the line to be. For example, <HR SIZE=1> will be a single-pixel "hairline" rule, whereas <HR SIZE=5> will be a wider rule.

Normally, horizontal rules span the width of the window. You can override this, however, with the WIDTH attribute, which allows you to specify the size of the line either as a relative percentage or as a precise pixel value. <HR WIDTH=250> draws a 250-pixel-wide line, whereas <HR WIDTH=50%> draws a line halfway across the window, no matter what size the window happens to be.

The SIZE and WIDTH attributes together turn the <HR> attribute into a useful tool for drawing any size rectangle you choose.

JUST A MINUTE

> It's the COLOR attribute that causes some disagreement between Netscape Navigator and Microsoft Internet Explorer. Navigator ignores it completely, and renders the rule as a transparent, three-dimensional indentation. Internet Explorer, however, obediently colors the rule solid green. Feel free to specify a COLOR attribute for any rule you draw, but keep in mind that only Internet Explorer users will see it.

Graphics Rules

If the rule color is important to your page layout, you might be better off using an ordinary GIF graphic element to simulate a rule. If you make the image fairly small and relatively narrow, say 3×300 pixels, it won't get in the way for most browser window widths.

You can also use small horizontal bars placed closely next to one another. One popular use of this technique is to create a "button bar" for navigation (see Figure 14.7). The best place to put such an element is at the very top of the screen so it can be most easily seen by people while your page is loading. You didn't forget to include the HEIGHT and WIDTH attributes, did you?

Figure 14.7.

Thin, side-by-side images create this navigation bar at the top of the page.

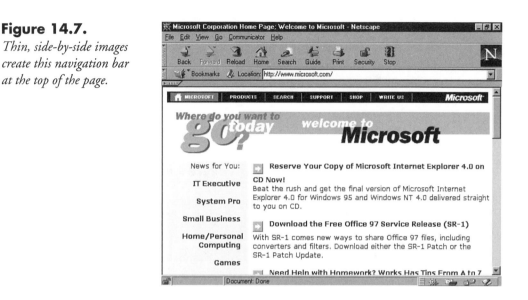

And, of course, you can use larger images to create the more decorative rules, consisting of birds on telephone wires and the like, that I'm sure you've seen on the Web.

JUST A MINUTE

You can use ALIGN="left" or ALIGN="right" in the <HR> tag, too. Horizontal rules are also affected by <DIV ALIGN="right"> and <DIV ALIGN="left">.

If you use rules, be aware that they can break up the overall appearance of the page and give it an old-fashioned look. Modern design usually uses white space and images to set off portions of the page. Nevertheless, rules are appropriate when used sparingly, and can add a bit of panache to your pages when used with a fine eye for overall effect.

COFFEE BREAK

The spacing and layout tricks in this hour provide that certain extra something to the ever-expanding 24-Hour HTML Cafe´:

http://www.mcp.com/sites/1-57521/1-57521-366-4/

I've also added some links from that page to especially well-designed sites to inspire your own efforts.

14

Summary

This hour provides some guidelines for designing attractive, highly readable Web pages. It also explains how to create and control blank space on your pages, eliminate borders from images, and draw customized rectangles and rules. You also saw how backgrounds can be used as a page layout device.

Table 14.2 summarizes the tags and attributes discussed in this hour.

Table 14.2. HTML tags and attributes covered in this hour.

Tag	Attribute	Function
`<IMG>`		Inserts an inline image into the document.
	`SRC="..."`	The address of the image.
	`ALIGN="..."`	Determines the alignment of the given image (see Hour 9, "Putting Images on a Web Page").
	`VSPACE="..."`	The space between the image and the text above or below it.
	`HSPACE="..."`	The space between the image and the text to its left and/or right.
	`WIDTH="..."`	The width, in pixels, of the image. If WIDTH is not the actual width, the image is scaled to fit.
	`HEIGHT="..."`	The height, in pixels, of the image. If HEIGHT is not the actual height, the image is scaled to fit.
	`BORDER="..."`	Draws a border of the specified value in pixels to be drawn around the image. If the images are also links, BORDER changes the size of the default link border.
` `		A line break.
	`CLEAR="..."`	Causes the text to stop flowing around any images. Possible values are RIGHT, LEFT, and ALL.
`<HR>`		A horizontal rule.
	`SIZE="..."`	The thickness of the rule, in pixels.
	`WIDTH="..."`	The width of the rule, in pixels or as a percentage of the document width.
	`ALIGN="..."`	How the rule will be aligned on the page. Possible values are LEFT, RIGHT, and CENTER.
	`COLOR="..."`	The color of the horizontal rule (Microsoft Internet Explorer only).

Q&A

Q I'd like to know exactly how wide the margins of a page are so I can line up my background and foreground images the way I want.

A Unfortunately, different browsers (and even the same browser on different types of computers) leave different amounts of space along the top and left side of a page, so you can't precisely line up foreground graphics with background images. Generally, you can expect the top and left margins to be 8 to 12 pixels.

Q I've seen pages on the Web with multiple columns of text, wide margins, and other types of nice layouts you didn't discuss. How were those pages made?

A Probably with the HTML table tags, which are discussed in Hour 16.

Quiz

Questions

1. How would you wrap text around the right side of an image, leaving 40 pixels of space between the image and the text?

2. How could you insert exactly 80 pixels of blank space between two paragraphs of text?

3. How would you write the HTML to draw a rule 20 pixels wide?

4. If you have a circular button that links to another page, how do you prevent a rectangle from appearing around it?

Answers

1. `<IMG SRC="myimage.gif" HSPACE=40 VSPACE=40 ALIGN="left">Text goes here.`

2. Create a small image that is all one color, and save it as `nothing.gif` with that color set to be transparent. Then put the following tag between the two paragraphs of text:

   `<IMG SRC="nothing.gif" WIDTH=1 HEIGHT=80>`

3. `<HR WIDTH=20>`.

4. Use the `BORDER=0` attribute, like this:

   `<A HREF="another_page.htm"><IMG SRC="circle.gif" BORDER=0></A>`

Activities

☐ Try creating a page with the wildest layout you can manage with the HTML tags you've learned so far. If you're resourceful, you should be able to create a staggered diagonal line of images, or place short sentences of text almost anywhere on the page.

14

Hour **15**

Image Maps

If you've read Hour 9, "Putting Images on a Web Page," you know how to make an image link to another document. (If you don't quite recall how to do it right now, it looks like this: `<A HREF="gohere.htm"><IMG SRC="image.gif"></A>`.) There are more powerful ways to use images than a simple link like this.

In this hour, you'll learn about

☐ When a picture is worth 1,000 words

☐ Making sense of images

☐ Client-side image maps: rectangular and non-rectangular regions

☐ Server-side image maps

☐ Combined client-side/server-side image maps

When a Picture Is Worth 1,000 Words

How many times have you grabbed pencil and paper to explain a complex idea by drawing a picture of it so you could point to the part you're talking about? Pictures transcend language barriers and avoid the issues of ambiguous terminology. Some navigational choices are so hard to describe in words that drawing a picture is the easiest way to handle the job, and HTML provides quite a few tools for getting a lot of information out of pictures.

You can subdivide an image into regions that link to different documents, depending on where someone clicks. This is called an *image map*, and any image can be made into an image map. A Web site with medical information might show an image of the human body and bring up different pages of advice for each body part, for example, or a map of the world could allow people to click on any country for regional information.

Many people use image maps to create a "navigation bar" that integrates icons for each page on their Web site into one cohesive image map.

Netscape Navigator and Microsoft Internet Explorer allow you to choose among several different methods for implementing image maps. Nowadays, all your image maps should probably be created using the latest method, which is called a client-side image map.

New Term   A *client-side* image map is a map that relies on the browser to interpret the map's defined, or "hot," areas. The old method, *server-side* maps, requested that information from the server, making the process take longer and making it less stable.

It's important to remember that some people can't or don't want to use image maps at all, for one reason or another, and you should always make available an alternate method of navigation on any page that uses them. Not only is it considerate toward persons with vision problems and those who surf with images turned off, but do you really want to prevent people from accessing your page because they don't have the latest browser?

For most sites, anyone should be welcome. For commercial sites, the potential of creating a customer far outweighs the battle about which browser is the best or which features you've "just got to have" to be "with it."

To sum it up: An image map is an image on a Web page that leads to two or more different links, depending on which part of the image someone clicks. Modern graphical Web browsers can use client-side image maps, but you can also create server-side image maps for compatibility with old browsers. Finally, you should always provide alternative textual navigation elements, even when the image map is easier to use, flashier, and just plain cooler.

Making Sense of Images

Unfortunately, computers aren't smart enough to look at a picture and understand it, so you need to have some way of telling them what part of the picture you're pointing at. You do this is by giving it the geometric coordinates of each significant region you want to use.

To make any type of image map, therefore, you'll need to figure out the numerical pixel coordinates of each region within the image that you want to be a clickable link. An easy way to do this is to open the image with Paint Shop Pro and watch the coordinates at the bottom of the screen as you use the rectangle selection tool to select a rectangular region of the image (see Figure 15.1). When the mouse button is down, the coordinates at the bottom of the screen show both the top-left and bottom-right corners of the rectangle, instead of just a single x,y position as shown here. Although client-side image maps can make use of non-rectangular regions, rectangles are common to all versions of both types of maps, so if your image can be described as rectanguler you'll be able to use either system.

Figure 15.1.

Paint Shop Pro can easily tell you the coordinates for image map regions so you don't have to muck about with special image-mapping utilities.

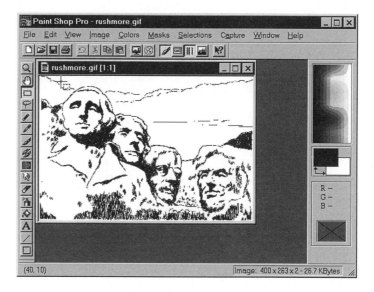

JUST A MINUTE

There are fancy programs that let you highlight a rectangle with your mouse and automatically spew out image map coordinates into a file, but they are rather cumbersome to use. You'll save the most time by ignoring the "time saver" programs and just locating the pixel coordinates in Paint Shop Pro or your favorite general-purpose graphics program.

You could use the image in Figure 15.1 as an image map, linking to four Web pages about the presidents immortalized on Mount Rushmore. To do so, first jot down the pixel coordinates of the top-left and bottom-right corners of each rectangular region shown in Figure 15.2. Just write the coordinates on a piece of paper for now; you'll see exactly how to put them into an HTML file momentarily.

Figure 15.2.

You don't have to draw anything that looks like this. I just made it to show you which regions in Figure 15.1 will become clickable links.

The coordinates are

    George Washington (region 1): 40,10 to 130,130
    Thomas Jefferson (region 2): 130,60 to 200,170
    Teddy Roosevelt (region 3): 201,120 to 270,240
    Abraham Lincoln (region 4): 280,120 to 380,250

To Do

You can take an image of your own and turn it into an image map as you read the following explanation:

1. For starters, choose a fairly large image that is visually divided into roughly rectangular regions.

2. If you don't have a suitable image handy, use Paint Shop Pro (or your favorite graphics program) to make one. One easy and useful idea is to put a word or icon for each of your important pages together into a button bar or signpost.

15

Creating Client-Side Image Maps

Once you have the coordinates written down, you're ready to create an HTML image map. Just after the <BODY> tag in your Web page, put

```
<MAP NAME="heads">
```

Now you need to type an <AREA> tag for each region of the image. Figure 15.3 shows how you would define the four regions of the Mount Rushmore image.

Figure 15.3.

The <MAP> *and* <AREA> *tags define the regions of an image map.*

```
<HTML><HEAD><TITLE>Mount Rushmore</TITLE></HEAD>
<BODY BGCOLOR="white" TEXT="black" LINK="black" VLINK="black">
<MAP NAME="heads">
<AREA SHAPE="RECT" COORDS="40,10,130,130" HREF="george.htm">
<AREA SHAPE="RECT" COORDS="131,60,200,170" HREF="thomas.htm">
<AREA SHAPE="RECT" COORDS="201,120,270,240" HREF="teddy.htm">
<AREA SHAPE="RECT" COORDS="280,120,380,250" HREF="abraham.htm">
</MAP>
<DIV ALIGN="center">
<H1>The Immortal Presidents</H1>
<IMG SRC="rushmore.gif" WIDTH=400 HEIGHT=263 USEMAP="#heads">
<P><A HREF="george.htm">Washington</A> |
<A HREF="thomas.htm">Jefferson</A> |
<A HREF="teddy.htm">Roosevelt</A> |
<A HREF="abraham.htm">Lincoln</A>
</DIV>
</BODY></HTML>
```

Rectangular Regions

Each <AREA> tag in Figure 15.3 has three attributes:

☐ SHAPE="RECT" indicates that the region is rectangular. You'll see how to create regions with other shapes later in this section.

☐ COORDS="40,10,130,130" gives the top-left and bottom-right corner coordinates for the rectangular region.

☐ HREF="george.htm" specifies the page that clicking on the region will link to. You can use any address or filename that you would use in an ordinary <A HREF> link tag.

After the <AREA> tags, you are finished defining the image map, so you insert a closing </MAP> tag.

To place the actual image map on the page, you use an ordinary <IMG> tag and add a USEMAP attribute:

```
<IMG SRC="rushmore.gif" USEMAP="#heads">
```

Use the name you put in the <MAP> tag (and don't forget the # symbol). In Figure 15.3, I also included WIDTH and HEIGHT attributes, as you should for any image on a Web page.

JUST A MINUTE

It is also possible to put the map definition in a separate file by including that file's name in the USEMAP attribute, like this:

`<IMG SRC="/thisthat.gif" USEMAP="maps.htm#thisthat">`

For instance, if you used the same image map on every page in your Web site, you could just put the <MAP> and <AREA> tags for it on one page instead of repeating it on every single page where it appears.

Figure 15.4 shows the image map in action. Notice that Netscape Navigator displays the link address for whatever region the mouse is moving over at the bottom of the window, just as it does for normal links. If someone clicked where the mouse cursor (the little hand) is shown in Figure 15.4, the page named george.htm would come up.

Figure 15.4.

The image map defined in Figure 15.3 as it appears on the Web page.

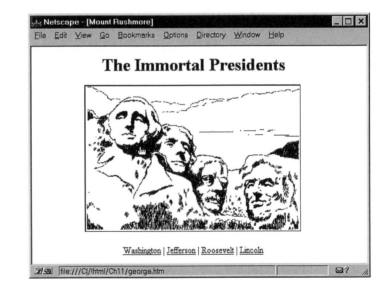

Notice that I included text links on this page that go to the same pages as the image map links do. This allows people who use text-mode and other image map-less Web browsers—or who don't want to wait for the image to finish loading—to access those pages. Remember that

15

there are a significant number of people, even some of those with the latest and greatest versions of half a dozen browsers at their fingertips, who surf with images turned off. Your page will only annoy them if you don't provide alternative navigational elements.

Non-Rectangular Regions

Some images don't lend themselves to being broken up into neat rectangular regions. The image in Figure 15.5, for example, would make a great image map, but the regions you would want to click on couldn't be defined just by specifying the top-left and bottom-right corners.

Figure 15.5.

To divide this image into regions, you need more shapes than just upright rectangles.

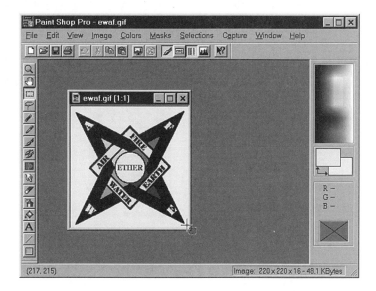

Fortunately, HTML image maps let you create polygonal regions with any number of corners. You can also define circular regions, which would be handy for the ETHER region in Figure 15.5.

I've sketched the clickable regions for this image map in Figure 15.6.

Figure 15.7 shows the HTML to define the actual image map, and Figure 15.8 shows the resulting Web page. To make polygonal regions, use SHAPE="poly" in the <AREA> tag, and put each of the corner points in the COORDS attribute. For circular regions, use SHAPE="circle" and put the center point and radius (in pixels) in the COORDS attribute.

Figure 15.6.

Triangular and circular regions would work much better than rectangular ones for the image in Figure 15.5.

Figure 15.7.

A page defining the image map regions shown in Figure 15.6.

```
<HTML><HEAD><TITLE>The Medieval Elements</TITLE></HEAD>
<BODY BACKGROUND="gradient.jpg">
<MAP NAME="elements">
<AREA SHAPE="poly" COORDS="217,215, 185,84, 109,159"
 HREF="earth.htm">
<AREA SHAPE="poly" COORDS="5,218, 139,185, 64,108"
 HREF="water.htm">
<AREA SHAPE="poly" COORDS="5,7, 33,141, 112,61"
 HREF="air.htm">
<AREA SHAPE="poly" COORDS="216,5, 86,39, 161,109"
 HREF="fire.htm">
<AREA SHAPE="circle" COORDS="111,111,30"
 HREF="ether.htm">
</MAP>
<A HREF="nomaps.htm">
<IMG SRC="ewaf.gif" WIDTH=220 HEIGHT=220
 BORDER=0 ALIGN="right" USEMAP="#elements" ISMAP></A>
<H2>The Medieval Elements</H2>
Scientific knowledge has progressed far beyond
the four "elements" of earth, water, air, and fire as an
explanation of objective physical phenomena.<P>
However, many people still view these four qualities
as essential elements of our subjective inner experience
of the world. Click on one of the elements to the right
to read more about it.
</BODY></HTML>
```

Figure 15.8.

*This is how the image
map in Figure 15.7
appears to a reader about
to click on the AIR link.*

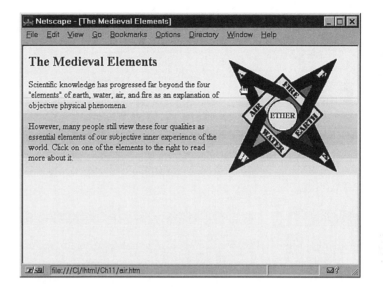

In addition to including text links on the page in Figures 15.7 and 15.8, I used a tricky little attribute of the <IMG> tag called ISMAP. If you put ISMAP in an image tag, you can also put an <A HREF> link around the image. That link will only work for older browsers that don't support client-side image maps. The nomaps.htm file I linked to might lead to a page of text links, or to an alternate entry into your site.

COFFEE BREAK

You can often avoid even the minimal hassle involved in creating an image map by breaking up the map into separate images and simply placing them next to each other on a Web page.

For an example, go to the page at

http://www.mcp.com/sites/1-57521/1-57521-366-4/

The three graphical links at the bottom of that page look like an image map, but they're actually just three regular old images with an <A HREF> tag around each of them. This is much simpler and has the big advantage that it can work with any browser, so if your image breaks up easily into rectangular regions you should consider using this alternative technique.

If you try this yourself, be careful not to put a space or line break between the <IMG> tags, or the images won't meet at the edges.

Wherever you can avoid image maps, do so; individual images are easier to maintain, and you can often use the pieces again in creative and useful ways. (Click on the links at the address I just gave you to see what I mean.)

COFFEE BREAK

I've prepared a little quiz to help you learn how to tell when image maps are necessary and when they aren't. Check it out by clicking on the Pop Quiz icon in the new image map at

`http://www.mcp.com/sites/1-57521/1-57521-366-4/`

Making a Server-Side Image Map

The original way to create an image map is to let the server computer where the Web page resides do all the work, and sometimes you have to do it that way. If the exact position (as opposed to general region) of the pointing device is important, client-side maps just won't do. Nonetheless, for many applications, it's not necessary to bother with server-side image maps anymore because it's easier and just as effective to provide text links for people using browsers that don't support client-side image maps. But there are an awful lot of people out there using these kinds of Web browsers, and it isn't really that hard to make your image maps work for them. Read the following explanation of what's involved and decide for yourself whether it's worth your time to provide server-side image maps.

When the user clicks an image that has been mapped this way, the browser program just sends the x,y coordinates of the mouse pointer's location to a special script on the server. Usually, this script is located in some subdirectory of `cgi-bin` on the server, and the HTML to implement the image map is just a normal anchor link.

```
<A HREF="/cgi-bin/imagemap/thisthat"><IMG SRC="thisthat.gif" ISMAP></A>
```

Simple. But when you install a Web page including such a link, you need to tell the image map script which parts of the image should be associated with which link addresses. This is normally done in a *map file*. Each line in the map file is simply the word `rect` followed by a URL address and two sets of x,y coordinates representing the top-left corner and the bottom-right corner of a region of the image. Some server scripts also support non-rectangular regions with the words `poly` and `circle` (or `round`), but you can't count on it without asking your Webmaster.

The first line in a map file begins with the word `default` followed by the URL address that should be used if the user happens to click outside any rectangular region defined by a `rect` line. A map file named `thisthat.map` might look like this:

```
default /top/this.htm
rect /top/this.htm 0,0,102,99
rect /top/that.htm 103,0,205,99
```

The final step in setting up a server-side image map is telling the image map script which map file to use for which image by adding a line to a system file named `imagemap.conf`. This file will already exist and includes entries for every image map defined on the server. You simply add a line with the name used in the `HREF` attribute of the `<A>` tag, a colon, and then the actual location and name of the associated map file. For example, the location of the map I just described is `HREF="/cgi-bin/imagemap/thisthat"`, and the map file is named `thisthat.map`. If this map file were in a directory named `/mapfiles`, the line in `imagemap.conf` would read

```
thisthat : /mapfiles/thisthat.map
```

All this isn't nearly as difficult as it might sound if you've never set up an image map before, but it can be a hassle, especially if your pages reside on somebody else's server and you don't have the rights to modify system files such as `imagemap.conf` yourself. What's worse, server-side image maps don't work at all on Web pages located on your hard drive, a CD-ROM, or most local networks.

There are also some variations in the exact syntax for image map implementation, depending on the software installed on your server, so if you move your pages to a different server, the image maps might not work anymore.

Fortunately, the latest versions of all the major browsers support the client-side image maps discussed earlier in this hour, where the association of links with specific regions in an image is handled by the browser itself instead of by a server script. This means that you can include image maps in your HTML files without imposing an additional burden on your Internet service provider's server, and you can be more certain that they will be processed correctly and dependably.

Combined Client-Side/Server-Side Image Maps

There is a way for you to provide client-side image maps that automatically switch to server-side image maps if the user's browser doesn't support client-side maps. With a single line of code, you can allow an image map to be interpreted either by the end user's software or by the server by including the `ISMAP` attribute in the `<IMG>` tag, and then including both a `USEMAP=` attribute and a `cgi-bin/imagemap` reference:

```
<MAP "#thisthat">
<AREA SHAPE="rect" COORDS="0,0,102,99" HREF="this.htm">
<AREA SHAPE="rect" COORDS="103,0,205,99" HREF="that.htm"></MAP>
<A HREF="/cgi-bin/imagemap/thisthat">
<IMG SRC="thisthat.gif" USEMAP="#thisthat" ISMAP></A>
```

Here, as with any unrecognized tag, browsers that don't support client-side image maps will simply ignore the <USEMAP> and <ISMAP> tags and treat the preceding code like an old-fashioned server-side image map.

Summary

This hour explains how to create image maps—links that lead to more than one place, depending on where you click on the image. You saw how to define rectangular and circular link regions within an image, as well as irregularly shaped polygonal regions. You also learned to provide an alternate navigation method for people using browsers that don't support the image map standard. Finally, you got a quick rundown on providing server-side image maps on most types of Web servers so that you can provide the best possible experience for all your users.

Table 15.1 is a summary of the tags and attributes covered in this hour.

Table 15.1. HTML tags and attributes covered in this hour.

Tag	Attribute	Function
<IMG>		Inserts an image into the document.
	ISMAP	This image is a clickable image map.
	SRC="..."	The URL of the image.
	USEMAP="..."	The name of an image map specification for client-side image mapping. Used with <MAP> and <AREA>.
<MAP>...</MAP>		A client-side image map, referenced by <IMG USEMAP="...">. Includes one or more <AREA> tags.
<AREA>		Defines a clickable link within a client-side image map.
	SHAPE="..."	The shape of the clickable area. Currently, rect, poly, and circle (or round) are the valid options.
	COORDS="..."	The left, top, right, and bottom coordinates of the clickable region within an image.
	HREF="..."	The URL that should be loaded when the area is clicked.

15

Q&A

Q I'd like to know exactly which browsers support client-side image maps and which ones support server-side image maps.

A All browsers that display graphics support server-side image maps. All versions of Netscape Navigator and Microsoft Internet Explorer since version 2.0 also support client-side image maps. Any other Web browser produced after 1995 probably supports client-side image maps, too.

Q My image maps with polygonal and circular regions don't seem to work correctly in Netscape 2.0. Why?

A Netscape Navigator version 2.0 and Microsoft Internet Explorer version 2.0 support only rectangular regions in client-side image maps. Only people using version 3.0 or later of these browsers will be able to click on non-rectangular regions.

Q I don't have Paint Shop Pro, and my graphics software doesn't tell me x,y coordinates. How do I figure out the coordinates for my image maps?

A Here's a sneaky way to do it using Netscape Navigator. Put the image on a page with the ISMAP attribute and an `<A>` tag around it, like this:

```
<A HREF="nowhere"><IMG SRC="myimage.gif" ISMAP></A>
```

When you view that page with Navigator, move the mouse over the image. You will see the coordinates in the message box at the bottom of the window.

Quiz

Questions

1. You have a 200×200-pixel image named `quarters.gif` for your Web page. When someone clicks in the top-left quarter of the image, you want him to get a page named `toplft.htm`. When he clicks on the top-right quarter, he should get `toprgt.htm`. Clicking in the bottom left should bring up `btmlft.htm`, and the bottom right should lead to `btmrgt.htm`. Write the HTML to implement this as a client-side image map.

2. If you wanted people using older browsers that don't support client-side image maps to get a page named `oldies.htm` when they click on any part of the image map, how would you modify the HTML you wrote for question 1?

3. How could you implement the effect described in question 1 without using image maps at all?

Answers

1.
```
<MAP NAME="quartersmap">
<AREA SHAPE="rect" COORDS="0,0,99,99" HREF="toplft.htm">
<AREA SHAPE="rect" COORDS="100,0,199,99" HREF="toprgt.htm">
<AREA SHAPE="rect" COORDS="0,100,99,199" HREF="btmlft.htm">
<AREA SHAPE="rect" COORDS="100,100,199,199" HREF="btmrgt.htm">
</MAP>
<IMG SRC="quarters.gif" WIDTH=200 HEIGHT=200
 USEMAP="#quartersmap">
```

2. Replace the <IMG> tag with

```
A HREF="oldies.htm">
<IMG SRC="quarters.gif WIDTH=200 HEIGHT=200 ISMAP
 USEMAP="#quartersmap"></A>
```

3. Use a graphics program such as Paint Shop Pro to chop the image into quarters, and save them as separate images named toplft.gif, toprgt.gif, btmlft.gif, and btmrgt.gif. Then type

```
<A HREF="toplft.htm"><IMG SRC="toplft.gif" WIDTH=100 HEIGHT=100 BORDER=0></
A><A
HREF="toprgt.htm"><IMG SRC="toprgt.gif"
WIDTH=100 HEIGHT=100 BORDER=0></A><BR>
<A HREF="btmlft.htm"><IMG SRC="btmlft.gif"
WIDTH=100 HEIGHT=100 BORDER=0></A><A
HREF="btmrgt.htm"><IMG SRC="btmrgt.gif"
WIDTH=100 HEIGHT=100 BORDER=0></A>
```

(Be careful to break the lines of the HTML inside the tags as shown above, to avoid introducing any spaces between the images.)

Activities

☐ If you have some pages containing short lists of links, see if you can cook up an interesting image map to use instead.

☐ Image maps are usually more engaging and attractive than a row of repetitive-looking icons or buttons. Can you come up with a visual metaphor related to your site that would make it easier—and maybe more fun—for people to navigate through your pages?

15

Hour 16

Advanced Layout with Tables

One of the most powerful tools for creative Web page design is the table, which allows you to arrange text and images into multiple columns and rows. This hour shows you how to build HTML tables and to control the spacing, layout, and appearance of the tables you create.

In this hour, you'll learn about

- ☐ Arranging pages
- ☐ Layout design
- ☐ The mechanics of table layout:
  - Table size
  - Alignment and spanning
  - Backgrounds and spacing
  - Nested tables
- ☐ Beyond tables: accessibility and the Web

Arranging Pages

Everything you read has structure to it, from the boring regimentation of a grocery list or a telephone book to the fresh and exciting pages of the latest, most hip magazine on your coffee table.

Okay, you know you could probably get the effect of a grocery list using HTML without too much trouble but how can you make your pages look sleek and elegant, the way the high fashion magazines do? Of course there's a secret to it. If you use HTML the way the original designers thought of it, the best you'll ever be able to do is create something that looks like a research paper, the digital equivalent of a dull typewritten page. That's just not good enough.

Graphic designers go to school for years to learn the straight dope on this, and you'll be learning this lesson in an hour, so pay close attention. The secret to getting and keeping the reader's interest is to keep the reader off balance, but not too much.

What?!! That's it? What about clear and informative? What does keeping people a little off balance have to do with that? Well, people love to be informed and we graphic arts people love to inform them but, like the farmer said who knocked his mule in the head with a two by four, you've got to get their attention first.

Symmetry is boring, plain and simple. It's great for those times when you're reading to extract a tiny bit of information from a swamp of data, such as when you look up a name in a phone book. In that case, symmetry works for you and the straightforward method of using neat little tables for data works fine. People are very good at seeing breaks in a pattern and the orderly progression of letters makes a pattern that causes the name you're looking for to jump out at you when you see it. However, few people read phone books for pleasure.

Many of the tricks of the graphic arts trade, when it comes right down to it, are ways to introduce little bits of asymmetry onto the page, from the line indentations of paragraphs to the drop caps, pull quotes, and asymmetric column layouts of your favorite magazine. Take out a popular magazine and really look at it. Most popular magazines take the page space available and break it down to a piece that is $1/3$ of the total and another $2/3$ of the total. Then, the designers switch the smaller half from side to side every so often and insert pictures and other elements and ratios to make it look less orderly than it really is. They often call it "movement," but we know now what it really is—a small inclination to the left or right that makes it look like the page elements might be going somewhere.

Tables help you break up the typographical space on your page so that you can attract people's attention and keep their interest just like the trendier magazines do. You can use the defined space on the page to lay out your information in ways that look a little off balance, but not wacky enough to confuse people. You can also use tables to impose strict order when you have

16

a problem that looks like a grocery list or telephone book, or when you want to convince people that you're stolid, upright, and boring, like a banker or stockbroker.

Thinking About Page Layout

Page layout is the organization of text and graphics on the page in a visually pleasing way that helps attract and hold the attention of the reader so that your message can be understood. A table is an arrangement of text and/or graphics into vertical columns and horizontal rows. As it happens, the human eye and brain are designed to easily grasp information arranged in horizontal or vertical lines so tables are almost ideal for all kinds of layouts.

16

To Do

To Do

As you read this hour, think about how arranging text into tables could benefit your Web pages. Here are some specific ideas to keep in mind:

☐ Of course, the most obvious application of tables is to organize tabular informa-tion, such as a multicolumn list of names and numbers. This is probably the least interesting as well, although it is very handy for that task and we will learn how to do this first.

☐ If you want more complex relationships between text and graphics than `<IMG ALIGN="left">` or `<IMG ALIGN="right">` can provide, tables can probably do it.

☐ Tables can be used to draw borders around text or around several graphics images, although this idea is overused on the Web and should probably be avoided as a rule. There is a wonderful book called *Visualizing Information* by Edward Tufte, in which he identifies most borders as "chart junk." He cautions creators of charts and tables to be subtle and not to overwhelm the eye but to help it. Borders are hardly subtle.

☐ Tables can be used to make subtle (or obvious) distinctions in background color that help the eye notice exceptions or keep track of large blocks of data.

☐ Whenever you need multiple columns of text, whether asymmetrical or not, tables are one answer.

For each of your pages that meets one of these criteria, try adding a table modeled after the examples in this hour. The "Activities" section at the end of this hour offers a couple of detailed suggestions along these lines, as well.

The Mechanics of Table Layout

To make tables, you have to start with a `<TABLE>` tag. Of course, you have to end your tables with the `</TABLE>` tag. If you want the table to have a border, which you rarely should, use a BORDER attribute to specify the width of the border in pixels. A border size of 0 will make the border invisible, which should be your own default choice when you are using a table as a page layout tool. Leaving the BORDER attribute out entirely also turns off borders, but space can be left on the page as if borders were present, which is not usually a good idea. For the examples in this hour, leave borders on so you can see what you're doing. However, in almost all cases you should turn them off before using tables on a production page.

There are a number of optional attributes you can specify in the <TABLE> tag, but these are discussed after you get the basics under your belt.

With the <TABLE> tag in place, the next thing you need is the <TR> tag. <TR> creates a table row, which contains one or more cells of information. To create these individual cells, use the <TD> tag. <TD> stands for table data; you place the table information after the <TD> tag.

In addition to <TABLE>, <TR>, and <TD>, there is a fourth tag, <TH>. It is used exactly like <TD>, and it identifies the cell as part of the heading of the table.

JUST A MINUTE

Because there was no visible difference between the <TD> and <TH> cells in some older browsers, many short-sighted Web page authors haven't bothered to use <TH>. This was and is a mistake. Browser technology has caught up with the tag, which is now rendered by the current versions of the major browsers in boldface, a handy shortcut, but is also crucial to new capabilities that will help make the Web more accessible for everyone. Don't be fooled by people who tell you that you can ignore this or that tag because "it's just the same." HTML tags were designed by very clever people who argued for weeks and months over every addition to the list. Believe me, if the tag exists, it's because there's a very good reason for it. You should try to use tags the way they were intended.

NEW TERM   A *cell* is a rectangular region that can contain text, images, and HTML tags. Each row in a table is made up of at least one cell.

You can create as many cells as you want, but each row in a table should have the same number of columns as the other rows. The example in Figures 16.1 and 16.2 shows a simple table using only these four tags. Pay particular attention to the way I lined up the tags, because this format makes it very easy to keep your tags in the right order.

Figure 16.1.

The <TABLE>, <TR>,
<TH>, *and* <TD> *tags are*
all you need to create
simple tables.

Figure 16.2.

The HTML table in
Figure 16.1 has three
rows with three cells
each.

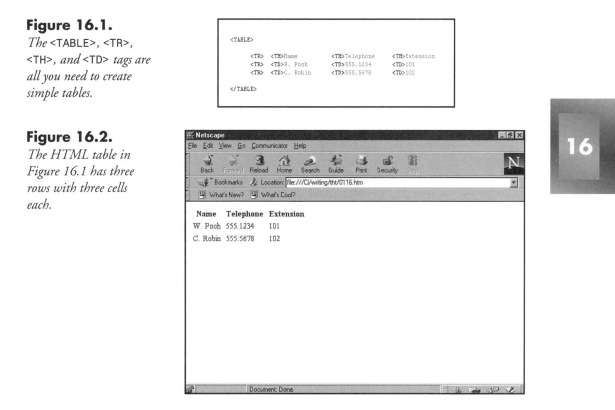

You can place virtually any other HTML element into a table cell. However, tags used in one cell don't carry over to other cells, and tags from outside the table don't apply within the table. For example, if you wrote

```
<FONT SIZE="5">
<TABLE>
  <TR> <TD><FONT SIZE="6">Hello </TD>World</FONT>
</tr>
</TABLE>
</FONT>
```

the word World would be normal-sized because neither the <FONT> tag outside the table nor the <FONT> tag from the previous cell affects it. To make both the words Hello and World larger than normal, you would need to type the following:

```
<TABLE>
  <TR> <TD><FONT SIZE="6">Hello</FONT>    <TD><FONT SIZE="6">World</FONT>
</TABLE>
```

Table Size

Ordinarily, the size of a table and the size of its individual cells automatically expand to fit the data you place into it. However, you can choose to control the exact size of the entire table by putting WIDTH and/or HEIGHT attributes in the <TABLE> tag. You can also control the size of each cell by putting WIDTH and HEIGHT attributes in the individual <TD> tags. The WIDTH and HEIGHT can be specified as either pixels or percentages. For example, the following HTML makes a table 500 pixels wide and 400 pixels high:

```
<TABLE WIDTH="500" HEIGHT="400">
```

To make the first cell of the table 20% of the total table width and the second cell 80% of the table width, you would type:

```
<TABLE WIDTH="80%">
  <TR> <TD WIDTH="20%">Skinny cell    <TD WIDTH="80%">Fat cell
</TABLE>
```

Alignment and Spanning

By default, anything you place inside a table cell is aligned to the left and vertically centered. You can align the contents of table cells both horizontally and vertically with the ALIGN and VALIGN attributes.

You can apply these attributes to either <TR> or <TD> tags. Alignment attributes assigned to <TR> tags apply to all cells in that row. Depending on the size of your table, you can save yourself a considerable amount of time and effort by applying these attributes at the <TR> level and not in each individual <TD> tag. The HTML code in Figure 16.3 uses VALIGN="top" to bring the text to the top of each cell and VALIGN="bottom" to bring the table images to the bottom of their cells. Figure 16.4 shows the result.

Figure 16.3.

Use ALIGN *and* VALIGN *to control the alignment of any row or individual cell.*

```
<TABLE>

        <TR ALIGN="Center">       <TH COLSPAN="3">PHONEBOOK

        <TR>    <TH>Name          <TH>Telephone       <TH>Extension
        <TR>    <TD>W. Pooh        <TD>555.1234        <TD>101
        <TR>    <TD>C. Robin       <TD>555.5678        <TD>102
        <TR>    <TD>W. Tigger      <TD COLSPAN="2">Unlisted

</TABLE>
```

16

Figure 16.4.

The HTML code in Figure 16.3 uses ALIGN="center" *to explicitly center the text in the top cell, although some browsers center* <TH> *cells by default.*

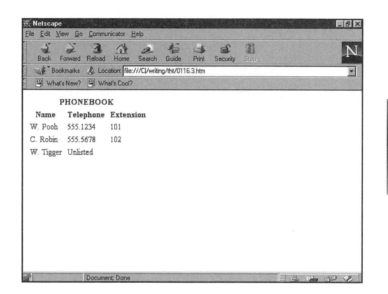

JUST A MINUTE

> The HTML 4.0 standard deprecates the use of ALIGN to control text alignment, preferring to use style sheets instead. Unfortunately, not all browsers support style sheets yet, so we're stuck with the old methods for a while and we'll largely ignore style sheets in these lessons for the sake of clarity and time. You should use style tags and attributes on production pages, however, in addition to now deprecated items, so that when the browsers catch up with the tags, your pages will be ready. I cover style sheets in more detail in Hour 17, "Using Style Sheets."

At the top of Figure 16.4, a single cell spans three columns. This is accomplished with the COLSPAN="3" attribute in the <TD> tag for that cell. As you might guess, you can also use the ROWSPAN attribute to create a cell that spans more than one row. You'll see examples of ROWSPAN later in this hour.

As you know, HTML ignores extra spaces between words and tags. However, you might find your HTML tables easier to read (and less prone to time-wasting errors) if you use spaces to indent <TR> tags a bit, as I did in Figure 16.3, and space out the <TH> and <TD> tags along a single line so that the format of the code mirrors the final form of the table.

Keeping the structure of rows and columns organized in your mind can be the most difficult part of creating complex tables, especially because the tiniest error can throw the whole thing into disarray. You'll save yourself time and frustration by sketching out your tables on graph paper before you start writing the HTML to implement them and by trying to keep all the elements of a single row on a single line in your code if at all possible. If included text might cause the line length to become unmanageable, lay out the table alone using this technique and then fill in the data later.

Backgrounds and Spacing

You can give an entire table—and each individual row or cell in a table—its own background, distinct from any background you might use on the Web page itself. You do this by placing a BGCOLOR and/or BACKGROUND attribute in the <TABLE>, <TR>, <TH>, or <TD> tags exactly as you would in the <BODY> tag (see Hour 13, "Backgrounds and Color Control"). To give an entire table a yellow background, for example, you would use <TABLE BGCOLOR="yellow">. In most browsers, BACKGROUND takes precedence over BGCOLOR, so for maximum safety you might want to argue both when using a background image. That way future browsers, if any, conforming strictly to HTML standards will show something, if not the image you had in mind. You can achieve nice effects using this trick, including the alternating white and pale green underlay that computer printouts use to make keeping track of lines easy.

JUST A MINUTE

Only users of Netscape Navigator and Microsoft Internet Explorer versions 3.0 or higher will see table background colors. Background images are handled differently in Microsoft IE and Navigator. Navigator 4.0 displays background images argued in the <TABLE> tag as if they had been called for in the individual <TH> or <TD> tags. Microsoft IE displays them as if they form a single background image behind the entire table. BACKGROUND= is not currently a part of the proposed HTML 4.0.

You can also control the space around the borders of a table with the CELLPADDING and CELLSPACING attributes. The CELLSPACING attribute sets the amount of space (in pixels) between table borders and table cells themselves. The CELLPADDING attribute sets the amount of space around the edges of information in the cells. Setting the CELLPADDING value to 0 causes all the information in the table to align as closely as possible to the table borders, possibly even touching the borders. CELLPADDING and CELLSPACING give you good overall control of the table's appearance.

You can see the effect of background color and spacing attributes in Figures 16.5 and 16.6. This table uses a 1 pixel-wide border, with 10 pixels of cell padding inside the cells and 5 pixels between the cells.

Figure 16.5.

This table uses background colors for individual cells, as well as cell padding and spacing controls.

```
<HTML>
<HEAD><TITLE>Tabula Rasa</TITLE></HEAD>
<BODY BGCOLOR="white">

<TABLE BORDER=1 CELLPADDING=10 CELLSPACING=5>
<TR VALIGN="top">
    <TD BGCOLOR="#FFB080"><I>Product</I></TD>
    <TD BGCOLOR="#FFB080"><I>Description</I></TD>
    <TD BGCOLOR="#FFB080"><I>Price</I></TD>
</TR>
<TR  VALIGN="top">
    <TD HEIGHT=110 VALIGN="bottom"><IMG SRC="table1.gif"></TD>
    <TD BGCOLOR="#FFFF80"><H2>Tabula Suprema</H2></TD>
    <TD BGCOLOR="#FFFF80"><H2>$795</H2></TD>
</TR>
<TR  VALIGN="top">
    <TD HEIGHT=110 VALIGN="bottom"><IMG SRC="table2.gif"></TD>
    <TD BGCOLOR="#FFFF80"><H2>Tabula Allegro</H2></TD>
    <TD BGCOLOR="#FFFF80"><H2>$675</H2></TD>
</TR>
<TR VALIGN="top">
    <TD HEIGHT=110 VALIGN="bottom"><IMG SRC="table3.gif"></TD>
    <TD BGCOLOR="#FFFF80"><H2>Tabula El-Cheapo</H2></TD>
    <TD BGCOLOR="#FFFF80"><H2>$295</H2></TD>
</TR>
</TABLE>

</BODY></HTML>
```

16

Figure 16.6.

Compare the spacing and overall aesthetics of this table (from the HTML in Figure 16.5) to the "plain" table in Figure 16.4.

Nested Tables

You can place an entire table within a table cell, and that separate table can possess any and all the qualities of any table you might want to create.

For example, the table in Figures 16.7 and 16.8 has no borders, but in its bottom-left cell, I included the entire table from Figure 16.6, which does have borders. Nested tables open up a vast universe of possibilities for creative Web page layout.

Figure 16.7.

The actual source for this HTML file contains all the text from the <TABLE> tag to the </TABLE> tag in Figure 16.5.

```
<HTML>
<HEAD><TITLE>Tabula Rasa</TITLE></HEAD>
<BODY BGCOLOR="white">
<TABLE>
<TR><TD>
      <IMG SRC="tabula.gif" ALIGN="left">
      <DIV ALIGN="center">
      <FONT COLOR="maroon">
      <H1>Tabula Rasa, Inc.</H1>
      <B>Antique tables<BR>for the modern home</B>
      </FONT></DIV>
      </TD>
      <TD ROWSPAN=2>
At Tabula Rasa, our mission is to locate and restore the
most beautiful tables in the world and sell them to you.
If you put one of our tables in your dining room, then you
can eat on it. Or if you don't want to get it dirty, you
could just put a vase with some flowers on it and eat in
front of the TV. In any case, guests and relatives are sure
to comment on your refined taste and obscene wealth
when they see your new antique table,
and you sure can't beat that feeling.<P>
So enough chit-chat. The bottom line is: You buy a table,
or we have our boys pay a little visit to your house once
or twice a week for the rest of your life. And trust me,
these guys are not vacuum salesmen. So hand over the credit
card and let's get this over with. You'll be glad you did.
We guarantee it.<P> <I>Tabula Rasa is a wholely owned
subsidiary of Cosa Nostra Furnishings Inc.</I>
</TD></TR>
<TR><TD>

            ...the table from Figure 16.5 goes here...

</TD></TR></TABLE>
</BODY></HTML>
```

Figure 16.8.

Nesting one table inside another lets you use different borders and spacing in different parts of your layout.

16

Netscape - [Tabula Rasa]

File   Edit   View   Go   Bookmarks   Options   Directory   Window   Help

Tabula Rasa, Inc.

**Antique tables
for the modern home**

Product	Description	Price
	Tabula Suprema	$795
	Tabula Allegro	$675
	Tabula El-Cheapo	$295

At Tabula Rasa, our mission is to locate and restore the most beautiful tables in the world and sell them to you. If you put one of our tables in your dining room, then you can eat on it. Or if you don't want to get it dirty, you could just put a vase with some flowers on it and eat in front of the TV. In any case, guests and relatives are sure to comment on your refined taste and obscene wealth when they see your new antique table, and you sure can't beat that feeling.

So enough chit-chat. The bottom line is: You buy a table, or we have our boys pay a little visit to your house once or twice a week for the rest of your life. And trust me, these guys are not vacuum salesmen. So hand over the credit card and let's get this over with. You'll be glad you did. We guarantee it.

Tabula Rasa is a wholely owned subsidiary of Cosa Nostra Furnishings Inc.

Document Done

COFFEE BREAK

The boring, conventional way to use tables is for tabular arrangements of text and numbers. But the real fun begins when you make the borders of your tables invisible, and use them as guides for arranging graphics and columns of text any way you please. For an example, take a look at

http://www.mcp.com/sites/1-57521/1-57521-366-4/

While I worked on building this table, I left the borders visible so I could make sure everything was placed the way I wanted. Then, before incorporating this table into the final Web page, I changed to BORDER="0" to make the lines invisible.

This page also links to a site called LOOK, which uses nontraditional layouts—and everything else we can pull out of the bag—to be eye-catching and distinctive, albeit without any actual informative content. You'll notice though, that the actual page uses a roughly two-thirds/one-third layout, so what might look a little chaotic actually has an underlying structure that is quite traditional. When you start being aware of it, you'll see this off-balance, but not too much. This sort of asymmetry is found almost everywhere you look, from advertisements to architecture and fine art. Your real-world site will probably be a bit more tame than the LOOK site, but of course some of you will start getting even crazier ideas.

You can also see how I incorporated some simple tables into the 24-Hour HTML Café site to enhance its aesthetics and functionality:

`http://www.mcp.com/sites/1-57521/1-57521-366-4/`

Beyond Tables: Accessibility and the Web

Tables are great, as you've seen, but they had one huge problem when they were first designed: Some people can't see them. One of the major changes made in HTML 4.0 is the addition of elements and attributes that make tables easier to use for everyone, not just people with graphical Web browsers and perfect vision but also for people who speak languages other than English or those based on the Roman alphabet.

It did this by the addition of elements and attributes to allow optional captions and titles, both row and column groups, language preference, and direction (to accommodate languages like Hebrew and Arabic which read from left to right). All of these additions will increase convenience and readability for everyone while making it possible for specialized audio or Braille browsers to organize tables and other features in a way that makes sense for people who navigate by touch or hearing.

Make no mistake, these changes are not just valuable for such specialized use; they affect everyone. The popularity of audio books is not restricted to blind people, but has become a huge industry. It won't be too long before you'll be able to surf the Web while tooling down the road in your car, having the text read to you and the pictures described, and selecting links by spoken command. Imagine being able to surf into the auto club and seek out sightseeing information as you speed along or imagine getting directions when you're lost—all without losing sight of the road. This is going to be very, very cool.

This has been such a huge change that we won't have time to look at everything in this short lesson, but we'll look at how the basic table elements we previously studied have been extended to make browsing easier. Don't be surprised if some of them look familiar, because they have been showing up in browsers piecemeal and non-standardized, but the exact syntax has changed slightly in some cases.

16

By this time you should be pretty good at deciphering HTML, so I'm going to offer the following snippets pretty much uncommented, as I think most of it is clear as it stands.

Captions

This tag is used within the <TABLE> tag and identifies a caption associated with the table:

```
<TABLE>
  <CAPTION>TELEPHONE BOOK</CAPTION>
  <TR> <TH>Name      <TH>Telephone <TH>Extension
  <TR> <TD>W. Pooh  <TD>555.1234  <TD>101
  <TR> <TD>C. Robin <TD>555.5678  <TD>102
</TABLE>
```

JUST A MINUTE

It's easy to feel overwhelmed sometimes by the many different tags you can use which have much the same appearance on the pages. The trouble lies in the limitations of browsers, or the browsers you happen to use, rather than in the tags themselves. Remember, tags capture meaning and function, not appearance, although many people are confused about this. The <CAPTION> tag is an excellent example; it's usually rendered as what looks like a simple centered title in most browsers. Some people advise you to use a simple <H> or <DIV> tag, or even simple text with a font change and centering. Don't do it! They may look the same but they will be a source of problems forever, as browsers evolve to use the tags in meaningful ways, and will rot your pages from the inside out, like a cancer.

Row Groupings

Several new elements—<THEAD>, <TFOOT>, and <TBODY> —have been added to the interior of tables to allow more control over the formatting of rows. Note that <THEAD> and <TFOOT> should both appear before <TBODY>, although logically <TFOOT> should follow. This is so the browser can render the footer, which might contain important identifying data, before proceeding with the body or bodies, which could be quite large. Some browsers may offer optional loading of the table itself based on the user's inspection of the caption, header, and footer text. These tags are logically associated with and contain <TR> elements so they should be associated with them in your code. This is a good format for clarity:

```
<TABLE>
   <THEAD>
        <TR> ...header stuff...
   <TFOOT>
        <TR> ...footer stuff...
   <TBODY>
        <TR> ...
        <TR> ...
```

```
<TBODY>
    <TR> ...
    <TR> ...
    <TR> ...
</TABLE>
```

Column Groupings

<COLGROUP> and <COL> allow you considerable control over the width and layout of columns, as well as make navigation easier for future browsers. Note that the WIDTH= attribute has moved from the <TH> and <TD> tags, and its use in those tags will be non-standard. These tags can only occur at the start of a table, after the optional caption element, as shown here:

```
<TABLE>
  <COLGROUP>
     <COL width="20">
     <COL width="0*">
     <COL width="3*">
  <COLGROUP align="center">
     <COL width="1*">
     <COL width="2*" align="char" char=".">
  <THEAD>
  <TR> ...
</TABLE>
```

This code snippet sets up five columns: the first 20 pixels wide, the second the minimal size needed to display the contained data, and the rest proportionally sized to use the rest of the available space as one half, one sixth, and one third of the remainder respectively. You figure out their portion of total left by adding up the asterisk items (six in this case) as a denominator and then sticking the individual asterisk item on top as a numerator. So, $3/6 = 1/2$, $1/6$, and $2/6 = 1/3$. The fourth column is centered. The last column uses another new attribute to align the contents on the decimal point, at last!

Element Changes

There are some important changes to tags and attributes that you'll need to be aware of:

☐ <TABLE>: The <TABLE> element has added quite a few new attributes and incorporated a few which may be familiar from other browsers, a few of which we'll list here in linear form (FRAME="...", RULES="...", CELLPADDING="...", and CELLSPACING="..."), and lots more. FRAME and RULES subsume and logically replace BORDER, although BORDER has been retained for backward compatibility. See the table at the end of this hour for further explanation.

☐ <TR>: It has added quite a few new or changed attributes as well, including several common to all the tags mentioned here but only cited once (LANG="...", DIR="...", ID="...", CLASS="...", and STYLE="..."), and some new or changed ones (ALIGN="...", CHAR="...", and CHAROFF="...").

These tags let you assign a language and direction to the element, which could affect indexing, font, reading direction (either left to right or right to left), quote method, decimal point, and other attributes that vary from language to language.

Also new are attributes that let you refer to various groupings of elements for the purpose of applying styles and the like, as well as an inline style attribute.

- [ ] CHAR: Assigns a character to align a table on, in which case you need to have an ALIGN="char" as well, which is a new argument. CHAROFF is an offset to be applied to the alignment character.

- [ ] <TH> / <TD>: Data and header cells have added new tags as well, including AXIS= and AXES=, which identify unique coordinates revealing the position of the cell in the surrounding table. These attributes could be used to automatically enter the contents into a database or furnish navigation "landmarks" for an audio browser.

In addition, various events deserve mention, including ONCLICK, ONDBLCLICK, ONMOUSEDOWN, ONMOUSEUP, ONMOUSEOVER, ONMOUSEMOVE, ONMOUSEOUT, ONKEYPRESS, ONKEYDOWN, and ONKEYUP. The names are fairly self explanatory.

An Example

This is an example of a multicolumn table using new tags and attributes:

```
<TABLE>
  <CAPTION>TELEPHONE BOOK</CAPTION>
<COLGROUP>
    <COL STYLE="Color: yellow">
    <COL STYLE="Color: white">
    <COL>
  <COLGROUP>
    <COL>
  <THEAD>
    <TR> <TH>Name      <TH>Telephone <TH>Extension <TH>Notes
  <TFOOT>
    <TR> <TD COLSPAN="4">Source: Pooh Corners Phone Directory, 1997
  <TBODY>
    <TR> <TD>W. Pooh  <TD>555.1234  <TD>101  <TD>No fixed bedtime
    <TR> <TD>C. Robin <TD>555.5678  <TD>102  <TD>Must be home by dark
</TABLE>
```

JUST A MINUTE

This code, although considered an accepted part of HTML 4.0, may not display correctly on any current browser, despite the claims of some. The definition of the footer treatment is a little ambiguous in the draft proposal, so everyone seems to have taken the easy route of rendering it merely as a consecutive row in the table, instead of rendering it for display and then filling in the body in between, as would be logically accurate.

Summary

In this hour, you learned to arrange text and images into organized arrangements of rows and columns called tables. You also learned how these things can be used to lay out the space on your pages in attractive ways that improve clarity and comprehension. You learned the four basic tags for creating tables and many optional attributes for controlling the alignment, spacing, and appearance of tables. You also saw that tables can be nested within one another for an even wider variety of layout options. This hour also presents how HTML 4.0 has made tables much more powerful and accessible for everyone, offering tools for organizing data in ways that can be meaningful to everyone.

Table 16.1 summarizes the tags and attributes covered in this hour.

Table 16.1. HTML tags and attributes.

Tag	Attribute	Function
`<TABLE>...</TABLE>`		Creates a table that can contain any number of rows (`<TR>` tags).
	`BORDER="..."`	Indicates the width in pixels of the table borders. (`BORDER=0`, or omitting the `BORDER` attribute, makes borders invisible.)
	`CELLSPACING="..."`	The amount of space between the cells in the table.
	`CELLPADDING="..."`	The amount of space between the edges of the cell and its contents.
	`WIDTH="..."`	The width of the table on the page, in either exact pixel values or as a percentage of page width.
	`BGCOLOR="..."`	Background color of all cells in the table that do not contain their own `BACKGROUND` or `BGCOLOR` attribute.
	`BACKGROUND="..."`	Background image to tile within all cells in the table that do not contain their own `BACKGROUND` or `BGCOLOR` attribute (Microsoft Internet Explorer 3.0 only).

16

Tag	Attribute	Function
	FRAME="..."	VOID ¦ ABOVE ¦ BELOW ¦ HSIDES ¦ LHS ¦ RHS ¦ VSIDES ¦ BOX ¦ BORDER
		This attribute specifies which sides of the frame that surrounds a table will be visible. Most are self-explanatory but VSIDES and HSIDES are the vertical and horizontal sides, respectively; LHS and RHS are the left and right hand sides, respectively; and BOX and BORDER are all four sides.
	RULES="..."	NONE ¦ GROUPS ¦ ROWS ¦ COLS ¦ ALL
		This attribute specifies which rules will appear between cells within a table.
<TR>...[</TR>]		Defines a table row, containing one or more cells (<TD> tags).
	ALIGN="..."	The horizontal alignment of the contents of the cells within this row. Possible values are LEFT, RIGHT, and CENTER.
	VALIGN="..."	The vertical alignment of the contents of the cells within this row. Possible values are TOP, MIDDLE, and BOTTOM.
	BGCOLOR="..."	Background color of all cells in the row that do not contain their own BACKGROUND or BGCOLOR attributes.
	BACKGROUND="..."	Background image to tile within all cells in the row that do not contain their own BACKGROUND or BGCOLOR attributes (Microsoft Internet Explorer 3.0 only).

16

continues

Table 16.1. continued

Tag	Attribute	Function
	LANG="..."	Defines this element as belonging to a certain language group which should be rendered, if possible, in an appropriate character set.
	DIR="..."	LTR ¦ RTL
		Defines this element as having a direction, which may be different from the default. This element should be rendered, if possible, in the direction indicated.
	ID="..."	Associates an ID with this element.
	CLASS="..."	Associates a class with this element.
	TITLE="..."	Associates a title with this element.
	STYLE="..."	Associates a style with this element.
<TD>...[</TD>]		Defines a table data cell.
	ALIGN="..."	The horizontal alignment of the contents of the cell. Possible values are LEFT, RIGHT, and CENTER.
	VALIGN="..."	The vertical alignment of the contents of the cell. Possible values are TOP, MIDDLE, and BOTTOM.
	ROWSPAN="..."	The number of rows this cell will span.
	COLSPAN="..."	The number of columns this cell will span.
	WIDTH="..."	The width of this column of cells, in exact pixel values or as a percentage of the table width.
	BGCOLOR="..."	Background color of the cell.
	BACKGROUND="..."	Background image to tile within the cell (Microsoft Internet Explorer 3.0+ and Netscape Navigator 4.0+ only).

16

Tag	Attribute	Function
<TH>...[</TH>]	Same as <TD>	Defines a table header cell which should be rendered and handled differently if possible. Latest versions of MSIE and Netscape Navigator render these cells in boldface.
<THEAD>...[</THEAD>]		Contains <TR> element(s) that should be grouped with the header. If present, this element must contain at least one <TR>. See the W3C document.
<TFOOT>...[</TFOOT>]		Contains <TR> element(s) which should be classed with the footer. If present, this element must contain at least one <TR>. (See the W3C document.)
<TBODY>...[</TBODY>]		Contains <TR> element(s) which should be grouped into a body. If present, this element must contain at least one <TR>. (See the W3C document.)

Q&A

Q **I made a big table, and when I load the page, nothing appears for a long time. Why the wait?**

A Because the Web browser has to figure out the size of everything in the table before it can display any part of it, complex tables can take a while to appear on the screen. You can speed things up a bit by always including WIDTH and HEIGHT tags for every graphics image within a table. Using WIDTH attributes in the <TABLE> and <TD> tags also helps.

Q **I've noticed that a lot of pages on the Web have tables in which one cell will change while other cells stay the same. How do they do that?**

A Those sites are using frames, not tables. Frames are similar to tables except that each frame contains a separate HTML page and can be updated independently of the others. The new "floating frames" can actually be put inside a table, so they can look just like a regular table even though the HTML to create them is quite different. You'll find out how to make frames in Hour 18, "Interactive Layout with Frames."

Q **The Microsoft Web site says there's a whole new table standard, and that they're the only ones that support it. Is that true?**

A Well, not exactly. The proposed HTML 4.0 standard introduces several new table tags, which are supported (in their current, unofficial form) by Internet Explorer 4.0. As we've seen previously, the primary uses of these extensions are to exert greater control over how tables are displayed and accessed, and to prepare the ground for advanced features that no current browser supports completely. Both Microsoft and Netscape support some features the way they were intended but also make room for their own "pet" tags and attributes, some of which are incompatible with the standard. While it's possible for both companies to say that they support the proposal, a proposal is not quite the same as a standard and supporting is not quite the same as adhering. Keep your eye on the Microsoft and Netscape Web sites (`http://www.microsoft.com` and `http://home.netscape.com`) for details about these new table tags.

But don't worry; the new standard will not make any of the table tags covered in this hour obsolete. They will all continue to work just as they do now.

Quiz

Questions

1. You want a Web page with two columns of text side by side. How do you create it?
2. You think the columns you created for question 1 look too close together. How do you add 30 pixels of space between them?

Answers

1. You can do it with the following table:
   ```
   <TABLE>
     <TR> <TD ALIGN="top">...First column...<TD ALIGN="top">...Second col-
   umn...
   </TABLE>
   ```

2. Add `CELLSPACING=30` to the `<TABLE>` tag. (Or you could use `CELLPADDING=15` to add 15 pixels of space inside the edge of each column.)

16

JUST A MINUTE

Note that the practice of laying out the elements horizontally, to mirror the format of the finished table as much as possible, makes even complex nested tables fairly easy to decipher. The format makes it clear that there is a single horizontal row in the first table, that the second cell has a nested table in it (which requires a "jog" in the format) with two rows of one cell each, and then a third cell.

16

Activities

☐ You can use a simple one-celled table with a border to draw a rectangle around any section of text on a Web page. By nesting that single-cell table in another two-column table, you can put a "sidebar" of text to the left or right side of your Web page. Outlined sections of text and sidebars are very common on printed paper pages, so you'll probably find uses for them on your Web pages, too.

☐ Do you have any pages where different visitors might be interested in different information? Use a table to present two or three columns of text, each with its own heading (and perhaps its own graphic). Then something of interest to everyone will be visible at the top of the page when it first appears.

PART

V

Style Sheets and Site Design

Hour

Hour 17

Using Style Sheets

Until the adoption of cascading style sheets, HTML was missing an important element. While rudimentary control of style with headers and font tags is possible, headers and font tags are also cumbersome and limited. Style sheets are the long-awaited solution for many of HTML's restrictions. The results include better font control, color management, margin control, and even the addition of special effects such as text shadowing.

In this hour, you'll learn

☐ What style sheets are

☐ How to use style sheets

☐ What types of style sheets are currently available

☐ About class and grouping

NEW TERM *Style sheet* refers to a combination of methods that allow you to control elements of style, such as headers, text, color, margins, and special effects. They have been used in desktop publishing for years. For the purposes of the Web, the introduction of style sheets is the solution to many style issues previously not addressed by HTML. When I refer to *style sheets* in this book, I am referring to the Web-based variety, unless otherwise noted.

There are three types of style sheets:

- ☐ **Inline.** The inline method allows you to take any HTML tag and add a style to it. Say I wanted to control a paragraph's font. I could simply add a `style="font: arial"` argument to the paragraph `<P>` tag, and the browser would display that paragraph using the font argued in my code.
- ☐ **Embedded.** The embedded method allows you to control a full page of HTML. Using the `<style>` tag, which is placed between the opening `<html>` and `<body>` tags, you insert detailed style attributes that will be applied to the entire page.
- ☐ **Linked.** Also referred to as an "external" style sheet, this is a powerful way of creating master styles that you can apply to an entire site! A main style sheet document is created and given the `.css` extension. This document contains the styles you want a single page or even thousands of pages to adopt. Any page that links to this document will take on the styles called for in that document.

So What's This Cascading Stuff?

The term *cascading* refers primarily to the fact that not only can multiple styles be used in an individual HTML page, but that the style sheet–compliant browser will follow an order— a *cascade*—to interpret style information.

This means that I can use all three style types and the browser will interpret the linked styles first, embedded second, and inline last. Even though I might have master styles applied to an entire site, I can control aspects of individual pages with embedded styles and individual areas within those pages with inline styles.

JUST A MINUTE

> This hour will get you started using style sheets right away, but they are extensive and if you enjoy what you do here, you will probably want to know more. A significant source of information on style sheets can be found at the World Wide Web Consortium's site at `http://www.w3.org/Style/`, and a search for `cascading style sheets` on any Web search engine such as infoseek (`http://www.infoseek.com/`) or AltaVista (`http://www.altavista.digital.com/`) will bring back plenty of extended information.
>
> Another excellent resource is *Laura Lemay's Web Workshop: Designing with Style Sheets, Tables, and Frames* by Molly E. Holzschlag (one of this book's authors!). This book will not only show you how to design with style sheets, but how to use other advanced HTML methods to get great-looking sites.

Style sheet syntax is somewhat different than standard HTML. The following sections take a closer look at how style sheets are created.

Using Inline Style

Inline styles require the `style` attribute, as follows:

```
<P STYLE="font: 14pt arial">
The text in this paragraph will display as 14 point text using the arial font.
</P>
```

You can add inline styles to any relevant HTML tag. Paragraphs, headers, horizontal rules, anchors, and table cells are all some of the candidates for inline style you can begin to play with.

JUST A MINUTE

> If you want to specify a style for only a part of a page rather than just the specific HTML tag in question, you can place a `style` attribute within a `<DIV>` (division) or `<SPAN>` tag. These tags specify a defined range of text, so everything between them will adopt the style you call for. The only difference between `<DIV>` and `<SPAN>` is that `<DIV>` forces a line break, while `<SPAN>` doesn't. Therefore, you should use `<SPAN>` to modify the style of any portion of text shorter than a paragraph.

Here's how a sample `style` attribute might look:

```
<P STYLE="color: green">This text is green, but
<SPAN STYLE="color: red"> this text is red.</SPAN>
Back to green again, but...</P>
<P>...now the green is over, and we're back to the default color for this page.
```

Figure 17.1 shows the results.

Figure 17.1.

An example of inline style sheets in action.

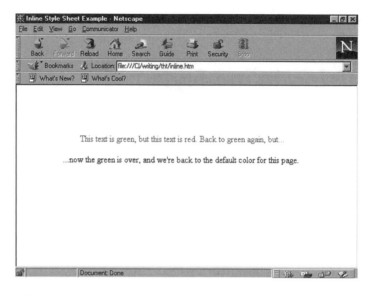

Embedded Style Sheets

Embedded styles use the `<STYLE>` tag, placed under the `</HEAD>` tag and before the `<BODY>` tag in a standard HTML document:

```
<HTML>
<HEAD>
<TITLE>Embedded Style Sheet Example I</TITLE>
</HEAD>
<STYLE>
BODY {background: #FFFFFF; color: #000000; margin-top: .25in;
margin-left: .75in; margin-right: .75in}
H1 {font: 14pt verdana; color: #0000FF}
P {font: 12pt times; text-indent: 0.5in}
A {color: #FF0000; text-decoration: none}
</STYLE>
```

As you can tell from this example, the style sheet is beginning to look quite a bit different than standard HTML, but it's not difficult to follow the logic. In this case, the page's body is calling for a background color; a text color; and top, left, and right margin spacing in inches.

Notice how the level-one heading (`<H1>`) calls for a font using the font's name as well as a literal point size. Here is a prime example of why cascading style sheets are so powerful—not only can I choose to control sizing in points, but you'll note that the margins and indentation in this style sheet example use inches. Pixels (`px`), percentage (`75%`), and centimeters (`cm`) can also be used.

Another interesting aspect of this style sheet includes the difference in fonts as defined by the header and paragraph style—they're different in color, indentation, and font face. With style sheets, gone are the days of having an HTML page littered with font tags and non-breaking spaces in order to achieve these variations. Style is handled in a nice, compact fashion.

The A (anchor) tag in the style sheet shows yet another very handy piece of syntax. The text-decoration: none string forces underlining to be removed from links, allowing for clean, attractive results. Figure 17.2 shows this embedded style example in action.

Figure 17.2.

An embedded style sheet example. Note the header and font face differences, the margins, and no underlines beneath the links.

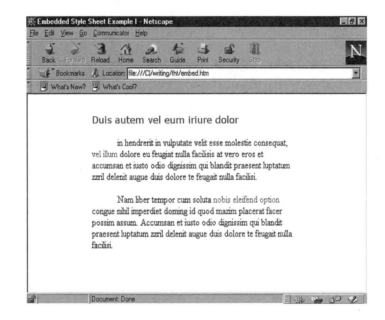

Linked Style Sheets

The external method of style sheets extends the concept of embedded style. All of the styles you might apply externally are coded exactly as you would for an embedded style sheet, but placed in a separate document that's given the extension of .css. If I wanted the styles I've selected for the preceding embedded example applied to numerous pages within my site, I simply create a document with the same information:

```
<STYLE>
BODY {background: #FFFFFF; color: #000000; margin-top: .25in;
margin-left: .75in; margin-right: .75in}
H1 {font: 14pt verdana; color: #0000FF}
P {font: 12pt times; text-indent: 0.5in}
A {color: #FF0000; text-decoration: none}
</STYLE>
```

Then save this document as a unique file—I'll call it my-style.css and make sure it's in the same directory as the pages that will contain this style.

Now I can proceed linking as many individual HTML pages to this document as I want, using the following syntax placed below the </TITLE> tag and above the </HEAD> tag:

```
<HTML>
<HEAD>
<TITLE>Linking to the External Style Sheet</TITLE>
<LINK rel=stylesheet href="my-style.css" type="text/css">
</HEAD>
```

All of the pages containing this link will adopt the styles I've called for in my-style.css, which you can see displayed in Figure 17.2. Yes, the results for this page are exactly the same as for the embedded example!

To Do

You can add style to any of your current HTML pages by creating a master style sheet and linking to it. Try it! If you want to go the distance, embed a slightly different style sheet into one of the pages linked to the master page, and add inline style to one section of a page. You'll see the cascade in action—with the inline style overpowering the embedded and master codes (see Figure 17.3).

Figure 17.3.

In this example, I've used three types of style sheets to achieve results. Note how it differs slightly from the embedded example in Figure 17.2.

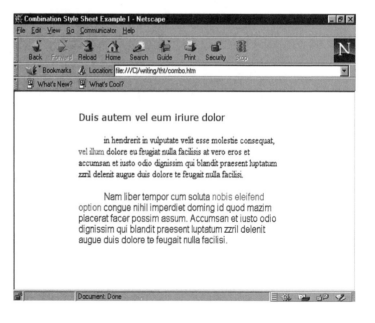

JUST A MINUTE

Be absolutely sure to view your style sheet pages in an appropriate browser, such as Internet Explorer 3.0 and above or Netscape 4.0 and above. Otherwise, all of your styles will disappear! You should always test your style sheet–enhanced pages without the style sheet to make sure they still look acceptable. To do this, use an older browser or just change the name of the style sheet temporarily so the browser can't find it.

Style Attributes

The following list describes some of the many attributes you can use with style sheets. These will help you get started:

☐ `font:` lets you set many font properties at once. You can specify a list of font names separated by commas. If the first is not available, the next will be tried, and so on. You can also include the words `bold` and/or `italic` and a font size. Each of these font properties can be specified separately with `font-family:`, `font-size:`, `font-weight: bold`, and `font-style: italic` if you prefer.

☐ `text-decoration:` is useful for turning link underlining off. Simply set text decoration to `none`. The values of `underline`, `italic`, and `line-through` are also supported.

☐ `line-height:` is also known in the publishing world as leading. This sets the height of each line of text—essentially the space between each line.

☐ `background:` places a color or image behind text, either with a color or a `url(address)` where `address` points to a background image tile. Note that this can be assigned not only to the `<BODY>` tag, but to any tag or span of text to "highlight" an area on a page.

JUST A MINUTE

One problem with fonts—and this holds true for standard HTML font tags as well as for style sheets—is that if the font face isn't resident on a user's machine, she will not see the font. This means you should select fonts that are fairly standard to common machines. Times and Garamond are the two serif fonts (fonts with little strokes on their face) common to PCs and Macintoshes, respectively. Arial and Helvetica are the sans serif companions. Does this mean you shouldn't have fun and use other font faces? Not at all! Just be sure to include these fonts within your string, so you can have some, if not total, control over what your site visitor will see.

Microsoft offers wonderful typographical information. Visit `http://www.microsoft.com/typography/` to find out more about where fonts on the Web are going!

17

Class and Grouping

Two other interesting aspects of style sheets include class and grouping. Class—as anyone who enjoys *Vogue* magazine knows—should be an inherent part of style. For the purposes of HTML style, class refers to ways of breaking down your style calls into very precise pieces. Whenever you want some of the text on your pages to look different than the other text, you can create what amounts to a custom-built HTML tag. Each type of specially formatted text you define is called a *style class*.

NEW TERM   A *style class* is a custom set of formatting specifications that can be applied to any passage of text in a Web page.

For example, suppose you wanted two different kinds of <H1> headings in your documents. You would create a style class for each one by putting the following text in the style sheet:

```
H1.decorative {font: 24pt Lucida Handwriting}
H1.sans {font: 18pt Arial}
```

To choose between the two style classes in an HTML page, you would use the class attribute, as follows:

```
<H1 class=decorative>We Live in Interesting Times</H1>
The old Chinese curse has come true!
<H1 class=sans>Read the Book!</H1>
An excellent book by Turing Minsky explains why.
```

The words We Live in Interesting Times appear in 24-point Lucida Handwriting, but the words Read the Book! appear in the 18-point Arial font instead. Note also how the text in between defaults to Times, because I haven't created a style sheet argument for it (see Figure 17.4). Therefore, the browser selects its own default body font.

Figure 17.4.

Note the differences in header styles, achieved here with the use of class.

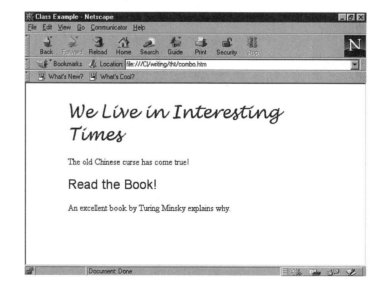

17

NEW TERM *Grouping* is the condensing of style-related tags and attributes. Consider the following non-grouped example:

```
P.1 {font: arial; font-size: 12pt; line-height: 14pt}
```

This example means that all paragraphs with the class of 1 will show up as a 12-point arial font with a line height of 14 points. I can group this class as follows:

```
P.1 {font: 12pt/14pt arial}
```

The style sheet action will be the same. Notice how I place the font size first, the line height after the forward slash, and then the name of the font. Grouping does require a specific order. More information can be found at the World Wide Web Consortium's site and in *Laura Lemay's Web Workshop: Designing with Style Sheets, Tables, and Frames.*

Summary

Style sheets can help expand your HTML knowledge into the realm of design. By offering control over typography, margins, line height, and other page attributes, you can quickly and easily add true style to your pages. Whether you decide to do this with inline, embedded, or linked style sheets is entirely up to you. It will all depend upon what your needs are and how detailed you want to get. This hour also helped you to understand that you can use all three, resulting in a cascade of options sure to give you exciting results!

Q&A

Q Can I set defaults for an entire page?

A Style sheets work on a concept known as *inheritance*. This means that if you set a BODY style first, every tag you place underneath it "inherits" that attribute. Simply said, what you place in the BODY is essentially the default value. So, load up the BODY tag with your global values, and set other specifications below.

Q Say I link a style sheet to my page that says all text should be blue, but there's a `<SPAN style="font-color: red">` tag in the page somewhere. Will that text come out blue or red?

A Red. Remember, inline styles always take precedence over a linked, external style sheet. Any style specifications you put between `<STYLE>` and `</STYLE>` tags at the top of a page will also take precedence over external style sheets (but not over inline styles later in the same page).

17

Q Can I link more than one style sheet to a single page?

A Sure. For example, you might have a sheet for typography and another one for margins and spacing. Just include a `<LINK>` tag for both.

Q When I pull up a page made with style sheets in my browser, I get a blank page. What's going wrong?

A Style sheet syntax is quite moody. Everything needs to be in the right order. If you look over your syntax carefully and find no problems there, look at the rest of your HTML—especially if you are also using tables on the page.

Q I was looking at some style sheets and I see that sometimes quotations are used around font names, sometimes they aren't. Why is this?

A If a font name is more than one word, use quotations. Otherwise, it isn't mandatory to do so. However, developing consistency in style is a good goal to aim for.

Q Where do I get more fonts?

A All computers come with standard fonts. You can get tons of common fonts on the Web, and on inexpensive CD-ROMs available at your computer store. For the purposes of style sheets, don't spend a lot of money or time on fonts. Use what you have.

Quiz

Questions

1. Create a linked style sheet to specify half-inch margins, 30-point blue Arial headings, and all other text in double-spaced 10-point blue Times Roman (or the default browser font).

2. If you saved the style sheet you made for question 1 as `main.css`, how would you apply it to a Web page named `intro.htm`?

3. Create a standard HTML page and add a 12-point Arial font to only one paragraph.

Answers

1. Here's what you need to input:

```
BODY {font: 10pt blue;
line-height: 20pt;
margin-left: 0.5in;
margin-right: 0.5in;
margin-top: 0.5in;
margin-bottom: 0.5in}
H1 {font: 30pt blue Arial}
```

17

2. Put the following tag between the `<head>` and `</head>` tags of the `intro.htm` document:

```
<LINK rel=stylesheet type="text/css" HREF="corporat.css">
```

3. The results:

```
<P style="font: 12pt arial">this text appears in 12 point arial</P>
```

Activities

☐ Develop a linked style sheet for your Web site, and apply it to all your pages. (Use inline styles for pages that need to deviate from it.) If you work for a corporation, chances it has already developed font and style specifications for printed materials. Get a copy of those specifications, and follow them for company Web pages, too.

Hour 18

Interactive Layout with Frames

One major limitation of HTML in the old days was that you could see only one page at a time. Frames overcome this limitation by dividing the browser window into multiple HTML documents. Similar to tables (discussed in Hour 16, "Advanced Layout with Tables"), frames allow you to arrange text and graphics into rows and columns of text and graphics.

In this hour, you'll learn about

- ☐ Why to use frames
- ☐ What frames are
- ☐ Creating a frameset document, the `<FRAME>` tag, linking frames, margins, borders, and scrolling
- ☐ Borderless frames and nested frames
- ☐ Inline frames
- ☐ Supporting frameless browsers

Why Use Frames?

Unlike table cells, a frame can contain links that change the contents of other frames (or its own contents). For example, one frame can display an unchanging table of contents while the other frames change based on which links the reader follows. This means that frames can be used for updating portions of the page while other portions remain constant, a potential savings in download time and a sure way to ensure that the user doesn't see an annoying, completely blank screen while moving from page to page on your site. Thus frames can be a means of ensuring smooth transitions and a continuous site identity without duplicating common elements on each page.

Also, frames, especially borderless frames, can be used to provide exact placement of graphics on the page and offer other formatting advantages. Unlike tables, frames can be set to resize dynamically within the browser, so your page might look better when divided into frames than it would if put into a table. Each design challenge is different, and frames are a powerful tool in your arsenal of techniques, not the one and only solution to every design problem you'll ever face.

In fact, the new features of HTML 4.0—including the new <OBJECT> tag, cascading style sheets, and even a close cousin of the traditional Netscape frame, the inline frame—have made the case for traditional frames less compelling in some cases. It's no longer true that frames are the only way to update portions of your page without affecting others, and style sheets have made some text and graphics placement problems trivial.

JUST A MINUTE

Frames are only supported by Netscape Navigator version 2.0 or later and Microsoft Internet Explorer version 3.0 or later. Also, they cause serious problems for some older browsers, and are difficult to make accessible for disabled access, not to mention the fact that some people just plain don't like them. It's important to provide alternate means to navigate your site, and it's not terribly difficult either. You'll see how to provide alternate content for other browsers in the "Supporting Frameless Browsers" section near the end of this hour.

Frames are basically a way of arranging and presenting several Web pages at once. You'll be able to learn the material in this hour faster if you have a few interrelated Web pages all ready before you continue. Here are some guidelines to help you work with frames:

To Do

1. If you have an index page or table of contents for your Web site, copy it to a separate directory folder so you can experiment with it without changing the original. Copy a few of the pages that the index links to as well.

2. As you read this hour, try modifying the sample frames I present to incorporate them into your own Web pages.

What Are Frames?

At first glance, Figure 18.1 may look like an ordinary Web page, but it is actually three separate Web pages all displayed in the same Netscape Navigator window. Each of these pages is displayed in its own frame, separated by horizontal bars.

Figure 18.1.

Frames allow more than one Web page to be displayed at once.

A frame is a rectangular region within the browser window that displays a Web page alongside other pages in other frames.

The main advantage of using frames becomes apparent when a reader clicks on one of the links in the bottom frame of Figure 18.1. The top and bottom frames will not change at all, but a new page will be loaded and displayed in the middle frame, as in Figure 18.2.

Figure 18.2.

Clicking on See Us Make It in Figure 18.1 brings up a new middle page but leaves the top and bottom frames the same.

Creating a Frameset Document

How did I make the site in Figures 18.1 and 18.2? First, I created the contents of each frame as an ordinary HTML page. These pages (shown in Figures 18.3 through 18.6) don't contain any tags that you haven't already seen in other hours.

Figure 18.3.

This page was designed specifically to fit in the top frame of Figures 18.1 and 18.2.

```
<HTML>
<HEAD><TITLE>Maple Syrup from Sandiwood Farm</TITLE></HEAD>
<BODY BACKGROUND="hboard.jpg">
<IMG SRC="corner1.gif" ALIGN="left">
<IMG SRC="corner2.gif" ALIGN="right">
<DIV ALIGN="center">
<FONT FACE="Lucida Handwriting" SIZE=2 COLOR="maroon">
<B>The Schlosser Family<BR>
<IMG SRC="swfarm.gif" ALT="Sandiwood Farm"><BR>
Wolcott, Vermont, USA</B></FONT>
</DIV>
</BODY></HTML>
```

18

Figure 18.4.

This ordinary Web page appears in the middle frame in Figure 18.1.

```
<HTML>
<HEAD><TITLE>Maple Syrup from Sandiwood Farm</TITLE></HEAD>
<BODY BACKGROUND="paper.jpg"
 TEXT="maroon" VLINK="red" LINK="red" ALINK="black">
<IMG SRC="maple.gif" ALIGN="left" HSPACE=10>
<FONT FACE="Lucida Handwriting" SIZE=4>
<H1>Pure Maple Syrup</H1> <H2>A Vermont Tradition</H2>
Every spring, when the snow turns to the texture of
granulated sugar and the warm morning sun melts the frost
on the window panes, the sugar maples come out of their
long winter's sleep. The result is one of Nature's most
sumptous delights - fresh maple sap, boiled down to a thick,
rich syrup as sweet as springtime itself.<P>
<IMG SRC="foods.gif" ALIGN="right">
<H2>It's Not Just for Breakfast!</H2>
Every Vermonter knows that if you save your maple syrup just
for pancakes, you're depriving yourself of a vast variety of
luscious, mapley treats: cookies, muffins, breads, and
almost any baked goods will truly come to life with the
special flavor of fresh syrup. Use a touch of maple instead
of vanilla in whipped cream or ice cream. Drizzle it over
hams and other meats, or add it to spicy sauces and curries
(in India, a very similar syrup is made from the sap of local
trees). Try a little in seltzer water for a healthy and
exotic refresher! And of course, nothing compares to the
Native American delicacies of blueberries and syrup in the
summer, and maple-flavored squash in the fall.<P>
<IMG SRC="mapleaf.gif" ALIGN="left" HSPACE=6>
<H2>A Wholesome, Healthy Treat</H2>
Vermont maple syrup is healthier and lower in calories than
refined sugar, and is better for the planet since it involves
less industrial waste in its production. We invite you to
<A HREF="makeit.htm">see how our family produces syrup at
Sandiwood farm</A> the traditional way, and
<A HREF="order.htm">order some of our fresh syrup</A>
for your own kitchen and table.<P>
</BODY>
</HTML>
```

Figure 18.5.

This is the bottom frame in Figure 18.1. Clicking on a link causes the contents of the middle frame to change.

```
<HTML>
<HEAD><TITLE>Maple Syrup from Sandiwood Farm</TITLE></HEAD>
<BODY BACKGROUND="hboard.jpg"
 TEXT="maroon" VLINK="red" LINK="red" ALINK="black">
<IMG SRC="corner3.gif" ALIGN="left">
<IMG SRC="corner4.gif" ALIGN="right">
<DIV ALIGN="center">
<FONT FACE="Lucida Handwriting" SIZE=4>
<A HREF="main.htm" TARGET="main">Pure Maple Syrup</A>
<IMG SRC="icon.gif" ALIGN="middle">
<A HREF="makeit.htm" TARGET="main">See Us Make It </A><BR>
<A HREF="order.htm" TARGET="main">Order Some!</A>
</DIV>
</BODY></HTML>
```

18

Figure 18.6.

This window contains five frames. (In Microsoft Internet Explorer, there would be no white lines between them.)

To put them all together, I used a special kind of page called a *frameset document.*

NEW TERM A *frameset* is the HTML command center for a framed page. It tells the page which pages to load, and where to load them. It is also referred to as a *frameset document* in this hour.

A frameset document tells the browser which pages to load and how to arrange them in the browser window. Figure 18.7 shows the frameset document for the Sandiwood Farm site in Figures 18.1, 18.2, and 18.6.

Figure 18.7.

If you load this frameset document in Netscape Navigator, you'll see the site in Figure 18.1.

```
<HTML>
<HEAD><TITLE>Maple Syrup from Sandiwood Farm</TITLE></HEAD>
<FRAMESET ROWS="80,*,80">
<FRAME SRC="banner.htm" SCROLLING=NO
 MARGINHEIGHT=4 MARGINWIDTH=4>
<FRAME SRC="main.htm" NAME="main">
<FRAME SRC="bottom.htm" SCROLLING=NO
 MARGINHEIGHT=4 MARGINWIDTH=4>
</FRAMESET>
</HTML>
```

In the code in Figure 18.7, there is a <FRAMESET> tag instead of a <BODY> tag. No tags that would normally be contained in a <BODY> tag can be within the <FRAMESET> tag. The <FRAMESET> tag in Figure 18.7 includes a ROWS attribute, meaning that the frames should be arranged on top of each other like the horizontal rows of a table. If you want your frames to be side-by-side, use a COLS attribute instead of ROWS.

You must specify the sizes of the ROWS or COLS, either as precise pixel values or as percentages of the total size of the browser window. You can also use an asterisk (*) to indicate that a frame should fill whatever space is available in the window. If more than one frame has an * value, the remaining space will be allotted equally between them.

In Figure 18.7, `<FRAMESET ROWS="80,*,80">` means to split the window vertically into three frames. The top and bottom frames will be exactly 80 pixels tall, and the middle frame will take up all the remaining space in the window. The top frame contains the document `banner.htm`, and the bottom frame contains `bottom.htm`. Because you can't predict the size of the window in which someone will view your Web page, it is usually safest to use percentages rather than exact pixel values to dictate the size of the rows and columns. For example, to make a left frame 20% of the width of the browser window with a right frame taking up the remaining 80%, you would type

```
<FRAMESET COLS="20%,80%">
```

An exception to this rule would be when you want a frame to contain a single image of a certain size; then you would specify that size in pixels and add a few pixels for the frame borders. This is the case in Figure 18.7, where the background images for the boards are exactly 80 pixels thick.

If you specify any frame size in pixels, there must also be at least one frame in the same frameset with a variable (*) width so that the document can be displayed in a window of any size.

The `<FRAME>` Tag

Within the `<FRAMESET>` and `</FRAMESET>` tags, you should have a `<FRAME>` tag indicating which HTML document to display in each frame. (If you have fewer `<FRAME>` tags than the number of frames defined in the `<FRAMESET>` tag, any remaining frames will be left blank.) You don't need to specify a closing `</FRAME>` tag.

Include a SRC attribute in each `<FRAME>` tag, with the address of the Web page to load in that frame. (You can insert the address of an image file instead of a Web page if you just want a frame with a single image in it.)

You can include any HTML page you want in a frame. For example, the middle frame of Figure 18.1 is listed in Figure 18.4. For smaller frames, however, it's a good idea to create documents specifically for the frames with the reduced display area for each frame in mind. The top frame in Figure 18.1, for instance, is listed in Figure 18.3. It is much shorter than most Web pages because it was designed specifically to fit in a frame 80 pixels tall.

Linking Frames

The real fun begins when you give a frame a name with the `<FRAME NAME>` attribute. You can then make any link on the page change the contents of that frame using the `<A TARGET>` attribute. For example, Figure 18.7 includes the following tag:

```
<FRAME SRC="main.htm" NAME="main">
```

18

This displays the main.htm page in that frame when the page loads, and names the frame main. (The frame name doesn't have to match the name of its contents; it just happens to in this example.)

In the bottom frame, listed in Figure 18.5, you will see the following link:

```
<A HREF="makeit.htm" TARGET="main">See us make it.</A><BR>
```

When the user clicks this link, makeit.htm is displayed in the frame named main (the middle frame). To accomplish this sort of interactivity before the invention of frames, you would have had to use complex programming or scripting languages. Now you can do it with a simple link!

If the TARGET="main" attribute hadn't been included, the makeit.htm page would be displayed in the current (bottom) frame instead.

To save space, I haven't listed the makeit.htm page in a figure; it's just a regular Web page with no special frame-related features. You can see what the top of it looks like in Figure 18.2, and see the whole site online at

```
http://www.mcp.com/info/1-57521/1-57521-366-4/
```

JUST A MINUTE

When you include the TARGET attribute in a link, you can use a few special frame names in addition to the names you have defined with FRAME NAME:

☐ _blank loads the link into a new, unnamed window.

☐ _self loads the link into the current frame, replacing the document now being displayed in this frame.

☐ _top loads the link into the entire browser window.

☐ _parent loads the link over the parent frame if the current frame is nested within other frames (This name is the same as _top unless the frames are nested more than one level deep).

Note that all other names beginning with an underscore (_) will be ignored.

Margins, Borders, and Scrolling

In addition to the NAME attribute, the <FRAME> tag can take the following special frame-related attributes:

☐ MARGINWIDTH: Left and right margins of the frame (in pixels).

☐ MARGINHEIGHT: Top and bottom margins of the frame (in pixels).

18

☐ SCROLLING: Display scrollbar for the frame? (yes or no).

☐ NORESIZE: Don't allow this frame to be resized by the user.

MARGINWIDTH and MARGINHEIGHT are pretty much self-explanatory, but each of the other attributes is discussed in detail in the next few paragraphs.

Normally, any frame that isn't big enough to hold all its contents will have its own scrollbar(s). The middle frames in Figures 18.1 and 18.2 are examples. If you don't want a particular frame to ever display scrollbars, you can put SCROLLING="NO" in the frame tag. Conversely, SCROLLING="YES" forces both horizontal and vertical scrollbars to appear, whether or not they are needed.

You might wonder why I included SCROLLING="NO" for the top and bottom <FRAME> tags in Figure 18.7. I did so because the images in those frames don't quite fit within the 80 pixels I allowed when you count the margin of the page, too. So Netscape Navigator displays scrollbars that scroll down only a few pixels, and have no real purpose. Rather than make the frame bigger (and take up valuable window real estate with empty margin space), I just turned off the scrollbars.

The only situation I can think of where you might want to use SCROLLING=YES is if some graphics won't line up correctly unless you can count on the scrollbars always being there. Chances are, you'll probably never need SCROLLING=YES.

18

People viewing your frames can ordinarily resize them by grabbing the frame border with the mouse and dragging it around. If you don't want anyone messing with the size of a frame, put NORESIZE in the <FRAME> tag.

Borderless Frames

The coolest use of frames has to be borderless frames. That's how you make your frames invisible at the same time, allowing you unprecedented control over the placement of elements on the page.

Both Microsoft Internet Explorer and Netscape Navigator allow you to control the size of the frame borders or eliminate the borders altogether. HTML 4.0 just allows you to turn off the borders.

Unfortunately, Microsoft and Netscape do not yet agree on how frame borders should be controlled, and W3C has combined and rejected features of both in its own solution, so you need to use three different sets of nonstandard HTML tags. For Microsoft Internet Explorer, you can make the borders disappear by including FRAMEBORDERS="NO" in the <FRAMESET> tag. This makes a frame document look just like a regular Web page, with no ugly lines breaking it up. The FRAMESPACING attribute also lets you specify the number of pixels between frames in a frameset.

For Netscape Navigator, use BORDER="0" in the <FRAMESET> tag to eliminate borders, or BORDER= followed by a number of pixels to change the size of the frame borders.

For HTML 4.0, use FRAMEBORDERS="0" in each adjacent <FRAME> tag. The border's numeric choices are 1 (the default value) and 0.

If you want borderless frames in all three, type FRAMEBORDERS="NO" BORDER="0" in your <FRAMESET> tag (see Figures 18.7 and 18.8), and FRAMEBORDERS="0" in all adjacent <FRAME> tags. Note that the location of the attribute has changed in the draft proposal and that you now have to type in three attributes in two different tags to account for most browsers.

Figure 18.8.

To create Figure 18.6, I used a <FRAMESET> within a <FRAMESET>.

```
<HTML>
<HEAD><TITLE>Maple Syrup from Sandiwood Farm</TITLE></HEAD>
<FRAMESET ROWS="80,*,80" FRAMEBORDER=NO BORDER=0>
<FRAME SRC="banner.htm"
 SCROLLING=NO MARGINHEIGHT=4 MARGINWIDTH=4>
<FRAMESET COLS="80,*,80" FRAMEBORDER=NO BORDER=0>
<FRAME SRC="side.htm">
<FRAME SRC="main.htm" NAME="main">
<FRAME SRC="side.htm">
</FRAMESET>
<FRAME SRC="bottom.htm"
 SCROLLING=NO MARGINHEIGHT=4 MARGINWIDTH=4>
</FRAMESET>

<NOFRAMES><BODY>
<H1>Sandiwood Farm</H1>
<H2>Pure Vermont Maple Syrup</H2>
Your Web browser doesn't support frames,
but you can still <A HREF="main.htm">
explore our Web pages the old-fashioned way.</A>
</BODY></NOFRAMES>
</HTML>
```

Nested Frames

By nesting one <FRAMESET> within another, you can create rather complex frame layouts. For example, the document shown in Figure 18.6 and listed in Figure 18.8 has a total of five frames. A COLS frameset is used to split the middle frame of the ROWS frameset into three pieces.

The two side pieces contain the simple page in Figure 18.9, which is nothing but a background tile. The net effect is to surround the changing middle frame with a static "wooden" picture frame.

18

HTML 4.0 has added the I-frame (inline frame) capability, which allows you to get around this rather cumbersome, but still effective, method.

Figure 18.9.

This is the side.htm *page, which is just a background tile with no foreground text or images.*

```
<HTML>
<BODY BACKGROUND="vboard.jpg">
</BODY>
</HTML>
```

Inline Frames

Now that inline frames are available in HTML 4.0, a lot of the more complex tricks are no longer needed. The nested frames "picture frame" effect I created in the preceding section can be accomplished more simply using a floating inline frame above an empty page with a background graphic. It's so easy to do, in fact, that I'll leave it as an exercise for your imagination.

Hint: Here is the only special code you'll need:

```
<IFRAME src="anydoc.html" width="300" height="100"
➥scrolling="auto" frameborder="1">
[ Your browser does not display inline frames. <A href="anydoc.html">
Select this link</A> to retrieve the referenced document. ]
</IFRAME>
```

This code snippet illustrates the tag used to display an inline frame, the most important change to the frame specification in HTML 4.0. If you use Internet Explorer, it might look strangely familiar. Note that you cannot resize an inline frame, so NORESIZE is not a valid argument.

This tag and its contents will display an inline frame in browsers that support this construct and, because browsers ignore tags they don't recognize, will display the included link text if inline frames are not supported. I included the text to show graphically when it would be displayed. On a production page, you'd want to make the message less obtrusive. After all, you're advertising yourself, not the companies who make new browsers.

Supporting Frameless Browsers

After the framesets in Figure 18.8, I included a complete Web page between the <BODY> and </BODY> tags. Notice that this doesn't appear at all in Figure 18.6. All Web browsers that support frames will ignore anything between the <NOFRAMES> and </NOFRAMES> tags.

To users of older Web browsers that don't support frames, the page listed in Figure 18.8 looks like Figure 18.10.

Figure 18.10.

This is what Figure 18.8 looks like when you view it with Netscape Navigator version 1.2, which doesn't support frames.

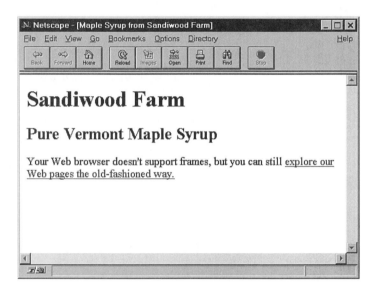

Because some browsers do not support frames, and some people don't like frames, it is both wise and thoughtful to include alternative content with the <NOFRAMES> tag, enabling these audiences. Every frame has a content document somewhere. It takes very little effort to provide a link to the primary content page or even to include the entire text of the main content page in the NOFRAMES section. This has the advantage of making sure your site is visible to everyone, not just those people who have the latest of everything and no circumstances that might preclude their use of frames in the first place.

JUST A MINUTE

Some Web page publishers actually produce two versions of their site—one with frames, and one without. You can save yourself that hassle by simply including links between all the pages that will appear in your primary frame.

For example, all the pages that appear in the middle frame in this hour's sample site are linked together with ordinary links (that don't use TARGET). You can get all the information from the site by starting at the main.htm page instead of the syrup.htm frameset document.

18

Summary

In this hour, you learned how to display more than one page at a time by splitting the Web browser window into frames. You learned to use a frameset document to define the size and arrangement of the frames, as well as which Web page or image will be loaded into each frame. You saw how to create links that change the contents of any frame you choose while leaving the other frames unchanged. You also discovered several optional settings that control the appearance of resizable borders and scrollbars in frames. Finally, you saw how to nest framesets to create complex frame layouts and how to use the <NOFRAMES> tag to ensure accessibility and ease of use for everyone.

Table 18.1 summarizes the tags and attributes covered in this hour.

Table 18.1. HTML tags and attributes covered in this hour.

Tag	Attribute	Function
`<FRAMESET>...</FRAMESET>`		Divides the main window into a set of frames, each of which can display a separate document.
	`ROWS="..."`	Splits the window or frameset vertically into a number of rows specified by a number (such as 7); a percentage of the total window width (such as 25%); or as an asterisk (*), which indicates that a frame should take up all the remaining space or divide the space evenly between frames (if multiple * frames are specified).
	`COLS="..."`	Works similar to ROWS except that the window, or frameset, is split horizontally into columns.
	`ONLOAD="..."`	Specifies a script to run when all frames have been loaded.

18

continues

Table 18.1. continued

Tag	Attribute	Function
	ONUNLOAD="..."	Specifies a script to run when all frames have been unloaded.
	FRAMESPACING="..."	Space between frames, in pixels For Microsoft Internet Explorer 3.0 only. Not an HTML 4.0 attribute.
	FRAMEBORDER="..."	Specifies whether to display a border for the frames. Options are YES and NO for Microsoft Internet Explorer 3.0 only. Note that the placement of this attribute has moved to the <FRAME> tag in HTML 4.0. The default action is to display borders.
	BORDER="..."	Size of the frame borders (in pixels) for Netscape Navigator only. Setting the value to 0 turns off borders. Not an HTML 4.0 attribute. The default action is to display borders.
<FRAME>		Defines a single frame within a <FRAMESET>.
	SRC="..."	The URL of the document to be displayed in this frame.
	NAME="..."	A name to be used for targeting this frame with the TARGET attribute in <A HREF> links.

18

Tag	Attribute	Function
	MARGINWIDTH="..."	The amount of space (in pixels) to leave to the left and right side of a document within a frame.
	MARGINHEIGHT="..."	The amount of space (in pixels) to leave above and below a document within a frame.
	SCROLLING="..."	Determines whether a frame has scrollbars. Possible values are YES, NO, and AUTO.
	NORESIZE	Prevents the user from resizing this frame (and possibly adjacent frames) with the mouse.
	FRAMEBORDER="..."	Specifies whether to display a border for the frame. Options are 1 and 0 for HTML 4.0; 1 stands for on and 0 stands for off. The default action is to display borders. Note that the placement of this attribute has changed in HTML 4.0 and that all adjacent frames must request no borders for the request to be effective. Not an MSIE 3.0 or Netscape attribute.
<IFRAME>...</IFRAME>		Creates an inline frame which can place content from another document into your page.
	WIDTH="..."	Sets the width of the frame in pixels.

18

continues

Table 18.1. continued

Tag	Attribute	Function
	`HEIGHT="..."`	Sets the height of the frame in pixels.
	`FRAMEBORDER="..."`	Sets the width of the border.
	`SCROLLING="..."`	Sets the scrolling
`<NOFRAMES>...</NOFRAMES>`		Provides an alternate document body in `<FRAMESET>` documents for browsers that do not support frames (usually encloses `<BODY>...</BODY>`).

Q&A

Q Once I have some frames, how do I get rid of them and go back to a single page again?

A Link to the page you want to display, and include `TARGET="_top"` in the `<A>` tag. This page will take up the entire browser window and eliminate all frames (unless the page you load is a frameset document, too).

Q Can I display other people's Web pages from the Internet in one frame and my own pages in another frame at the same time? What if those sites use frames, too?

A You can load any document from anywhere on the Internet (or on an intranet) into a frame. If the document is a frameset, its frames will be sized to fit within the existing frame you load it into.

For example, you could put a hotlist of your favorite links in one frame, and have the pages that those links refer to appear in a separate frame. This makes it easy to provide links to other sites without risking that someone will get lost and never come back to your site. Note, however, that if any link within that site has `TARGET="_top"`, it will replace all your frames. In fact, this is a good trick in itself, and doesn't depend on JavaScript or any other language. Simply create a button near the top of your page. Label it Escape from Frames or some such thing, and you've supplied a way for people to escape from frame tyranny without making the decision for them.

You should also be aware that framing somebody else's pages so they appear to be part of your own site may get you in legal trouble. Several major lawsuits are pending on this exact issue, so be sure to get explicit written permission from anyone whose pages you plan to put within one of your frames (just as you would if you were putting images or text from their site on your own pages).

Q Can I prevent people from putting my pages in their frames, and making my lovely pages look like part of their sleazy site?

A Yes. To "frame-proof" any page, put the following "secret code" in the `<BODY>` tag:

```
<BODY onLoad="if (self != top) top.location = self.location">
```

The page will then always appear by itself, with no other frames visible, even if the link that called it up was within a frame. (This is JavaScript, by the way. See Hour 22, "Applets, ActiveX, and Objects," and Hour 23, "Using Scripts to Alter Elements," to learn more JavaScript magic tricks.)

Q Can I make my pages appear in two separate browser windows instead of two frames within the same window?

A Yes. Just put `TARGET="_blank"` in any `<A>` link tag to open a new browser window for the page the link leads to. The contents of the current browser window won't change, although they probably will be hidden behind the new window when it appears.

Q Do I need to put a `<TITLE>` in all my frames? If I do, which title will be displayed at the top of the window?

A The title of the frameset document is the only one that will be displayed. But it's a good idea to give titles to all your pages just in case somebody opens one by itself, outside any frame.

Quiz

Questions

1. How would you write the HTML to list the words stegosaurus, brontosaurus, tyrannosaurus rex, triceratops, and pterodactyl in a frame taking up the left 25% of the browser window, and make it so that clicking on each name brings up a corresponding Web page in the right 75% of the browser window?

18

Answers

1. You need seven separate HTML documents. The first document is the frameset:

```
<HTML><HEAD><TITLE>Dinosaurs</TITLE></HEAD>
<FRAMESET COLS="25%,75%">
<FRAME SRC="index.htm">
<FRAME SRC="stegosaurus.htm" NAME="mainframe">
</FRAMESET>
</HTML>
```

Next, you need the index.htm document for the left frame:

```
<HTML><HEAD><TITLE>Dinosaurs Index</TITLE></HEAD>
<BODY>
Pick a dinosaur:<P>
<A HREF="stegosaurus.htm" TARGET="mainframe">stegosaurus</A><P>
<A HREF="brontosaurus.htm" TARGET="mainframe">brontosaurus</A><P>
<A HREF="tyrannosaurus_rex.htm" TARGET="mainframe">tyrannosaurus_rex</A><P>
<A HREF="triceratops.htm" TARGET="mainframe">triceratops</A><P>
<A HREF="pterodactyl.htm" TARGET="mainframe">pterodactyl</A><P>
</BODY></HTML>
```

Finally, you need the five HTML pages named tyrannosaurus rex.htm, triceratops.htm, stegasaurus.htm, brontosaurus.htm, and pteradactyl.htm. These will contain the information about each dinosaur.

Activities

☐ Design a page using frames with a border, then, without the border. What do you personally think the advantages to each are? The disadvantages?

18

Hour 19

Creating HTML Forms

Up to this point, everything in this book has focused on getting information out to others. (E-mail links, introduced in Hour 8, "Intra-Page and E-mail Links," are the one exception.) But HTML is a two-way street; you can also use your Web pages to gather information from the people who read them.

In this hour, you'll learn about

- ☐ What forms are
- ☐ How forms work
- ☐ Form design
- ☐ Creating a form:
  - Text input
  - Identifying the data
  - Checkboxes
  - Radio buttons
  - Selection lists
  - Text areas
  - Submit!

Custom submit buttons

Including hidden data

☐ New features of HTML 4.0 forms

What Forms Are

Web forms allow you to receive feedback, orders, or other information from the readers of your Web pages. If you've ever used a Web search engine such as Lycos or Excite, you're familiar with HTML forms. Product order forms are also an extremely popular use of forms. Forms allow you to subtly influence the sorts of information your users provide, as well as offer ease of use and convenience for quickly selecting from lists of options or entering complex data with a few keystrokes.

This hour shows you how to create your own forms and the basics of how to handle form submissions.

An HTML form is the part of a Web page that includes areas where readers can enter information to be sent back to you, the publisher of the Web page.

How Forms Work

Before you learn the HTML tags to make your own forms, you should understand how the information that someone fills out on a form makes its way back to you. You also need to have the person who runs your Web server computer set it up to process your forms.

Every form must include a button for the user to submit the form. When someone clicks on this button, all the information they have filled in is sent (in a standard format) to an Internet address that you will specify in the form itself. HTML 4.0 also adds many options for including different kinds of actions in your forms. You could call local scripts that perform error-checking for each field, use scripts to announce audible directions for filling out the fields, navigate directly to an input field with a keystroke, and many other new and exciting capabilities.

Of course, the most important use for forms is still to allow you to collect the data at some point. For that information to get to you, you have to put a special forms-processing program at that address.

Almost all Internet service provider companies that offer Web page hosting also provide preprogrammed scripts to their customers for processing forms. The most common thing that such a script would do is forward the information from the form to your e-mail address, although it might also save the information to a file on the Web server or format the form data to make it easier for you to read.

It's also possible to set things up so that much of the form information can be interpreted and processed automatically. For example, server software exists to authorize a credit card transaction automatically over the Internet, confirm an order to the customer's e-mail address, and enter the order directly into your company's in-house database for shipment. Obviously, setting up that sort of system can get quite complex, and it's beyond the scope of this book to explain all the things you could do with form data once it has been submitted.

Before you start building your first form, you should do the following:

To Do

1. Ask your Internet service provider what they offer for form-processing scripts and what exact address your forms should send their information to. In the next hour, you'll see where and how to put that address into your forms.

2. If you run your own Web server computer, the server software probably came with some basic form-processing scripts. Consult your documentation to set them up properly and find out the address on your server where each is located.

3. If you have a choice of several forms-processing scripts, I recommend starting with the script to simply send the "raw" form data to your e-mail address. The example in this hour uses such a script. You can experiment with fancier scripts later.

Once you have the address of your forms-processing script, you're ready for the rest of this hour. As usual, I recommend that you create a form of your own as you read through my examples.

Designing a Form

Before you start coding, spend a little time thinking about what sort of information you need and how you can help your reader fill in the information most easily. Drawing the layout on a piece of paper will help you organize the fields into logical groups and tell you whether the form seems clear and easy to use. A little time spent on this front-end design will save lots of time later dealing with correcting wrongly entered data and probably will help keep your readers happy with you to boot!

Creating a Form

Every form must begin with a <FORM> tag, which can be located anywhere in the body of the HTML document. The <FORM> tag normally has two attributes, METHOD and ACTION:

```
<FORM METHOD="post" ACTION="/cgi/generic">
```

Nowadays, the METHOD is almost always "post", which means to send the form entry results as a document. (In some special situations, you may need to use METHOD="get", which submits the results as part of the URL header instead. For example, "get" is sometimes used when submitting queries to search engines from a Web form. If you're not yet an expert on forms, just use "post" unless someone tells you to do otherwise.)

The ACTION attribute specifies the address of the program or script on the server computer that will process the information a user enters on a form. This is the address that your service provider or Web server manager should be able to give you, as mentioned in the previous "To Do" section. If you are a programmer, you can also write your own scripts in any language supported on the server.

The form in Figures 19.1 and 19.2 includes every type of input that you can currently use on HTML forms. Figure 19.3 is the same form as it might look after someone fills it out. As you read through the rest of this hour, refer to these figures for an example of each type of input element.

Figure 19.1.

All parts of a form must fall between the <FORM> *and* </FORM> *tags.*

```
<HTML><HEAD><TITLE>Get Me Rich Quick</TITLE></HEAD>
<BODY>
<H2>Get Me Rich Quick</H2>
<FORM METHOD="post" ACTION="/htbin/generic">

<INPUT TYPE="hidden" NAME="cant_see_me"
        VALUE="the user won't see this">
<PRE>Check this checkbox if you want to send me money: <INPUT
TYPE="checkbox" NAME="checkme" CHECKED>

Enter your credit card number in this text box: <INPUT
TYPE="text" NAME="cardnum" SIZE=20>
Expiration date: <INPUT TYPE="text" NAME="ext" SIZE=5>

Select the card type with these radio buttons:
<INPUT TYPE="radio" NAME="payment" VALUE="v" CHECKED> Visa
<INPUT TYPE="radio" NAME="payment" VALUE="m"> MasterCard
<INPUT TYPE="radio" NAME="payment" VALUE="d"> Discover

Choose the amount of your contribution from
this scrolling list: <SELECT
NAME="howmuch" SIZE=3>
   <OPTION SELECTED> $1,000,000
   <OPTION>$100,000
   <OPTION>$10,000
   <OPTION>$1,000
   <OPTION>$100
   <OPTION> Whatever</OPTION>
</SELECT>

Pick your reason from this pull-down list: <SELECT
NAME="why">
   <OPTION SELECTED> You deserve it
   <OPTION> I don't deserve it
   <OPTION> I'm rich
   <OPTION> I'm stupid
   <OPTION> I love you
   <OPTION> What the heck
</SELECT>

Enter any comments in this text area:<BR>
<TEXTAREA NAME="comments" rows=4 cols=40>
Gosh, this is a rare privilege.
Thanks and enjoy the dough.</TEXTAREA>
</PRE>
<INPUT TYPE=submit VALUE="    I Submit!    ">
<INPUT TYPE=reset  VALUE="Never Mind.">
</FORM>
</BODY></HTML>
```

19

Figure 19.2.

The form listed in Figure 19.1 uses every type of HTML form input element.

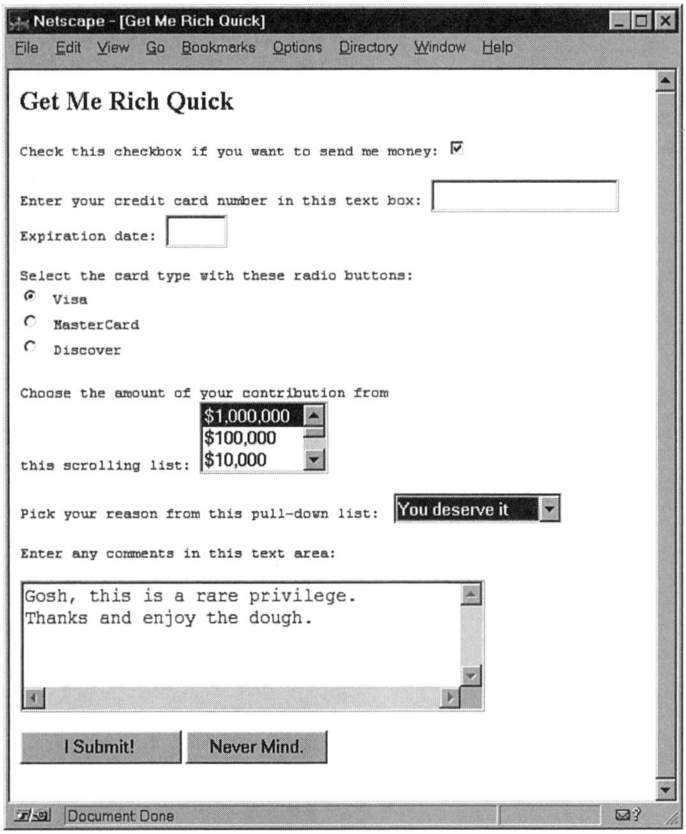

TIME SAVER

Notice that most of the text in Figure 19.2 is monospaced. Monospaced text makes it easy to line up a form input box with the box above or below it, and makes your forms look neater. To use monospaced text throughout a form, enclose the entire form between <PRE> and </PRE> tags. Using these tags also relieves you from having to put <BR> at the end of every line because the <PRE> tag puts a line break on the page at every line break in the HTML document.

19

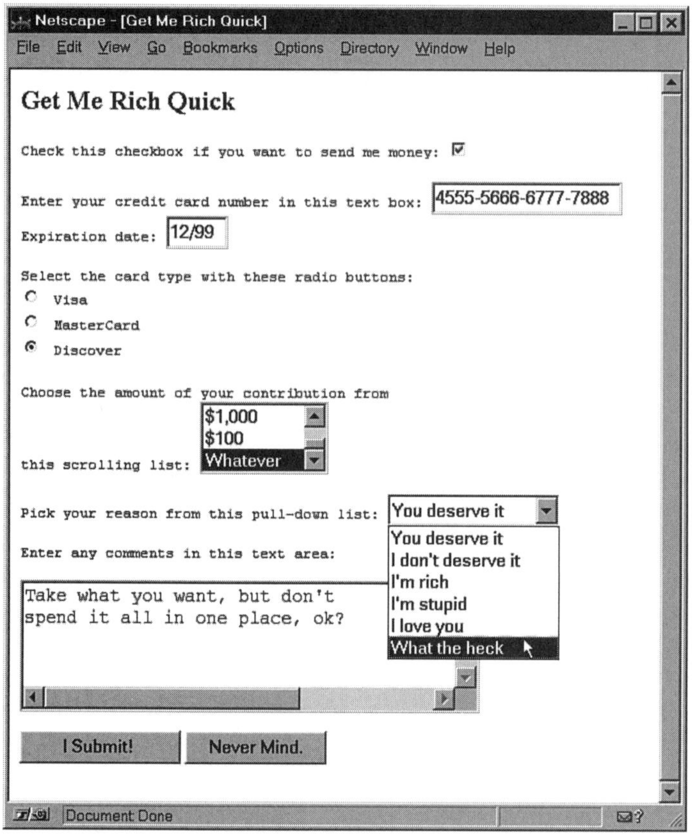

Figure 19.3.

Visitors to your Web site fill out the form with their mouse or keyboard, and then click the Submit button.

Text Input

To ask the user for a specific piece of information within a form, use the <INPUT> tag. This tag must fall between the <FORM> and </FORM> tags, but it can be anywhere on the page in relation to text, images, and other HTML tags. For example, to ask for someone's name you could type the following:

```
What's your first name? <INPUT TYPE="text" SIZE=20 MAXLENGTH=30
➥NAME="firstname">
What's your last name? <INPUT TYPE="text" SIZE=20 MAXLENGTH=30 NAME="lastname">
```

The TYPE attribute indicates what type of form element to display, such as a simple one-line text entry box in this case. (Each element type is discussed individually in the following sections.)

19

The SIZE attribute indicates approximately how many characters wide the text input box should be. If you are using a proportionally spaced font, the width of the input will vary depending on what the user enters. If the input is too long to fit in the box, most Web browsers will automatically scroll the text to the left.

MAXLENGTH determines the number of characters the user is allowed to type into the text box. If someone tries to type beyond the specified length, the extra characters won't appear. You may specify a length that is longer, shorter, or the same as the physical size of the text box. SIZE and MAXLENGTH are only used for TYPE="text" because other input types (checkboxes, radio buttons, and so on) have a fixed size.

JUST A MINUTE

> If you want the user to enter text without it being displayed onscreen, you can use <INPUT TYPE="password"> instead of <INPUT TYPE="text">. Asterisks (***) are then displayed in place of the text the user types. The SIZE, MAXLENGTH, and NAME attributes work exactly the same way for TYPE="password" as for TYPE="text".

Identifying the Data

No matter what type of input element it is, you must give a name to the data it gathers. You can use any name you like for each input item, as long as each one on the form is different. When the form is sent to the server script, each data item is identified by name.

For example, if the user entered Jane and Doe in the text box previously defined under the "Text Input" section, the server script would receive a document including the following:

```
firstname='Jane'
lastname='Doe'
```

If the script mails the raw data from the form submission to you directly, you would see these two lines in an e-mail message from the server. The script might also be set up to format the input into a more readable format before reporting it to you.

Figure 19.4 is a sample e-mail message from the form in Figure 19.3. Notice that each data element is identified by the name given to it in Figure 19.1. Your server script might present the data in a different format than that shown in Figure 19.4, but it should include all the same information.

19

Figure 19.4.

Clicking on the I Submit! button in Figure 19.3 causes this information to be sent to a server script. (The script may then be e-mailed to you.)

```
From: nobody@shore.net
Date: Mon, 9 Dec 1996 22:15:29 -0500 (EST)
To: dicko@shore.net
Subject: Web page form

cant_see_me='the user won'\''t see this'
checkme='on'
cardnum='4555-5666-6777-7888'
ext='12/98'
payment='d'
howmuch='Whatever'
why='What the heck'
comments='Take what you want, but don'\''t
spend it all in one place, ok?'
```

Checkboxes

The simplest input type is a checkbox, which appears as a small square the user can select or deselect by clicking on it. A checkbox doesn't take any attributes other than NAME:

```
<INPUT TYPE="checkbox" NAME="baby" VALUE="yes"> Baby Grand Piano
<INPUT TYPE="checkbox" NAME="upright"> Upright Piano
```

Selected checkboxes appear in the form result sent to the server script as follows:

```
baby='yes'
```

Blank (deselected) checkboxes do not appear in the form output result at all. If you don't specify a VALUE attribute, the default VALUE of "on" is used.

JUST A MINUTE

You can use more than one checkbox with the same name but with different values, as in the following code:

```
<INPUT TYPE="checkbox" NAME="pet" VALUE="dog"> Dog
<INPUT TYPE="checkbox" NAME="pet" VALUE="cat"> Cat
<INPUT TYPE="checkbox" NAME="pet" VALUE="iguana"> Iguana
```

If the user checked both cat and iguana, the submission result would include the following:

```
pet='cat'
pet='iguana'
```

Radio Buttons

Radio buttons, where only one choice can be selected at a time, are almost as simple to implement as checkboxes. Just use TYPE="radio" and give each of the options its own INPUT tag, as in the following code:

```
<INPUT TYPE="radio" NAME="card" VALUE="v" CHECKED> Visa
<INPUT TYPE="radio" NAME="card" VALUE="m"> MasterCard
```

The VALUE can be any name or code you choose. If you include the CHECKED attribute, that button will be selected by default. (No more than one button with the same name can be checked.)

If the user selected MasterCard from the preceding radio button set, the following would be included in the form submission to the server script:

```
card='m'
```

If the user didn't change the default CHECKED selection, card='v' would be sent instead.

Selection Lists

Both scrolling lists and pull-down pick lists are created with the <SELECT> tag. This tag is used together with the <OPTION> tag:

```
<SELECT NAME="extras" SIZE=3 MULTIPLE>
<OPTION SELECTED> Electric windows
<OPTION> AM/FM Radio
<OPTION> Turbocharger
</SELECT>
```

No HTML tags other than <OPTION> should appear between the <SELECT> and </SELECT> tags.

Unlike the text input type, the SIZE attribute here determines how many items show at once on the selection list. If SIZE=2 had been used in the preceding code, only the first two options would be visible, and a scrollbar would appear next to the list so the user could scroll down to see the third option.

Including the MULTIPLE attribute allows users to select more than one option at a time, and the SELECTED attribute makes an option selected by default. The actual text accompanying selected options is returned when the form is submitted. If the user selected Electric windows and Turbocharger, for instance, the form results would include the following lines:

```
extras='Electric windows'
extras='Turbocharger'
```

JUST A MINUTE

If you leave out the SIZE attribute or specify SIZE=1, the list will create a pull-down pick list. Pick lists cannot allow multiple choices; they are logically equivalent to a group of radio buttons. For example, another way to choose between credit card types would be

```
<SELECT NAME="card">
<OPTION> Visa
<OPTION> MasterCard
</SELECT>
```

19

Text Areas

The `<INPUT TYPE="text">` attribute mentioned earlier only allows the user to enter a single line of text. When you want to allow multiple lines of text in a single input item, use the `<TEXTAREA>` and `</TEXTAREA>` tags instead. Any text you include between these two tags will be displayed as the default entry. Here's an example:

```
<TEXTAREA NAME="comments" ROWS=4 COLS=20 WRAP="virtual">
Please send more information.
</TEXTAREA>
```

As you probably guessed, the ROWS and COLS attributes control the number of rows and columns of text that fit in the input box. Text area boxes do have a scrollbar, however, so the user can enter more text than fits in the display area. The WRAP attribute is a "Netscapeism" and is set to `"off"` by default, but it is thoughtful to include this attribute set either to `"virtual"`, which sends the text as one line but keeps it inside the window, just like a word processor, or to `"physical"`, which inserts line breaks. This compensates for a flaw in the way Netscape chose to display this kind of input. Microsoft IE doesn't pay any attention to this tag but behaves sensibly to begin with, wrapping the text properly on entry.

JUST A MINUTE

> Some older browsers do not support the placement of default text within the text area. In these browsers, the text may appear outside the text input box.

Submit!

Every form must include a button that submits the form data to the server. You can put any label you like on the submit button with the VALUE attribute:

```
<INPUT TYPE="submit" VALUE="Place My Order Now!">
```

A gray button will be sized to fit the label you put in the VALUE attribute. When the user clicks the button, all data items on the form are sent to the program or script specified in the FORM ACTION attribute.

Normally, this program or script generates some sort of reply page and sends it back to be displayed for the user. If no such page is generated, the form remains visible, however.

You may also optionally include a button that clears all entries on the form so users can start over again if they change their minds or make mistakes. Use this line:

```
<INPUT TYPE="reset" VALUE="Clear This Form and Start Over">
```

19

This has the disadvantage, however, of requiring the user to click on one or the other instead of being able to just press the enter key. Reset is kind of a useless feature as well, assuming that the user didn't fill in the form by leaning her elbow on the keyboard. The data entered on the form has no life beyond the page until, or if, you submit it.

Custom Submit Buttons

You can combine forms with all the HTML bells and whistles you've learned in this book, including backgrounds, graphics, text colors, tables, and frames. When you do so, however, the standard submit and reset buttons may start looking a little bland.

Fortunately, there is an easy way to substitute your own graphics for those buttons. To use an image of your choice for a submit button, type

```
<INPUT TYPE="image" SRC="button.gif" NAME="buttonxy">
```

The image named button.gif will appear on the page, and the form will be submitted whenever someone clicks on that image. You can also include any attributes normally used with the <IMG> tag, such as BORDER or ALIGN.

JUST A MINUTE

When the form data is sent to the server, the exact pixel coordinates of the click will be included as a data item with the name you specify in <INPUT NAME>. For example, the line in the previous paragraph might send

buttonxy="12,40"

Normally, you should ignore this information, but some server scripts use it to make the button into an image map.

There is no specific form type for a graphical reset button, but you can achieve the same effect by putting an image link to the current page, like this:

```
<A HREF="thispage.htm"><IMG SRC="cancel.gif" BORDER="0"></A>
```

JUST A MINUTE

The BORDER attribute is required to ensure that the image and simulated reset buttons look the same on the page. You could also make a text link that cancels the form and proceeds to another page (ignoring all information the user has entered so far) simply by linking to that other page. For example:

<A HREF="nodice.htm">Click here to cancel.</A>

19

Figures 19.5 and 19.6 show a jazzed-up version of the "Get Me Rich Quick" form, which uses customized submit and reset buttons.

Figure 19.5.

The last <INPUT> tag on this page creates a custom graphical submit button. The <IMG> tag after it resets the form.

```
<HTML><HEAD><TITLE>Get Me Rich Quick</TITLE></HEAD>
<BODY BACKGROUND="moneybk.gif" TEXT="red">
<DIV ALIGN="center">
<IMG SRC="getrich.gif" ALT="Get Me Rich Quick">
<P>
<FORM METHOD="post" ACTION="/htbin/generic">
<INPUT TYPE="hidden" SIZE=32 NAME="mail_to" VALUE="dicko">
Check here if you want to send me money:
<INPUT TYPE="checkbox" NAME="checkme" CHECKED><P>

<TABLE BORDER=2 CELLPADDING=20>
<TR><TD>
 Credit card number<BR>
 <INPUT TYPE="text" NAME="cardnum" SIZE=20><P>
 Exp. Date <INPUT TYPE="text" NAME="ext" SIZE=5>
</TD><TD>
 <INPUT TYPE="radio" NAME="payment" VALUE="v" CHECKED>
 Visa<P>
 <INPUT TYPE="radio" NAME="payment" VALUE="m"> MasterCard<P>
 <INPUT TYPE="radio" NAME="payment" VALUE="d"> Discover
</TD></TR>
<TR><TD>
 Amount of your contribution<P>
 <SELECT NAME="howmuch" SIZE=3>
  <OPTION SELECTED> $1,000,000
  <OPTION>$100,000
  <OPTION>$10,000
  <OPTION>$1,000
  <OPTION>$100
  <OPTION> Whatever</OPTION>
 </SELECT>
</TD><TD>
 Justification:
 <SELECT NAME="why">
  <OPTION SELECTED> You deserve it
  <OPTION> I don't deserve it
  <OPTION> I'm rich
  <OPTION> I'm stupid
  <OPTION> I love you
  <OPTION> What the heck
 </SELECT>
</TD></TR>
</TABLE>
<P>
<INPUT TYPE="image" SRC="takeit.gif" NAME="submitted"
 BORDER=0 ALIGN="top">
<A HREF="getrich2.htm">
<IMG SRC="forget.gif" BORDER=0 ALIGN="top"></A>
</FORM>
</DIV>
</BODY></HTML>
```

Figure 19.6.

The HTML in Figure 19.5 combines graphics, tables, and form input elements on this Web page.

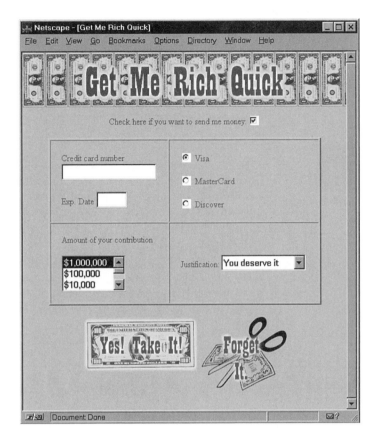

Including Hidden Data

If you want to send certain data items to the server script that processes a form, but you don't want the user to see them, you can use the INPUT TYPE="hidden" attribute. This attribute has no effect on the display at all; it just adds any name and value you specify to the form results when they are submitted.

You might use this attribute to tell a script where to e-mail the form results. For example, Figure 19.5 includes the following input element:

```
<INPUT TYPE="hidden" NAME="mail_to" VALUE="dicko">
```

which adds the following line to the form output:

```
mail_to='dicko'
```

19

For this attribute to have any effect, someone must create a script or program to read this line and do something about it. My Internet service provider's form script uses this hidden value to determine where to e-mail the form data. (My account name with them is dicko.)

Most scripts require at least one or two hidden input elements. Consult the person who wrote or provided you with the script for details. You can also use hidden items to indicate which of the many similar forms a particular result came from.

COFFEE BREAK

The most common mistake many companies make when putting the first order form on the Internet is the same one all too often made on paper order forms: leaving out a key piece of information. To save yourself the embarrassment of an incomplete order form, you might want to start with the sample form at

`http://www.mcp.com/sites/1-57521/1-57521-366-4/`

This is just your basic, run-of-the-mill product order form with credit card information, name, address, and so forth. Use it as a starting template and then add your own products, graphics, and unique information. Don't forget to change the `<FORM ACTION>` to the address of your own server script!

New Features of HTML 4.0 Forms

Because this book is about teaching you how to use HTML 4.0, this hour wouldn't be complete without including some information about the many new and exciting features that HTML 4.0 will make possible when browser support is widely available.

A lot of the new features involve things that were "forgotten" when HTML was being designed—things like accessibility for the vision- or dexterity-impaired, what to do if your mouse doesn't work or you don't have a mouse to begin with, how to group fields into logically-related categories, or even methods to explain what input is needed for a field before the user sends it off.

JUST A MINUTE

Remember, these changes will only be viewable in a browser compatible with HTML 4.0, such as Internet Explorer 4.0, or Netscape 4.0. I'll just give you an example of the sorts of things that can be done using a few new tags and attributes. I explain the new features more fully in Table 19.1.

19

Here's an example using the <FIELDSET>, <LEGEND>, and <LABEL>, which are all additions to HTML 4.0:

```
<FORM action="..." method="post">
<FIELDSET>
  <LEGEND align="top" accesskey="P">Personal Information</LEGEND>
  <LABEL for="last" accesskey="L">Last Name: </LABEL>
    <INPUT name="lastname" type="text" tabindex="1"
➥onfocus="audibleprompt(surname)" id="last">
  <LABEL for="first" accesskey="G">Given Name: </LABEL>
    <INPUT name="givenname" type="text" tabindex="2"
➥accesskey="G" onfocus="audibleprompt()" id="first">
</FIELDSET>
<FIELDSET>
  <LEGEND align="top" accesskey="S">Sexr</LEGEND>
  <LABEL for="msex" accesskey="M">Male</LABEL>
    <INPUT name="gender" type="radio" value="male" tabindex="3" id="msex">
</INPUT>
  <LABEL for="fsex" accesskey="F">Female</LABEL>
    <INPUT name="gender" type="radio" value="female" tabindex="3" id="fsex">
</INPUT>
</FIELDSET>
<FIELDSET>
  <LEGEND align="top" accesskey="R">Request for Subscription</LEGEND>
  Would you like to receive our newsletter?
  <LABEL for="news" accesskey="Y">Yes</LABEL>
    <INPUT name="newsletter"
      type="radio"
      value="Yes" tabindex="4" id="news"></INPUT>
  <LABEL for="nonews" accesskey="N">No</LABEL>
    <INPUT name="newsletter"
      type="radio"
      value="No" tabindex="4" id="nonews"></INPUT>
</FIELDSET>
</FORM>
```

In the preceding form, the fields are grouped into logical classifications, and the user can navigate to any field or classification by entering the initial letter of the field name from the keyboard. On the Mac, the user would hold down the CMD key and type the letter, while on the PC she would hold down the ALT key. The fields can also be tabbed through in a specified order. Further, when the first and last name fields have focus, a script that plays an audible prompt is called. This could be expanded to perform error-checking on the client-side so that required fields were all filled in with reasonable data before the form is sent to your server for processing.

Of course these aren't all the new features of HTML 4.0, but they will help get you started on what you can do when the new browsers become available that support the extended feature set.

19

Summary

This hour demonstrates how to create HTML forms, which allow readers of your Web pages to enter specific information and send it back to you.

You also found that you need to set up a script or program to process form data before you actually create a form. Your Internet service provider or server software vendor can help you do this.

You saw an example of some of the many new features HTML 4.0 will provide. These new features build on the basic technology for creating forms and are not a replacement for the basics. Therefore, your practice on pre-HTML 4.0 features, coupled with knowledge of what's around the next bend, will help you to prepare for the future with knowledge you can use today.

Table 19.1 summarizes the HTML tags and attributes covered in this hour.

Table 19.1. HTML tags and attributes.

Tag	Attribute	Function
`<FORM>...</FORM>`		Indicates an input form.
	`ACTION="..."`	The address of the script to process this form input.
	`METHOD="..."`	How the form input will be sent to the server. Normally set to POST, rather than GET.
`<INPUT>`		An input element for a form.
	`TYPE="..."`	The type for this input widget. Possible values are CHECKBOX, HIDDEN, RADIO, RESET, SUBMIT, TEXT, or IMAGE.
	`NAME="..."`	The name of this item, as passed to the script.
	`VALUE="..."`	For a text or hidden item, the default value; for a checkbox or radio button, the value to be submitted with the form; for reset or submit buttons, the label for the button itself.

19

Tag	Attribute	Function
	SRC="..."	The source file for an image.
	CHECKED	For checkboxes and radio buttons, this indicates that this item is checked.
	SIZE="..."	The width, in characters, of a text input region.
	MAXLENGTH="..."	The maximum number of characters that can be entered into a text region.
	ALIGN="..."	For images in forms, this determines how the text and image will align (same as with the <IMG> tag).
	ID="..."	Assigns an alphanumeric ID to an element that can be referenced by another element.
	DISABLED	The field cannot be changed and is not submitted with the form.
	READONLY	The field cannot be changed but is submitted with the form.
	ONFOCUS="..."	Script to be performed when the element gets focus.
	ONBLUR="..."	Script to be performed when the element loses focus.
	TABINDEX="..."	Ordinal value representing the order in which the tab key will change the focus.
<TEXTAREA>...</TEXTAREA>		Indicates a multiline text entry form element. Default text can be included.
	NAME="..."	The name to be passed to the script.
	ROWS="..."	The number of rows this text area displays.
	COLS="..."	The number of columns (characters) this text area displays.

continues

19

Table 19.1. continued

Tag	Attribute	Function
	ID="..."	Assigns an alphanumeric ID to an element that can be referenced by another element.
	DISABLED	This field cannot be changed and is not submitted with the form.
	READONLY	This field cannot be changed but is submitted with the form.
	ONFOCUS="..."	Script to be performed when the element gets focus.
	ONBLUR="..."	Script to be performed when the element loses focus.
	TABINDEX="..."	Ordinal value representing the order in which the tab key will change the focus.
	WRAP="..."	Indicates whether the browser should wrap the text in the window. Should almost always be either PHYSICAL or VIRTUAL. Default is OFF. Required for Netscape only.
<SELECT>...</SELECT>		Creates a menu or scrolling list of possible items.
	NAME="..."	The name that is passed to the script.
	SIZE="..."	The number of elements to display. If SIZE is indicated, the selection becomes a scrolling list. If no SIZE is given, the selection is a pop-up menu.
	MULTIPLE	Allows multiple selections from the list.
<OPTION>		Indicates a possible item within a <SELECT> element.
	SELECTED	With this attribute included, the <OPTION> will be selected by default in the list.

Tag	Attribute	Function
	VALUE="..."	The value to submit if this `<OPTION>` is selected when the form is submitted.
	ID="..."	Assigns an alphanumeric ID to an element that can be referenced by another element.
	DISABLED	The field cannot be changed and is not submitted with the form.
	READONLY	The field cannot be changed but is submitted with the form.
	ONFOCUS="..."	Script to be performed when the element gets focus.
	ONBLUR="..."	Script to be performed when the element loses focus.
	TABINDEX="..."	Ordinal value representing the order in which the tab key will change the focus.

HTML 4.0 Tags

Tag	Attribute	Function
`<LABEL>...</LABEL>`		Assigns a control label to an element.
	FOR="..."	A clickable label is associated with the referenced radio button or checkbox, or other controls are assigned to an element.
	DISABLED	The field cannot be changed and is not submitted with the form.
	READONLY	The field cannot be changed but is submitted with the form.
	ONFOCUS="..."	The script to be performed when the element gets focus.
	ONBLUR="..."	The script to be performed when the element loses focus.
	ACCESSKEY="..."	The value of a keyboard shortcut key to access this element.

19

continues

Table 19.1. continued

Tag	Attribute	Function
`<FIELDSET>...</FIELDSET>`		Groups related elements together.
`<LEGEND>...</LEGEND>`		Creates a description of a group of related elements.
	`ACCESSKEY="..."`	The value of a keyboard shortcut key to access this element.

Q&A

Q I've heard that it's dangerous to send credit card numbers over the Internet. Can't thieves intercept form data on its way to me?

A It is possible to intercept form data (and any Web pages or e-mail) as it travels through the Internet. If you ask for credit card numbers or other sensitive information on your forms, you should ask the company who runs your Web server about "secure" forms processing. There are several reliable technologies for eliminating the risk of high-tech eavesdroppers, but it may cost you quite a bit to implement the security measures.

To put the amount of risk in perspective, remember that it is much more difficult to intercept information traveling through the Internet than it is to look over someone's shoulder in a restaurant or retail store. Unless you service hundreds of credit card transactions per day, it will probably never be worth it to a would-be thief to bother tapping in to your forms data. Of the billions of dollars lost to credit card fraud each year, so far exactly zero has been from "unsecure" Internet transactions.

Q Can I put forms on a CD-ROM, or do they have to be on the Internet?

A You can put a form anywhere you can put a Web page. If it's on a disk or CD-ROM instead of a Web server, it can be filled out by people whether or not they are connected to the Internet. Of course, they must be connected to the Internet (or your local intranet) when they click on the submit button or the information won't get to you.

Quiz

Questions

1. What do you need to get from the people who administer your Web server computer before you can put a form on the Internet?

2. Write the HTML to create a "guestbook" form that asks someone for his name, sex, age, and e-mail address.

3. If you had created an image named sign-in.gif, how would you use it as the submit button for the guestbook in Question 2?

Answers

1. The Internet address of a script or program that is set up specifically to process form data.

2. Here's what you need to type to create a guestbook:

```
<HTML><HEAD><TITLE>My Guestbook</TITLE></HEAD>
<BODY>
<H1>My Guestbook: Please Sign In</H1>
<FORM METHOD="post" ACTION="/cgi/generic">
Your name: <INPUT TYPE="text" NAME="name" SIZE=20><P>
Your sex:
<INPUT TYPE="radio" NAME="sex" VALUE="male"> male
<INPUT TYPE="radio" NAME="sex" VALUE="female"> female<P>
Your age: <INPUT TYPE="text" NAME="age" SIZE=4><P>
Your e-mail address:
<INPUT TYPE="text" NAME="email" SIZE=30><P>
<INPUT TYPE="submit" VALUE="Sign In">
<INPUT TYPE="reset" VALUE="Erase">
</FORM>
</BODY></HTML>
```

3. Replace <INPUT TYPE="submit" VALUE="Sign In"> with

```
<INPUT TYPE="image" SRC="sign-in.gif" NAME="signxy">
```

Activities

☐ You should make a form using all of the different types of input elements and selection lists to make sure you understand how each of them works.

Hour 20

Organizing and Managing a Web Site

The first nineteen hours of this book led you through the design and creation of your own Web pages and the graphics to put on them. Now it's time to stop thinking about individual Web pages and start thinking about your Web site as a whole.

In this hour, you'll learn about

☐ Organizing a Web site for clarity

Appearance

Site structure

Navigational elements

Common mistakes

☐ Web site maintenance

Documentation

Managing change

Advanced maintenance issues

Organizing a Web Site for Clarity

This hour shows you how to organize and present multiple Web pages so that people will be able to navigate among them without confusion, and ways to make your Web site memorable enough to visit again and again.

Appearance

The overall appearance of your site is the face you present to the world. How will people recognize your site if it shows different faces depending on where you are? One of the most important design decisions is creating and maintaining a professional image that makes it clear that each and every page is what you or your company wants to present as its best work, reflecting the values and mission of the site owner.

This means you don't have Fozzie Bear saying "Whacka, Whacka!" on the entry page of a stock brokerage, or anywhere inside, however much of a Fozzie fan you may be. On your Muppet Adoration home page, it might be just the thing!

Site Structure

By this point in the book, you should have enough knowledge of HTML to produce most of your Web site. You have probably made a number of pages already, and perhaps even published them online.

As you read this hour, think about how your pages are organized now and how you can improve that organization. Don't be surprised if you decide to do a redesign that involves changing almost all of your pages—the results are likely to be well worth the effort!

Organizing a Simple Site

For many companies and individuals, building and organizing an attractive and effective Web site doesn't need to be a complex task. The Web page shown in Figure 20.1, for example, does its job quietly with a single graphics image and two short lists of links.

The goal of the home page in Figure 20.1, like the goal of many Web sites today, is simply to make the organization "visible" on the Internet. Many people today immediately turn to the World Wide Web when they want to find out about an organization or find out whether a particular type of organization exists at all. A simple home page should state enough information so that someone can tell whether they want to find out more. It should then provide both traditional address and telephone contact information and an electronic mail address.

The beauty of the Web is that a simple, short list like the "Materials currently available online from the GMWS" in Figure 20.1 can lead to a surprising wealth of information. Clicking on the first link on that list brings up the page in Figure 20.2, which in turns leads to a dozen more articles.

Figure 20.1.

This home page establishes a presence on the Internet with a minimum of fuss.

Netscape - [The Green Mountain Waldorf School]

File Edit View Go Bookmarks Options Directory Window Help

The Green Mountain Waldorf School

To enable the mind
To fire the imagination
To fortify the will
To quicken the initiative for life.
—Rudolf Steiner

The Green Mountain Waldorf School, located in Wolcott, Vermont, USA, provides a wholistic education to children throughout North Central Vermont, from the capitol city of Montpelier to the rural "Northeast Kingdom". Programs include a parent/child morning garden for two-and-a-half through four year olds and their parents, a kindergarten for children aged four through six years, a state accredited elementary school with first through sixth grades, and summer programs offering "adventures in art and nature" to children aged seven through seventeen. A wide variety of adult education workshops, artistic activities, visiting lecturers, study groups, and community events are also sponsored by the school.

A federated member of the Association of Waldorf Schools of North America, the Green Mountain Waldorf School is one of over 600 independent schools throughout the world which base their programs on the educational philosophy of Rudolf Steiner.

For more information about Waldorf education and the Green Mountain Waldorf School, please contact us at:

e-mail: GMWS@netletter.com

phone: 802-888-2828
fax: 802-888-3009

GMWS, RR 1 Box 4885, Wolcott, VT 05680 USA

Materials currently available online from the GMWS:

- Head, Heart, Hands: A Waldorf Family Newsletter
- The "un-TV" Guide: How and why to discover the joys of family life without television.

Other online links related to Waldorf education:

- Frequently Asked Questions about Waldorf Education
- Waldorf Education (Rudolf Steiner College)
- Glenn Karisch's Waldorf Education Page
- Waldorf Schools in North America
- Waldorf Schools Worldwide
- Waldorf Schools' E-mail Addresses

Document: Done

20

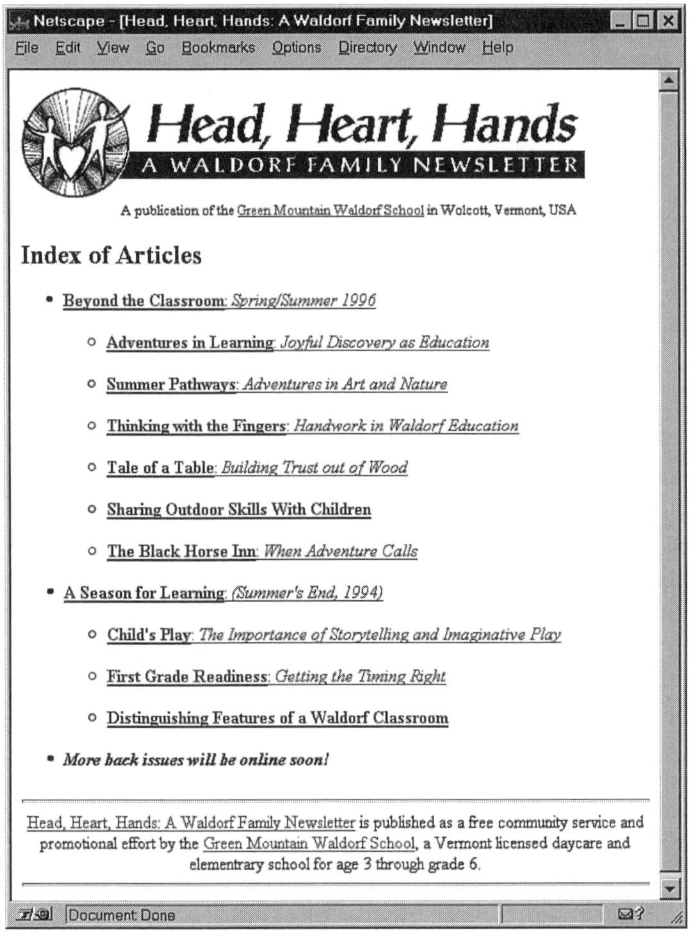

Figure 20.2.

Simple black-and-white graphics and a straight-forward table of contents make this index page fast to view and easy to use.

Having seen all the fancy graphics and layout tricks in Part III, "Web Page Graphics," you may be tempted to forget that a good old-fashioned outline is often the most clear and efficient way to organize a Web site. If you aren't selling visually oriented products or trying to prove that you're an artist, a list like the one in Figure 20.2 may be the best way to guide people through a relatively small Web site.

Organizing a Larger Site

For more complex sites, the techniques presented in Part III can both help organize and improve the looks of your site when used consistently throughout all of your pages. To see how you can make aesthetics and organization work hand-in-hand, let's look at how an existing site was recently redesigned for both better appearance and clearer organization.

20

The home page in Figure 20.3 is neatly organized into four categories of pages, accessible through the four regions of the image map or through the text links below them. The text on the page provides the essential information that someone would need to figure out what the site is about and whether or not they might be interested in looking further.

Figure 20.3.

This site has nice graphics and good organization, but you can do even better.

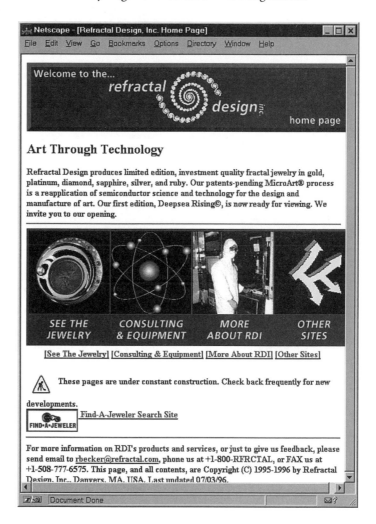

Navigational Elements

Figure 20.4 shows one of the pages you would get if you clicked on the image map in Figure 20.4. The banner at the top provides a strong visual relationship to the original page, and an icon at the bottom makes it easy to navigate back to the home page for further exploration.

Figure 20.4.

*If you click on CON-
SULTING & EQUIP-
MENT in Figure 20.3,
you get this page.*

If you produced pages similar to the ones in Figures 20.3 and 20.4 as your first site, you'd probably be proud, and rightly so. But you can use the techniques you've learned in this book to do even better.

Figure 20.5 is a more recent look at the same company's home page, and Figure 20.6 is the corresponding update of another page on the site. These differ from Figures 20.3 and 20.4 in several important ways, most of which you can apply to your own pages as well.

Figure 20.5.

A souped-up version of Figure 20.3 looks sharper, loads faster, and presents more key information immediately.

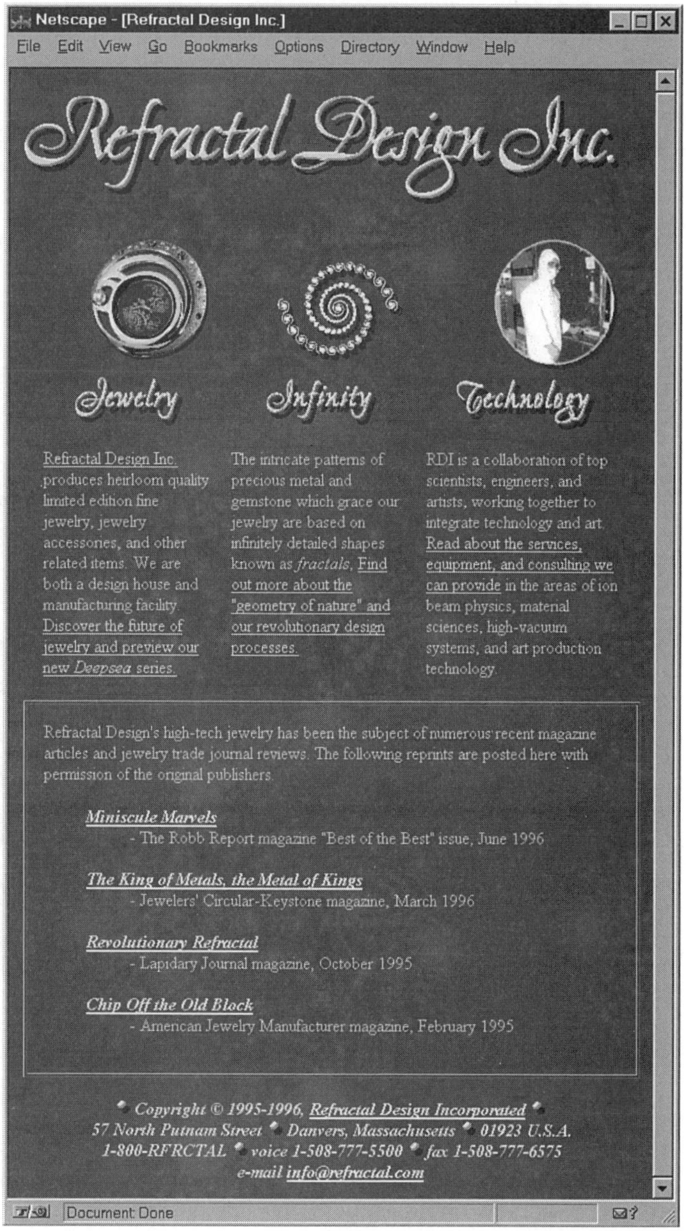

Figure 20.6.

Though this page has about the same text content as Figure 20.4, it has a stronger look and more navigation aids.

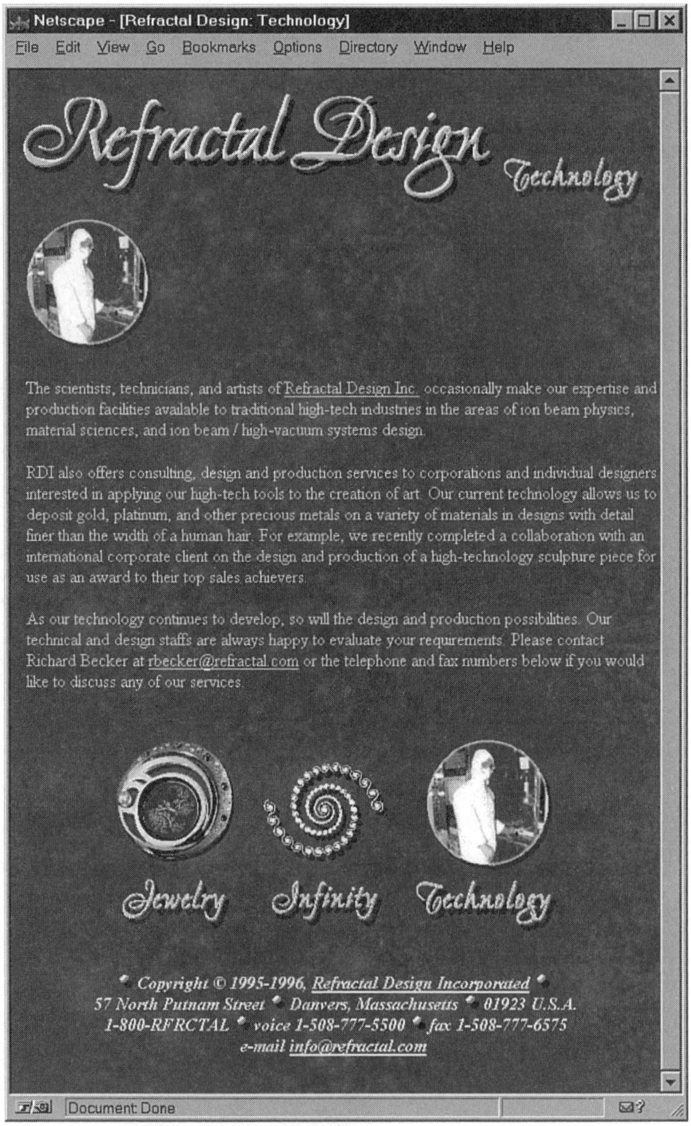

1. The new background and graphical titles provide a more appropriate mood and provide even more of a visual identity throughout the site than the blue banner graphic did.

2. All text and foreground graphics on the new home page load in less than eight seconds using a 28.8Kbps modem (the background takes an extra four seconds to

appear). The old home page takes over 25 seconds to finish loading, due to the large image map.

3. Use of a table provides people with more information about where they will go if they click on the three main links. Quite a bit of text that was "buried" in other pages before is now visible on the first screen that people see.

4. The prominent OTHER SITES link was removed. It is seldom a good business strategy to immediately refer visitors out the door.

5. The Under Construction sign was removed. People expect sites to be updated, but if your site is missing enough key information to need an Under Construction sign, it probably isn't ready to be put on the Internet yet.

6. The most compelling information that potential customers should see (the list of magazine articles and reviews) was moved to the home page. A table border separates it from the other text.

All these changes to the home page help bring more of the company's message to the intended audience more quickly and clearly. Yet some more subtle changes also make it considerably faster and easier to navigate around all the pages of the site.

The same graphics that appear on the home page are used as topic headers on each subsequent page. This has the double benefit of providing an immediate sense of where you are within the site and making the pages load almost instantly. (Web browsers will remember the graphics so they won't have to download them for the second page.) Those same graphics are also used as navigation buttons at the bottom of each page. Reusing navigation graphics as headers is a great trick that can be incorporated into almost any Web site.

Perhaps the most important change in the site is the choice of organizational headings. Think carefully about the main divisions of your site and the icons or headings you choose to represent those divisions. Your site will be much more compelling if they embody the primary message you want to convey to your audience.

Common Mistakes

Some of the following are common mistakes made by coders—newcomers *and* professionals!

Fracturing the Site

How many times have you been on a site that has sections that have a completely different appearance as soon as you leave the entry page? Historically, many large Web sites were created by merging individual departmental sites into one whole. Unfortunately, they sometimes look like it. Just as a business uses coordinated logos and advertising to project a consistent image, your site should clearly reflect the identity of the owner, even if the owner is an individual. Unrelated elements should be either ruthlessly excised or recreated to achieve a smooth transition between sections and a common means of navigation.

20

"Ransom Note" Font Selection

Just as word processors encouraged some people to sprinkle their documents with inappropriate fonts, style sheets and graphical text elements have allowed some people to make their pages read like a kidnapper's ransom note, with strange fonts pasted onto the page and without thought about what the font says about the company.

"Found" Graphics

In the same way, using random graphics from the Web can be a false economy. Other media invest a lot of time trying to achieve a look that says, "This is a Cosmo ad" or "This is a New Yorker illustration." You should, too. There are many inexpensive CD-ROMs that contain huge selections of related images drawn using the same techniques. Use them.

Too Many Links

No matter how well you design the physical pages, if there are too many ways to get from here to there, people will become confused, like they might in a carnival house of mirrors. Navigation should be straightforward and easy to understand from the very first page. As people continue into the site, there should be a clear method of going back to the entry so they can follow another path.

Mish Mash Architecture

Just as too many links can be confusing, even on a site with good structure overall, a site whose structure resembles a drunkard's walk will be confusing to the casual surfer, even if the links are fairly well defined. Try to keep the structure relatively flat; every time you need a link to continue, a few of your users will give up and go away unless there is something there on the link page that is worth seeing in its own right. There's an art to giving enough of a teaser to get people to come inside without making the entry page so busy that you can't see the forest for the trees. Look at a magazine cover or a newspaper front page for some ideas.

Web Site Maintenance

Because Web sites can be (and usually should be) updated frequently, creating pages that can be easily maintained is essential. This hour shows you how to add comments and other documentation to your pages so that you, or anyone else on your staff, can understand and modify your pages. It also shows you how to make one page automatically load another, and how to forward visitors to pages that have moved.

Documentation

One of the two most important items of documentation for any Web site is the site map, a logical diagram of the entire site, showing how pages are related to each other and the comments embedded in the HTML code for each page.

20

Site Maps

Site mapping tools are very commonly automated and several are freely available, including the Site Map tool included with the latest version of NCSA Mosaic, available at

```
http://www.ncsa.uiuc.edu/SDG/Software/WinMosaic/HomePage.html
```

But the best way to start out is with a piece of paper or a stack of 3×5 cards. If you can't figure it out on a piece of paper, your site is probably too complicated to use easily! Automated tools can help you understand an existing site, but you should use that knowledge to help simplify it, not struggle to maintain something complicated that your visitors will be confused by.

You've already started thinking about organization, but now is the time to put that organization down on paper. In fact, you should probably go through the process of thinking, writing down, and then rethinking several times in designing and maintaining your site.

Comments

Whenever you type an HTML page, keep in mind that you or someone else will almost certainly need to make changes to it someday. Simple text pages are easy to read and revise, but complex Web pages with graphics, tables, and other layout tricks can be quite difficult to decipher. Keep your pages neat and tidy while you're coding them or you are likely to be sorry later on.

For example, it isn't at all obvious from looking at the HTML in Figure 20.7 what the resulting page would actually look like. Even if you looked at the graphics files, it would take some serious brain work to figure out how they are being arranged on the page.

The HTML in Figure 20.8 will make exactly the same Web page as that in Figure 20.7— but it sure is easier to tell how in Figure 20.8! Actually formatting the text of your HTML is one way to make your pages easier to read and revise, and Figure 20.8 is much better than Figure 20.7 in that regard.

Even more importantly, Figure 20.8 uses the HTML comment tag (`<!-- {anything} -->`) to add plain-English explanations of the unusual tricks and potentially confusing tags. These are likely to be very helpful to anyone who might need to make changes to this page in the future, even if that person is the page's original author.

Anything you type in an HTML file between the `<!--` and `-->` sequences will not appear on the actual Web page. Only when someone selects View | Source or edits the HTML file with a text editor will he see your comments. Both Figures 20.7 and 20.8 will look like Figure 20.9 when viewed in a Web browser.

20

Figure 20.7.

This will produce a nice-looking page, but the HTML itself is a mess.

```
<HTML><HEAD><TITLE>Dick Oliver's Home Page</TITLE></HEAD>
<BODY BACKGROUND="strip.gif" TEXT="white" LINK="red"
VLINK="red" ALINK="white"><IMG SRC="dickani.gif">
   . . . <IMG SRC="dickog.gif"><BR>  .<P>
So what can you do when you're too dumb to become a
physicist or mathematician, and not quite crazy enough
to qualify for free food at the asylum?
Write books, I figure. And software. And what the heck
maybe some newsletters and Web pages, too. But enough
about me already. On to these far more interesting topics:<BR>
<DIV ALIGN="center"><TABLE><TR><TD><IMG SRC="see.gif"></TD>
<TD><FONT COLOR="cyan"><I>See...</I></FONT><BR>
<A HREF="family.htm"><FONT COLOR="cyan">My family</FONT></A>
<BR><A HREF="house.htm"><FONT COLOR="cyan">My house</FONT></A>
<BR><A HREF="hotlist.htm"><FONT COLOR="cyan">My hotlist</FONT>
</A></TD><TD><IMG SRC="hear.gif"></TD><TD>
<FONT COLOR="yellow"><I>Hear...</I></FONT><BR>
<A HREF="hello.wav"><FONT COLOR="yellow">My voice</FONT></A>
<BR><A HREF="brillig.RA"><FONT COLOR="yellow">My favorite poem
</FONT></A><BR><A HREF="erica.RA"><FONT COLOR="yellow">
My daughter</FONT></A></TD><TD><IMG SRC="get.gif"></TD><TD>
<FONT COLOR="red"><I>Get...</I></FONT><BR><A HREF="news.htm">
My newsletter</A><BR><A HREF="books.htm">My books</A><BR>
<A HREF="inquirer.htm">My foolishness</A></TD></TR></TABLE><P>
Happy? Disgusted? Lonely? Enlightened? Just plain stupid?<BR>
Why not send some e-mail to
<A HREF="mailto:DICKO@netletter.com"><FONT COLOR="#00FF00">
DickO@netletter.com</FONT></A> to tell me about it?<P>
</DIV></BODY></HTML>
```

JUST A MINUTE

Note for Microsoft Internet Explorer users: Microsoft reintroduced a non-standard <COMMENT>...</COMMENT> tag pair that was used in NCSA Mosaic for backward-compatibility; you rarely see this on the Net anymore, other than on a few Microsoft pages. Browsers other than Microsoft IE and NCSA Mosaic (and a few other browsers based on NCSA Mosaic or predating the tag, such as Lynx) will display the text between these tags as if the tags were ignored, which they are. This behavior can be useful only in very limited ways.

Furthermore, many browsers implement comments incorrectly, sometimes stopping at the first > they see. As a general rule, it's best to limit comments to a single line if there are any enclosed HTML tags (in fact, it's best to avoid enclosing HTML tags in comments) and don't depend on strict enforcement of the rules regarding comments, under which <!> is an empty comment, <!------> is not a comment, and <!--------> is (for reasons too complicated to explain in the short space here and which the programmers who make browsers have trouble coping with as well).

Figure 20.8.

Both this HTML and the HTML in Figure 20.7 produce the same results. But this page is much easier to maintain.

```
<HTML><HEAD><TITLE>Dick Oliver's Home Page</TITLE></HEAD>
<COMMENT><!--   Background is white on top
                and black on bottom
--></COMMENT>
<BODY BACKGROUND="strip.gif"
      TEXT="white" LINK="red" VLINK="red" ALINK="white">
<IMG SRC="dickani.gif" ALT="Dick Oliver">
<COMMENT><!--   The periods will be invisible, since they
                are white on a white background.
--></COMMENT>
. . .
<IMG SRC="dickog.gif" ALT="Welcome to the Land of DickO">
<BR>  <P>
<COMMENT><!--   Now we should be over the black part of
                the background, so white text will show up.
--></COMMENT>
So what can you do when you're too dumb to become a
physicist or mathematician, and not quite crazy enough
to qualify for free food at the asylum?
Write books, I figure. And software. And what the heck
maybe some newsletters and Web pages, too. But enough
about me already. On to these far more interesting topics:<BR>
<COMMENT><!--   A 6-column, 1-row table with eye, ear, and
                hand next to the links to see, hear, and get.
--></COMMENT>
<DIV ALIGN="center">
<TABLE><TR>
<TD><IMG SRC="see.gif"></TD>
<TD>
   <COMMENT><!--   Microsoft Internet Explorer 3 won't show
                   the font color set below. (It will show red
                   for all links.) Only Netscape 3 will.
   --></COMMENT>
   <FONT COLOR="cyan"><I>See...</I></FONT><BR>
   <A HREF="family.htm">
     <FONT COLOR="cyan">My family</FONT></A><BR>
   <A HREF="house.htm">
     <FONT COLOR="cyan">My house</FONT></A><BR>
   <A HREF="hotlist.htm">
     <FONT COLOR="cyan">My hotlist</FONT></A>
</TD>
<TD><IMG SRC="hear.gif"></TD>
<TD>
   <FONT COLOR="yellow"><I>Hear...</I></FONT><BR>
   <A HREF="hello.wav">
     <FONT COLOR="yellow">My voice</FONT></A><BR>
   <A HREF="brillig.RA">
     <FONT COLOR="yellow">My favorite poem</FONT></A><BR>
   <A HREF="erica.RA">
     <FONT COLOR="yellow">My daughter</FONT></A>
</TD>
<TD><IMG SRC="get.gif"></TD>
<TD>
   <FONT COLOR="red"><I>Get...</I></FONT><BR>
   <COMMENT><!--   The VLINK color is red, so no need
                   for FONT COLOR here.
   --></COMMENT>
   <A HREF="news.htm">My newsletter</A><BR>
   <A HREF="books.htm">My books</A><BR>
   <A HREF="inquirer.htm">My foolishness</A>
</TD>
</TR></TABLE>
<P>
Happy? Disgusted? Lonely? Enlightened? Just plain stupid?<BR>
Why not send some e-mail to
<A HREF="mailto:DICKO@netletter.com">
<FONT COLOR="#00FF00">DickO@netletter.com</FONT></A>
to tell me about it?
<P></DIV>  <COMMENT><!-- End of centered region --></COMMENT>
</BODY></HTML>
```

20

Figure 20.9.

The comments in Figure 20.8 don't show up on the actual Web page. The page in Figure 20.7 also looks just like this.

It will be well worth your time now to go through all the Web pages you've created so far and add any comments that you or others might find helpful when revising them in the future.

1. Put a comment explaining any fancy formatting or layout techniques before the tags that make it happen.

2. Use a comment just before an `<IMG>` tag to briefly describe any important graphic whose function isn't obvious from the `ALT` message.

   Of course, for accessibility it *should* be obvious.

3. Always use a comment (or several comments) to summarize how the cells of a table are supposed to fit together visually.

4. If you use hexadecimal color codes (such as `<FONT COLOR="#8040B0">`), insert a comment indicating what the color actually is (bluish-purple).

5. Indenting your comments (as I did in Figure 20.8) helps them to stand out and makes both the comments and the HTML easier to read. Don't forget to use indentation in the HTML itself to make it more readable, too.

20

6. Last but not least, always document who created or changed the code on the page and when this was done. If a question does arise, it may be very handy to be able to ask whoever did it why they did what they did, just in case.

Managing Change

Web sites change. That's a given. How you handle the changes marks the difference between a tyro and a professional Web designer. One of the most courteous things you can do when rearranging a site is to put a small referral page in the old location, telling people who may have bookmarked the old site where to find the new location. This is often done by means of a CGI (Common Gateway Interface) script so that actual physical pages don't have to be maintained and the pages are generated on-the-fly when people try to access them. Although CGI scripts are beyond the scope of this book, it's thoughtful to leave a page behind when you move. It's much like sending out a change of address card to your friends when you change your snail-mail address.

Later in this hour, I talk about one way you can use the <META... > tag to help make it even more convenient for most modern browsers, but you should always, at a minimum, include the new entry page as well as the new equivalent of the old page (if any) as links on a very simple and easy to read "*XYZ* Site has moved" page. After a few months or years, the referral page can be deleted if this seems like a good idea. Some large sites keep their referral pages active indefinitely.

We've already mentioned the amateurishness of perpetual Under Construction signs, but a referral page may be the only place you could legitimately use one. The only time a user will see it is when she stumbles "behind the scenes," and it might be appropriate to apologize for the inconvenience.

Advanced Maintenance Issues

There are a few advanced tags that you may occasionally see in the <HEAD> section of Web pages, many of which are either directly or indirectly related to automating maintenance of your page. These tags are listed in Table 20.1 so that you'll have some general idea what they're for, just in case you ever encounter them. However, most of them are never used by most Web page authors today, so you don't need to worry about learning them now. In the future, they will become more and more important, as browsers and site maintenance tools begin to support the features they make possible.

The <META> tag deserves special mention because it can be used for a wide variety of purposes. The most common (and arguably the most nifty) of these purposes is to make any page automatically load any other page after an amount of time you choose. The secret incantation you need to put in the head of your page to perform the trick looks like this:

```
<META HTTP-EQUIV="Refresh" CONTENT="5; nextpage.htm">
```

20

Put the number of seconds to wait before loading the next page where I put 5 in the line above, and put the address of the next page to load instead of *nextpage.htm*.

You can also use <META> to specify any information about the document you want, such as the author or a page ID number. How and why you do this is beyond the scope of this introductory book, and very few Web page authors ever use the <META> tag for anything other than automatically loading a new page. The advantage of this tag is that you can associate a name with the provided information so an automated tool can extract it at a later date. You most often see the <META> tag used on larger sites.

Table 20.1. Advanced HTML tags.

Tag	Function
<BASE>	Used to explicitly override the address where this page resides. Handy if you move a page temporarily and don't want to update the new path to referenced images and other pages, but seldom actually used.
<META>	Automatically loads a new page after a specified time interval (see previous paragraphs), or specifies advanced technical information, related to the page, that may be used for Web site automation. The <META> tag is an ideal place to put information such as the name of the author or owner of a page, the creation date, copyright information, and so on.
<ISINDEX>	Indicates that this document is a CGI script that allows searches. Deprecated in HTML 4.0. Use <INPUT> instead. See "Forms" in Hour 19, "Creating HTML Forms."
<LINK>	Indicates a link from this document to one or more others that can be used by an automated tool of some sort, as opposed to <A>, which marks a user action element in the body.
<NEXTID>	Indicates the *next* document to this one (as might be defined by an automated tool to manage HTML documents in series). <NEXTID> is considered obsolete and should not be used.
<STYLE>	A very new tag used to define style sheet specifications for a document. Refer to Hour 6, "Font Control and Special Characters," for more information on style sheets. This is a very important tag that not only allows considerable control over the appearance of your pages, but can be used to centralize the appearance of an entire site, allowing changes to be performed globally by editing a single file.

Tag	Function
`<SCRIPT>`	A relatively new tag, used to insert programming scripts directly into a Web page. See Hour 22, "Applets, ActiveX, and Objects," for more information. This is another way to allow the appearance and functionality of a page, even HTML itself, to be changed on-the-fly, extending your design capabilities beyond the limits of static code. This tag is not confined to the header and is closely related to the `<OBJECT>` and `<APPLET>` tags discussed elsewhere.

Summary

This hour has given you examples and explanations to help you organize your Web pages into a coherent site that is informative, attractive, and easy to navigate.

This hour also discussed the importance of making your HTML easy to maintain and introduced the `<COMMENT>` tag to help you toward that end. Finally, a few tags that you don't need to know were mentioned just in case you see them in someone else's documents and wonder what they are. One of these was the `<META>` tag, which can be used to make a page automatically load another page.

Table 20.2 summarizes the tags covered in this hour.

Table 20.2. HTML tags covered in Hour 20 (see also Table 20.1).

Tag	Attribute	Function
`<!--...-->`		The official way of specifying comments. The text in the comment won't be displayed by Web browsers. This is the method mandated by Internet standards bodies.
`<COMMENT>...</COMMENT>`		An old way to create a comment to be seen only by Web page authors. The text in the comment may or may not be displayed, depending on the browser.

20

Q&A

Q I've seen pages that ask viewers to change the width of their browser window or adjust other settings before proceeding beyond the home page. Why?

A The idea is that the Web page author can offer a better presentation if he has some control over the size of the reader's windows or fonts. Of course, nobody even bothers to change their settings, so these sites always look weird or unreadable. You'll be much better off using the tips you learn in this book to make your site readable and attractive at any window size and a wide variety of browser settings.

Q How many major categories or *navigation buttons* should my site have?

A Generally, no more than seven, because psychological tests have shown many times that people have difficulty keeping track of more than seven choices at a time. If your site has more than seven pages, use subcategories—preferably with each set of subcategories on its own page.

Q Won't lots of comments and spaces make my pages load slower when someone views them?

A All modems compress text when transmitting it, so adding spaces to format your HTML doesn't usually change the transfer time at all. You'd have to type hundreds of words of comments to cause even one extra second of delay when loading a page. It's the graphics that slows pages down, so squeeze your images as tight as you can (refer to Hour 11, "Making Pages Display Quickly"), but use text comments freely.

Quiz

Questions

1. What are three ways to help people stay aware that all your pages form a single site?

2. What two types of information should always be included in the first home page that people encounter at your site?

3. If you wanted to say, "Don't change this image of me. It's my only chance at immortality," to future editors of a Web page, but you didn't want people who view the page to see that message, how would you do it?

4. Suppose you recently moved a page from `http://mysite.com/oldplace/thepage.htm` to `http://mysite.com/newplace/thepage.htm`, but you're not quite sure whether you're going to keep it there yet. How would you automatically send people who try the old address to the new address, without any message telling them there was a change?

20

Answers

1. (a) Using consistent background, colors, fonts, and styles.

   (b) Repeat the same link words or graphics on the top of the page the link leads to.

   (c) Repeat the same small header, buttons, or other element on every page of the site.

2. (a) Enough identifying information so that they can immediately tell the name of the site and what the site is about.

   (b) Whatever the most important message you want to convey to your intended audience is, stated directly and concisely.

3. Put the following just before the `<IMG>` tag:

```
<!-- Don't change this image of me.
  It's my only chance at immortality. -->
```

4. Put the following page at `http://mysite.com/oldplace/thepage.htm`:

```
<HTML><HEAD><META HTTP-EQUIV="Refresh" CONTENT="0; http://mysite.com/
newplace/thepage.htm></HEAD>
</HTML>
```

   To accommodate people using older browsers that don't support `<META>`, it would be a good idea to also include the following just before the `</HTML>` tag:

```
<BODY><A HREF="http://mysite.com/newplace/thepage.htm">Click here to get
the page you're after.</A></BODY>
```

Activities

☐ As an exercise in possibilities, surf on over to "The 10 Types of Web Page Design" at `http://gate.cks.com/~patrick/types.html` and see whether you can organize (or at least imagine) your site as it would look as each of these types.

☐ Grab a pencil (the oldfangled kind), and sketch out your Web site as a bunch of little rectangles with arrows between them. Then sketch a rough overview of what each page will look like by putting squiggles where the text goes and doodles where the images go. Each arrow should start at a doodle-icon that corresponds to the navigation button for the page the arrow leads to. This can give you a good intuitive grasp of which pages on your site will be easy to get to and how the layout of adjacent pages will work together—all before you invest time in writing the actual HTML to connect the pages together.

20

PART VI

Dynamic Web Pages

Hour

Hour 21

Embedding Multimedia in Web Pages

Multimedia is a popular buzzword for sound, motion video, and interactive animation. This hour shows you how to include audiovisual and interactive media in your Web pages.

In this hour, you'll learn about

- [ ] Multimedia madness
- [ ] Multimedia resources
- [ ] Doing multimedia:

    MIME-compliant multimedia

    Multimedia in Microsoft Internet Explorer

    Multimedia in Netscape Navigator

- [ ] Multimedia in HTML 4.0

    The `<OBJECT>` tag

Multimedia Madness

The first thing you should be aware of is that computer multimedia is still in its youth, and Internet multimedia is barely in its infancy. The infant technology's rapid pace of growth creates three obstacles for anyone who wants to include audiovisual material in a Web page:

☐ There are many incompatible multimedia file formats to choose from, and none have emerged as a clear industry standard yet.

☐ Most people do not have fast enough Internet connections to receive high-quality audiovisual data without a long wait.

☐ Each new Web browser version that comes out uses different HTML tags to include multimedia in Web pages.

The moral of the story: Whatever you do today to implement a multimedia Web site, plan on changing it before too long. The good news is that you can sidestep all three of these obstacles to some extent today, and they are all likely to become even easier to overcome in the near future. This hour shows you how to put multimedia on your Web pages for maximum compatibility with the Web browser versions that most people are now using. It then introduces you to the new standard way that Web page multimedia will be handled in the future.

JUST A MINUTE

> The Microsoft ActiveX controls and Java applets discussed in Hour 22, "Applets, ActiveX, and Objects," can be used with many of the same types of media files discussed in this hour. Be sure to read Hour 22 before you make any final decisions about how you will incorporate multimedia into your Web site.

Multimedia Resources

Before you see how to place multimedia on your Web pages in any way, you need to have some multimedia content to start with.

Creating multimedia of any kind is a challenging and complicated task. If you're planning to create your own content from scratch, you'll need far more than this book to become the next crackerjack multimedia developer. Once you've got some content, however, this hour will show you how to place your new creations into your Web pages.

For those of us who are artistically challenged, a number of alternative ways to obtain useful multimedia assets are available. Aside from hiring an artist, here are a few suggestions:

☐ The Web itself is chock-full of useful content of all media types, and stock media clearinghouses of all shapes and sizes now exist online. See the hotlist at the 24-Hour HTML Café (`http://www.mcp.com/sites/1-57521/1-57521-366-4/`) for links to some of the best stock media sources on the Web.

☐ Don't feel like spending any money? Much of the material on the Internet is free. Of course, it's still a good idea to double-check with the accredited author or current owner of the content; you don't want to get sued for copyright infringement. In addition, various offices of the U.S. government generate content which, by law, belongs to all Americans. (Any NASA footage found online, for instance, is free for you to use.)

☐ Check out the online forums and Usenet newsgroups that cater to the interests of videographers. As clearly as possible, describe your site and what you want to do with it. Chances are you'll find a few up-and-coming artists who'd be more than happy to let thousands of people peruse their work online.

Doing Multimedia

The following sections show you how to add some audio and video to a Web page in four different ways:

☐ The "old way" for maximum compatibility with all Web browsers

☐ The "Microsoft way" that works best with Microsoft Internet Explorer 2.0 and 3.0

☐ The "Netscape way" that's best for Netscape Navigator 2.0 and 3.0

☐ The "new way" that works with versions 4.0 and later of Microsoft Internet Explorer and Netscape Navigator.

For the examples in this hour, I created a Web page allowing hungry Web surfers a chance to preview the daily menu for a (fictitious) seafood restaurant. A picture of a lobster was modified to create a short video. We then recorded and mixed a voice-over with some music in the background. All this was done with readily available software and hardware costing less than $200 (not counting the computer).

JUST A MINUTE

In this hour's sample page, I use Windows AVI video and WAV sound files. For better compatibility with non-Windows computers, you could use Apple's QuickTime audio/video, the Real Audio/Real Video format or any other video format supported by today's Web browsers. In this hour, the procedures shown for incorporating the files into your Web pages are the same, no matter which file format you choose.

21

MIME-Compliant Multimedia

The simplest and most reliable option for incorporating a video or audio file into your Web site is to simply link it in with <A HREF>, exactly as you would link to another HTML file. (Refer to Hour 3, "Linking to Other Web Pages," for coverage of the <A> tag.) Browsers use a standard called MIME (Multipurpose Internet Mail Extensions) to identify files as they are downloaded and decide how best to display them. Every file has a MIME type, even the Hypertext Markup Language (HTML) used to create your pages. The MIME type for HTML is text/html. So adding support for a new MIME type is just a matter of having the browser figure out how to handle it.

For example, the following line could be used to offer an AVI video of a Maine lobster:

```
<A HREF="lobstah.avi">Play the lobster video.</A>
```

When someone clicks on the words Play the lobster video, the lobstah.avi video file will be transferred to his or her computer. Whichever helper application or plug-in the user has installed to handle AVI files (MIME type: video/avi) will automatically start as soon as the file has finished downloading.

JUST A MINUTE

In case you're not familiar with helper applications (or helper apps for short), they are the external programs that a Web browser calls upon to display any type of file that it can't handle on its own. You can see what helper apps your browser is set up to use by selecting Options | General Preferences | Helpers in Netscape Navigator 3.0 or selecting View | Options | Programs | File Types in Microsoft Internet Explorer 3.0.

Plug-ins are a special sort of helper application that is specifically designed for tight integration with Netscape Navigator. You'll read more about plug-ins under the "Multimedia the Netscape Way" section later in this hour.

Multimedia in Microsoft Internet Explorer

The following multimedia techniques apply to Microsoft's Internet Explorer, especially version 3.0 and above.

Video

In Hour 9, "Putting Images on a Web Page," you learned to use the <IMG> tag. Microsoft Internet Explorer 3.0 also allows you to include AVI videos in a Web page with <IMG>.

The HTML code to include the video can be as simple as

```
<IMG DYNSRC="lobstah.avi" WIDTH=160 HEIGHT=120>
```

21

The DYNSRC stands for dynamic source, and tells Explorer that this is a motion video file instead of just a still SRC image. If you include both SRC and DYNSRC attributes in an IMG tag, then older browsers that don't support DYNSRC will simply display the SRC image instead.

Two more new attributes can be used along with DYNSRC in an IMG tag, too. CONTROLS displays a set of controls beneath the video clip. LOOP=INFINITE makes the video automatically repeat forever, while LOOP=n plays the video *n* times and then stops (for example, LOOP=3 would play three times). Naturally, you can also use any of the standard IMG attributes, such as ALIGN, BORDER, and so on.

COFFEE BREAK

Figures 21.1 and 21.2 include an AVI video clip embedded in a Web page using <IMG DYNSRC>. You can see the video by viewing this page with Microsoft Internet Explorer 3.0 or 4.0 at http://www.mcp.com/sites/ 1-57521/1-57521-366-4/

Figure 21.1.

This page includes embedded video and audio that will be played only by Microsoft Internet Explorer.

```
<HTML>
<HEAD><TITLE>The DownEast Restaurant</TITLE></HEAD>
<BODY BACKGROUND="wicker.jpg">
<DIV ALIGN="center">

<BGSOUND SRC="lobstah8.wav">
<A HREF="lobstah.avi">
   <IMG SRC="lobstah.jpg" DYNSRC="lobstah2.avi" LOOP=INFINITE
   WIDTH=160 HEIGHT=120 ALIGN="left" BORDER=0>
</A>

<FONT COLOR="red"><H1>The DownEast Restaurant</H1>
<H3>Portland, Maine</H3>
<H2><I>"Come DownEast, 'n have a Feast"</I></H2></FONT>
<BR CLEAR="all">
</DIV>
<HR><B>~Today's Catch~</B><P>
Fresh lobstah (a three-poundah!),  <B>$14.95</B><P>
Scrod and potatahs, baked in buttah,  <B>$10.95</B><P>
Heaping plattah of steamed clams,
fresh outtah th' mud,  <B>$12.95</B><P>
<HR><B>Come on ovah! The food's wicked good!</B>
</BODY></HTML>
```

To make the lobster video in the DownEast Restaurant sample page available to users who don't have Internet Explorer, I enclosed the <IMG> tag with an <A HREF> link and included the words "CLICK ME!" in the SRC image, as you can see in Figure 21.3.

Figure 21.4 shows what happens when a Netscape Navigator 3.0 user clicks on the image. The first frame of the AVI video appears, and users can click on it to play the video (or right-click for a menu of playback options, as seen in Figure 21.4). Users of other browsers see

21

whatever AVI viewer their software was configured to use, or they may be given the chance to save the AVI file to disk if no viewer is available.

Figure 21.2.

The page listed in Figure 21.1. (The lobster looks like an ordinary image when printed in this book, but it's a short video.)

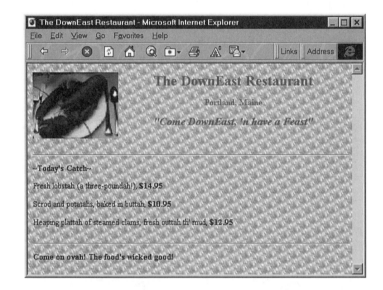

Figure 21.3.

Users of Netscape (and other browsers) see a still image, which they can click for the AVI video. This is the same page as seen with Explorer 3.0 in Figure 21.2.

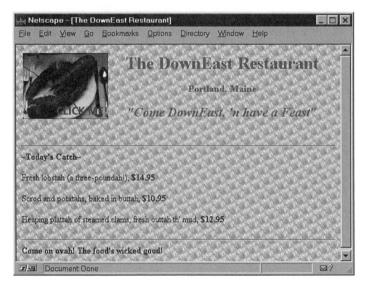

Figure 21.4.

Clicking on the image in Figure 21.3 lets users play the video using whatever AVI-compatible plug-in or helper app they have installed.

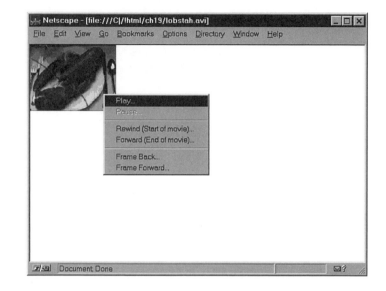

JUST A MINUTE

Note that DYNSRC begins playing video clips as soon as they begin downloading, but users whose browsers don't support DYNSRC have to wait until the video is completely done downloading before they begin to see it.

Audio

Video files embedded with `<IMG DYNSRC>` can include soundtracks, but Microsoft Internet Explorer also lets you specify a background sound for a page like this:

```
<BGSOUND SRC="lobstah.wav">
```

The background sound may or may not synchronize exactly with video content on the page, but when synchronization isn't important to you, BGSOUND can offer several advantages. Not only does the background sound usually start playing sooner than video, but you can include more than one video on the page, and use BGSOUND to provide a master soundtrack for all of them.

Multimedia in Netscape Navigator

While Microsoft opted to add the DYNSRC attribute to the old familiar `<IMG>` tag, Netscape chose instead to introduce an entirely new tag called `<EMBED>`.

21

The <EMBED> tag enables you to place any type of file directly into your Web page. In order for the media to appear on the Web page, however, every user must have a plug-in that recognizes the incoming data type and knows what to do with it. A plug-in is like a helper application that is fused into Navigator itself; it adds a new set of display capabilities directly into the browser.

The plug-ins that come bundled with Netscape Navigator 3.0 can handle most common media types, including WAV, AU, MPEG, MID, EPS, VRML, and many more. Many other plug-ins are also available from other companies to handle almost any type of media file.

TIME SAVER

> Netscape maintains a Web page that lists all registered plug-ins and plug-in developers. To check out the current assortment, head to this page:
>
> `http://home.netscape.com/comprod/products/navigator/version_2.0/`
> `plugins/index.html`
>
> The Plug-ins Development Kit, available for free from Netscape, allows developers to create new plug-ins for their own products and data types (for more information, see Netscape's Web site at `http://`
> `home.netscape.com/`).

The following line of HTML would embed a video clip named `lobstah.avi` at the current position on the page, as long as visitors to the page have an AVI-compatible plug-in or helper app:

```
<EMBED SRC="lobstah.avi">
```

Notice that, like the <IMG> tag, <EMBED> requires a SRC attribute to indicate the address of the embedded media file. Also like <IMG>, the <EMBED> tag can take ALIGN, WIDTH, and HEIGHT attributes. The SRC, WIDTH, HEIGHT, and ALIGN attributes are interpreted by the browser just as they would be for a still image. However, the actual display of the video is handled by whichever plug-in or helper app each user may have installed.

The <EMBED> tag also enables you to set any number of optional parameters, which are specific to the plug-in or player program. For instance, the page in Figure 21.5 includes the following:

```
<EMBED SRC="lobstah.avi" WIDTH=160 HEIGHT=120 ALIGN="left"
 AUTOPLAY="true" LOOP="true" ONCURSOR="play">
```

AUTOPLAY, LOOP, and ONCURSOR are not standard attributes of the <EMBED> tag, so the browser simply hands them over to the plug-in program to interpret. AUTOPLAY="true" and LOOP="true" are specific to the Netscape Navigator 3.0 LiveVideo plug-in (they tell it to automatically play the video as soon as it loads, and to play it over again each time it finishes).

Figure 21.5.

The <EMBED> tag embeds multimedia files directly into a Web page in Netscape Navigator.

```
<HTML>
<HEAD><TITLE>The DownEast Restaurant</TITLE></HEAD>
<BODY BACKGROUND="wicker.jpg">
<DIV ALIGN="center">

<BGSOUND SRC="lobstah8.wav">
<EMBED SRC="lobstah2.avi" WIDTH=160 HEIGHT=120 ALIGN="left"
 AUTOPLAY="true" LOOP="true" ONCURSOR="play">
<NOEMBED>
  <A HREF="lobstah.avi">
    <IMG SRC="lobstah.jpg" DYNSRC="lobstah2.avi" LOOP=INFINITE
       WIDTH=160 HEIGHT=120 ALIGN="left" BORDER=0>
  </A>
</NOEMBED>

<FONT COLOR="red"><H1>The DownEast Restaurant</H1>
<H3>Portland, Maine</H3>
<H2><I>"Come DownEast, 'n have a Feast"</I></H2></FONT>
<BR CLEAR="all">
</DIV>
<HR><B>~Today's Catch~</B><P>
Fresh lobstah (a three-poundah!),  <B>$14.95</B><P>
Scrod and potatahs, baked in buttah,  <B>$10.95</B><P>
Heaping plattah of steamed clams,
fresh outtah th' mud,  <B>$12.95</B><P>
<HR><B>Come on ovah! The food's wicked good!</B>
</BODY></HTML>
```

If a user happens to have the CoolFusion AVI viewer plug-in (from Iterated Systems, Inc. at `http://www.iterated.com`), CoolFusion will interpret the `ONCURSOR="play"` command to mean that whenever the user passes the mouse cursor over the video it should restart. If a user has a different AVI plug-in, or no plug-in at all for handling AVI files, this attribute will do nothing. (Refer to the Web pages of each plug-in developer for information on the commands that their plug-in will accept as attributes in the `<EMBED>` tag.)

If a suitable plug-in can't be found for an `<EMBED>` tag, the Windows 95 versions of both Netscape Navigator and Microsoft Internet Explorer may embed an OLE-compliant application to play the media file. For example, Figure 21.7 shows the same page as Figure 21.6 viewed with Microsoft Internet Explorer 3.0. The Windows Media Player application is embedded directly in the Web page.

Basically, when Navigator and Explorer encounter an `<EMBED>` tag, they try their hardest to find some way to embed the media file directly in the Web page. As a Web page author, you can't predict what plug-in or helper application will be selected, but you can at least put some instructions on the Web page telling your audience where to download a suitable player.

21

Figure 21.6.

With the appropriate Navigator plug-in installed, AVI files appear on the Web page just as if AVI support were built in to Netscape Navigator.

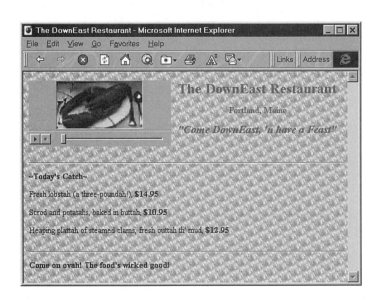

Figure 21.7.

Microsoft Internet Explorer may embed a separate helper application to play a media file in an <EMBED> tag.

JUST A MINUTE

Embedded helper apps only work in Windows 95 and Windows NT. They will not function for Macintosh or UNIX users. Visit http://www.microsoft.com/ie/ for more information on Macintosh IE-related news, and http://home.netscape.com/ to see what changes come about for Netscape browser plug-ins for the Mac.

21

> Also, you should not confuse this use of Windows object linking and
> embedding (OLE) with the ActiveX controls discussed in the next hour—
> even though they do rely on the same underlying OLE technology.

You can use <EMBED> with any type of audio, video, or interactive multimedia files as long as
your audience has the correct player software installed.

Unfortunately, you as a Web page author have no control over or knowledge of which file
types and applications people who visit your pages will have configured on their computers,
or even how many visitors will be using a Microsoft Windows operating system. So the exotic
uses of <EMBED> are probably best left to corporate intranets or other situations where the page
publisher has some control over the intended audience's computer setup.

Graceful Fallback

Because Netscape knew that its browser would be the first (and perhaps only) browser to
support the <EMBED> tag, they provided an easy way to include alternate content for other
browsers. Immediately following an <EMBED> tag, you can specify any amount of HTML code
for other browsers, between the <NOEMBED> and </NOEMBED> tags. For example, Figure 21.5
contains the following code:

```
<BGSOUND SRC="lobstah8.wav">
<EMBED SRC="lobstah.avi" WIDTH=160 HEIGHT=120 ALIGN="left"
 AUTOPLAY="true" LOOP="true" ONCURSOR="play">
<NOEMBED>
<A HREF="lobstah.avi">
 <IMG SRC="lobstah.jpg" DYNSRC="lobstah2.avi" LOOP=INFINITE
  WIDTH=160 HEIGHT=120 ALIGN="left" BORDER=0>
 </A>
</NOEMBED>
```

Here's how this will work in various browsers:

☐ Netscape Navigator 3.0 or 4.0 sees only the EMBED tag and ignores everything
between <NOEMBED> and </NOEMBED>. It ignores the Microsoft-specific <BGSOUND> tag.
(If the Netscape LiveMedia plug-in is installed, it interprets AUTOPLAY and LOOP as
discussed earlier. If the CoolFusion plug-in is installed, it interprets the ONCURSOR
command.)

☐ In Netscape Navigator 2.0, if no AVI-compatible plug-in is installed, users may see
an unsightly puzzle-piece icon and a message saying Plug-in Not Loaded. If they
click on the Get the Plug-in button, they will be taken to a page on Netscape
Corporation's Web site explaining how to get and install plug-ins and helper apps.

☐ Microsoft Internet Explorer 3.0 or 4.0 looks in the Windows file type Registry for a
player for the <EMBED> tag. If it can't find one, it plays the video specified in <IMG
DYNSRC> with its internal video player. It also plays the sound in the <BGSOUND> tag.

21

☐ Microsoft Internet Explorer 2.0 sees the `<BGSOUND>` and IMG tags. It plays the `lobstah8.wav` sound file in the background and displays the `lobstah.jpg` image. I added the words CLICK ME! to this image so that users with an AVI helper app can click on the image to play the `lobstah.avi` video clip specified in the A HREF attribute.

☐ Most other browsers see only the IMG SRC attribute and display the `lobstah.jpg` still image. If they have an AVI-compatible helper application installed, they can click on the image to see the video play in a separate window.

☐ Netscape Navigator version 1.2 is a special problem case because it recognizes the `<EMBED>` tag, but not the `<NOEMBED>` tag. It displays both the image specified in IMG SRC and an embedded OLE display or, more often, a broken image icon resulting from a failed attempt to display the `<EMBED>` tag. Clicking on the CLICK ME! image will still launch an AVI helper app if one is available.

To thicken the plot, some people who already have the software they need to view your EMBED media files may see a message announcing boldly "Warning: There is a possible security hazard here," which appears in Figure 21.8. What this message really means is that the user has a helper app available on his system that can display the media file, and Netscape Navigator (version 2.0 or higher) is about to run it. The alarmist tone of the message is very unfortunate, because the likelihood of having any security risk is actually no greater than any other time a helper app is invoked or a page is displayed.

Figure 21.8.

This alarmist message may appear in Netscape Navigator before users can see your innocent media files.

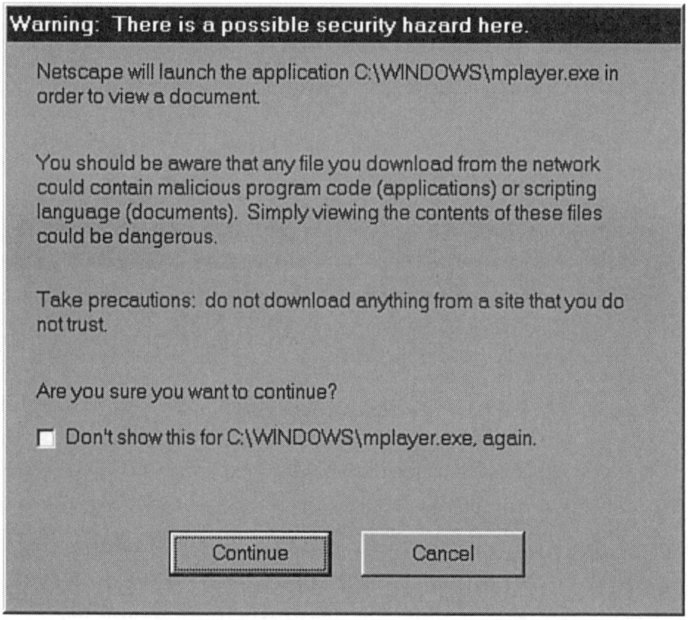

Warning: There is a possible security hazard here.

Netscape will launch the application C:\WINDOWS\mplayer.exe in order to view a document.

You should be aware that any file you download from the network could contain malicious program code (applications) or scripting language (documents). Simply viewing the contents of these files could be dangerous.

Take precautions: do not download anything from a site that you do not trust.

Are you sure you want to continue?

☐ Don't show this for C:\WINDOWS\mplayer.exe, again.

Continue   Cancel

Some novice users are sure to become convinced that they must click Cancel or risk having the monitor blow up, but what you really want them to do is click Continue so they can watch a totally harmless video clip.

Unfortunately, there's really nothing you can do as a Web page author to control whether this message appears, or any of the configuration options discussed in the next few pages. However, you should still be aware of what users may see so you can intelligently choose if and when to use the <EMBED> tag, and what sort of caveats to offer along with your embedded media.

Multimedia in HTML 4.0

Both Microsoft's <IMG DYNSRC> and Netscape's <EMBED> tag have come under fire for a number of reasons, both technical and political. At present, it looks nearly certain that they will be made obsolete very soon by a new tag called <OBJECT>, which has the blessing of Netscape, Microsoft, and the official World Wide Web Consortium (W3C) standards-setting committee.

The <OBJECT> Tag

The <OBJECT> tag will do everything Netscape wants the <EMBED> tag to do, plus a lot more.

You can read more about the <OBJECT> tag, including an example of its use, under "ActiveX Controls" in Hour 22. As of this writing, the exact usage of <OBJECT> is still under revision by the standards committee, so you should also keep an eye on the W3C pages at `http://www.w3.org/pub/WWW/` for more information. The current location of the draft specification is

`http://www.w3.org/TR/WD-html40-970708/cover.html`

The <OBJECT> tag is very powerful. It can be used to call programs just as the now deprecated <APPLET> tag does, but can also provide its own graceful fallback position. In the following code fragment, an object first calls an independent video display program written in Python (a programming language) that requires no data; if that doesn't work for some reason, it then attempts to display an MPEG video. Then it tries to display an ordinary GIF file and finally, if all else fails, a text description will be displayed by any browser which doesn't recognize the <OBJECT> tag. In reality, you would probably want to move the GIF into the inner content as well.

```
<OBJECT title="Over the Rainbow"                         classid="http://
➥www.oz.org/rainbow.py">
<OBJECT data="http://www.oz.org/rainbow.mpeg" type="application/mpeg">
<OBJECT src="http://www.oz.org/rainbow.gif">
Dorothy and her friends in Oz
</OBJECT>
</OBJECT>
</OBJECT>
```

21

This behavior is designed into the structure of the tag, which ignores its contents unless it fails. It will recursively fail until it finds a task that it can do. The value of this approach will be obvious to anyone who has been frustrated by yet another Plug-in not Loaded! message when viewing web pages.

JUST A MINUTE

> Unfortunately, the 4.0 versions of Microsoft Internet Explorer interpret the <OBJECT> tag somewhat unreliably, because they were released before the official standard for the tag was approved. The fact that most people are still using earlier browser versions has also slowed widespread use of the <OBJECT> tag.

Of course anything can be called by means of this sort of mechanism, including audio files, video, animated interactive displays, images such as are now referenced using the IMG attribute, or features no one has even thought of yet. It's a very cool and elegant solution to the vexing problem of multimedia confusion described at the top of this hour.

Summary

In this hour, you've seen how to embed video and sound into a Web page. But remember that the <EMBED> tag, and its successor, the <OBJECT> tag, can be used to include a vast array of media types besides just Windows AVI and WAV files. Some of these media types are alternative audio and video formats that aim to achieve greater compression, quality, or compatibility than the Windows standard formats. Others, such as Shockwave and QuickTime VR, add a variety of interactive features that old-fashioned audiovisual media types lack.

Table 21.1 summarizes the tags discussed in this hour.

Table 21.1. HTML tags and attributes covered in Hour 21.

Tag	Attribute	Function
<IMG>		Normally inserts an image, but Microsoft Internet Explorer also supports the inclusion of AVI video with the following attributes. (All <IMG> attributes covered in Hour 9 can also be used with DYNSRC video.
	SRC="..."	The URL of the image to be shown by browsers that can't show video.

Tag	Attribute	Function
	DYNSRC="..."	The address of a video clip in the Windows AVI format (dynamic source).
	CONTROLS	Used to display a set of video playback controls.
	LOOP="..."	The number of times a video clip will loop. (-1 or INFINITE means to loop indefinitely.)
	START="..."	When a DYNSRC video clip should start playing. Valid options are FILEOPEN (play when a page is displayed) or MOUSEOVER (play when a mouse cursor passes over the video clip).
<BGSOUND>		Plays a sound file as soon as the page is displayed (in Microsoft Internet Explorer version 2.0 or higher only).
	SRC="..."	The URL of the WAV, AU, or MIDI sound file to embed.
	LOOP="..."	The number of times a video clip will loop. (-1 or INFINITE means to loop indefinitely.)
<EMBED>		Embeds a file to be read or displayed by a Netscape plug-in application.
	SRC="..."	The URL of the file to embed.
	WIDTH="..."	The width of the embedded object in pixels.
	HEIGHT="..."	The height of the embedded object in pixels.
	ALIGN="..."	Determines the alignment of the media window. Values are the same as for the <IMG> tag.
	VSPACE="..."	The space between the media and the text above or below it.
	HSPACE="..."	The space between the media and the text to its left or right.

21

continues

Table 21.1. continued

Tag	Attribute	Function
	BORDER="..."	Draws a border of the specified size in pixels around the media.
<NOEMBED>...</NOEMBED>		Alternate text or images to be shown to users who do not have a plug-in installed or are using browsers that don't recognize the <EMBED> tag.
<OBJECT>...</OBJECT>		Inserts images, videos, Java applets, ActiveX controls, or other objects into a document.
	CODEBASE="..."	Specifies the base URL used when the object requires code. Not all rendering mechanisms require this attribute.
	CLASSID="..."	Specifies the URL (location) of a rendering mechanism.
	CODETYPE="..."	Specifies the Internet Media Type (MIME-Type) of data expected by the rendering mechanism specified by the CLASSID attribute. This attribute is optional, but recommended.
	DATA="..."	Specifies the URL (location) of the data to be rendered.
	TYPE="..."	Specifies the Internet Media Type (MIME-Type) for the file specified by the DATA= attribute. This attribute is optional, but recommended. If no explicit value is given for this attribute, the browser should attempt to determine the type of the data to be rendered.
	DECLARE	When present, this boolean attribute makes the current <OBJECT> definition a declaration only. The object must be instantiated by a subsequent <OBJECT> definition referring to this declaration.

Tag	Attribute	Function
	STANDBY="..."	Specifies a message that a user agent may render while loading the object's implementation and data.
	ALIGN="..."	texttop | middle | textmiddle | baseline | textbottom | left | center | right
		Deprecated. Specifies the position of the object with respect to its surrounding context. Whenever possible, it is recommended that this tag be replaced by stylesheet alignment controls.
	TITLE="..."	Specify a title for the object.
	SRC="..."	Specify the URL (location) of a data file that can be decoded and rendered by the browser itself.

Q&A

Q I hear a lot about "streaming" video and audio. What does that mean?

A In the past, video and audio files took minutes and sometimes hours to retrieve through most modems, which severely limited the inclusion of video and audio on Web pages. The goal that everyone is moving toward is streaming video or audio, which will play while the data is being received. This means you will not have to completely download the clip before you can start to watch it.

Streaming playback is now widely supported through Microsoft Internet Explorer's built-in features and Netscape Navigator plug-ins. The examples in this hour use Windows AVI and WAV audio files to demonstrate both streaming and the old-fashioned download-and-play methods of delivering audiovisual media.

Q How do I choose between video formats such as QuickTime, Windows AVI, RealVideo, and MPEG? Is there any significant difference between them?

A QuickTime is the most popular format among Macintosh users, though QuickTime players are available for Windows 3.1 and Windows 95 as well. Similarly, AVI is the format of choice for Windows users, but you can get AVI players for the Macintosh. However, both QuickTime and AVI are almost certain

21

to be eclipsed by MPEG as the online video standard of choice within the next couple of years. MPEG-1 is best for Internet transmission because it is far more compact than MPEG-2. Unfortunately, few people have MPEG-compatible players installed now.

So how do you choose? If your audience is mostly Windows users, pick AVI. If it includes a significant number of Mac users, pick QuickTime. If cross-platform compatibility is essential, consider the RealVideo format—though only those who download special software from www.real.com will be able to see that format. In any case, plan to switch to MPEG eventually.

Q **When I say I want multimedia on my Web pages, everybody tells me to get Shockwave. What is it, and do I need it?**

A Macromedia Director is the most popular multimedia development platform, both for CD-ROMs and on the Internet. The online player for Director files is called Shockwave, and you should certainly take a look at it if you're serious about creating your own Web page multimedia. See Macromedia's site at http://www.macromedia.com for more information.

(There are also many other excellent multimedia development tools available—too many to list in this hour!)

Quiz

Questions

1. What's the simplest way to let the widest possible audience see a video on your Web site?

2. Write the HTML to insert a video clip named thevideo.avi that will be seen only by users of Microsoft Internet Explorer 3.0 and 4.0. Users of other browsers should see an image named standin.gif instead. While you're at it, make the video automatically play when the page loads and repeat as long as the page is showing.

3. Write the HTML to embed a video file named myvideo.avi into a Web page so that both Netscape Navigator and Microsoft Internet Explorer users will be able to see it, and users of other browsers would see an image linking to it.

4. What tag will soon replace both <IMG DYNSRC> and <EMBED> and work with future versions of all major Web browsers?

Answers

1. Just link to it, like this:

```
<A HREF="myvideo.avi">My Video</A>
```

2. ```
<IMG DYNSRC="thevideo.avi" SRC="standin.gif"
START="fileopen" LOOP="infinite">
```

3. Use the following HTML:
```
<EMBED SRC="myvideo.avi">
<NOEMBED>
<A HREF="myvideo.avi"><IMG SRC="theimage.gif"></A>
</NOEMBED>
```

4. `<OBJECT>`

# Activities

☐ If you include multimedia elements that require special players, you might need a special page to help people understand and set up what they need to make the most of your site. A link to that page should be prominently located near the top of your home page, steering newcomers aside just long enough to give them a clue.

☐ The techniques and tags covered in this hour for embedding media also work with Virtual Reality Modeling Language (VRML) files. To find out how you can use VRML to put interactive three-dimensional scenes and objects in your Web pages, check out the VRML home page at

`http://home.netscape.com/eng/live3d/howto/vrml_primer_index.html`

21
```

Hour 22

Applets, ActiveX, and Objects

Congratulations! You've got HTML under your belt, and you're ready to graduate from the school of Web publishing and enter the advanced world of Web development.

In this hour, you'll learn about

- ☐ Beyond the passive page
- ☐ CGI and Perl scripting
- ☐ Plug-in power
- ☐ Custom programming
- ☐ Strong Java
- ☐ ActiveX controls

Beyond the Passive Page

The World Wide Web of the past was simply a way to present information, and browsing wasn't much different from sitting in a lecture hall, watching a blackboard, or staring at an overhead projector screen. But today's Web surfer is looking for interactive, animated sites that change with each viewer and each viewing.

To achieve that level of interactivity, this hour introduces a number of ways you can go beyond passive text and graphics into the dynamic world of modern Web site development.

It would take a book many times the length of this one to teach you all the scripting and programming languages that can be used to create interactive programs for the Web. However, you can easily learn the HTML to incorporate prewritten programs into your Web pages.

CGI and Perl Scripting

Until very recently, there were only two ways to enhance the functionality of a Web browser. You could write and place programs on the Web server computer using the CGI (Common Gateway Interface) to manipulate documents as they were sent out using Perl or another programming language, or you could write and install programs on the user's computer to manipulate or display documents as they were received, either as a *helper application* or as a *plug-in*.

You can still do both of these things, and they may still be the most powerful and flexible means of enhancing Web pages. Unfortunately, both involve a high level of expertise in traditional programming languages (such as C++) and knowledge of Internet transfer protocols and operating system architecture. If you're not fortunate enough to already be an experienced UNIX or Windows programmer, as well as something of a Net guru, you're not going to start cranking out cool Web applications tomorrow (or the next day, or the next).

On the server side, simplified scripting languages like Perl can flatten the learning curve quite a bit. Many people who don't consider themselves real programmers can hack out a (CGI) script to process Web forms or feed animations to a Web page without too many false starts.

Plug-in Power

With visual programming tools such as Visual Basic, you can learn to produce a respectable client-side helper application fairly quickly as well. Your browser can use this application to render your special task on the client side, but the interface is sometimes not very user friendly. Before dashing into the inside lane, though, I do need to tell you about one very new way to enhance the Web that is not any easier than the old ways. It is, however, even more powerful when used well. I'm referring to Netscape Navigator plug-ins, which are custom helper applications designed especially to extend Netscape's capabilities. The Live3D, LiveAudio, and LiveVideo capabilities that are built in to Netscape Navigator 3.0 and 4.0 are actually accomplished through plug-ins, for example.

You're probably familiar with some of the more popular plug-ins, such as Shockwave and Acrobat. Because these programs (which are usually written in C++) have direct access to both the client computer's operating system and Netscape's data stream, they are usually faster, more user-friendly, and more efficient than any other program you can create. They can draw directly to the Netscape window, making their output seem as though it were embedded into a Web page, or they can process invisibly in the background.

All this power comes at a price, however. Like any helper application, the user must manually download and install your plug-in, and you must write a completely separate plug-in for every operating system you want to support. And woe betide you if your plug-in is distributed with a bug in it. Because plug-ins run at the machine level, they can easily crash Netscape and/or the user's computer if they malfunction.

Therefore, developing plug-ins is not for the faint of heart. Yet the lure of power has seduced many a programmer before, and if you can call yourself a programmer without blushing, you too may find it well worth the effort. All in all, writing and debugging a plug-in is still considerably less daunting than developing a full-blown business application.

But there is an easier way, and because this hour is intended to take you on the fast track to Web development, I have to recommend that you avoid the old ways until you run into something that you just can't accomplish any other way.

Custom Programming

Suppose you just want your Web order form to add up totals automatically when customers check off which products they want. This is not rocket science. Implementing it shouldn't be either. You don't want to learn UNIX or C++ or the Windows 95 Applications Programming Interface. You don't want to compile and install half a dozen extra files on your Web server, or ask the user to download your handy-dandy calculator application. You just want to add up some numbers. Or maybe you just want to change a graphic according to the user's preferences, or the day of the week, or whatever. Maybe you want to tell a random joke every time somebody logs on to your home page. Until now, there really was no simple way to do these simple things.

Inline scripting languages such as JavaScript, which you'll learn more about later, are one way to accomplish these things with relative ease, but JavaScript and its competitors have limitations. For one thing, they're sometimes slow and don't actually do many things you might really want them to. The answer to this dreary situation is (bad pun coming!) to wake up and smell the coffee.

Strong Java

Complex applications of any kind are poorly suited for inclusion in HTML pages by means of a scripting language such as JavaScript. There are only so many lines of code you want to wade through to see the Web page itself.

When you outgrow JavaScript, does that mean you'll need to return to server-side scripting or applications programming? No. JavaScript is just the baby sister of a more robust and powerful language called Java. Like JavaScript, Java is especially designed for the Web. And like JavaScript scripts, Java programs install and run automatically whenever a Web page is loaded. However, unlike JavaScript, Java programs are compiled into a more compact and efficient form (called bytecodes) and stored in a separate file from the Web pages that may call them.

Java also includes a complete graphics drawing library, security features, strong type checking, and other professional-level programming amenities that serious developers need. The biggest limiting factor with Java mini-applications (called applets) is that they must be small enough so that downloading them won't delay the display of a Web page by an intolerable amount. Fortunately, Java applets are extremely compact in their compiled form and are often considerably smaller than the images on a typical Web page.

Best of all, the syntax of Java is nearly identical to JavaScript, so you can cut your teeth on JavaScript and easily move to Java when you need or want to.

You'll find many ready-to-use Java applets on the Web, and Figure 22.1 shows how to include one in a Web page. The following HTML inserts a Java applet named `RnbText.class` (which must be placed in the same directory as the Web page) with the `<APPLET>` tag. This applet makes some text wiggle like a wave while rainbow colors flow through it, as shown in Figure 22.2.

JUST A MINUTE

In the new HTML 4.0 standard, the `<APPLET>` tag is officially deprecated, which means that it is on its way to becoming obsolete. Don't worry too much about it, though; `<APPLET>` will continue to be a part of HTML for years to come, although you should certainly start thinking about changing over. The `<OBJECT>` tag that replaces it is discussed at the end of this hour. However, most people are still using earlier versions of Web browsers that require the `<APPLET>` tag and the current (4.0) versions of both Netscape Navigator and Microsoft Internet Explorer still support `<APPLET>`. So you should continue to use `<APPLET>` until all of your intended audience switches to HTML 4.0-compatible browsers, which, realistically, may be never for some.

22

Figure 22.1.

Java applets are pre-written programs that you place on your Web page with the <APPLET> tag.

```
<HTML>
<HEAD><TITLE>Hawaiian Hard Drive</TITLE></HEAD>
<BODY BACKGROUND="hhd.jpg">
<DIV ALIGN="center">
<IMG SRC="hhd2.gif" ALT="Hawaiian Hard Drive"><BR>
<APPLET CODE="RnbText.class" WIDTH=580 HEIGHT=50>
<PARAM NAME="text"
 VALUE="H a w a ii's  C o m p u t e r  N e w s">
</APPLET>
<P></DIV>
<FONT SIZE=4>The mission of the Hawaiian Hard Drive
newspaper and Web site are to inform a broad range of
computer users and the general general public of the
latest trends in the computer market. Through our writers
and advertisers, you'll find out about software, hardware,
applications  and other areas of interest.<P>
<DIV ALIGN="center">
<HR SIZE=10>
<APPLET CODE="RnbText.class" WIDTH=230 HEIGHT=50>
<PARAM NAME="text" VALUE="F e a t u r e s">
</APPLET>
<P><B><A HREF="webpages.htm">Making Your Own Web Page</A><BR>
<A HREF="virus.htm">A Computer Virus Primer</A><BR>
<A HREF="copyrite.htm">Software Copyright Protection</A><BR>
<P>
</FONT>
<HR SIZE=10>
<A HREF="mailto:PDeptula@aol.com">PDeptula@aol.com</A>
</ADDRESS><P>
All stories are copyright, 1995-1996 by their authors.<BR>
The Java Applet on this page was designed by
<A HREF="http://www.crl.com/~integris">
Integris Network Services</A>.<P>
</DIV>
</BODY></HTML>
```

```
<APPLET CODE="RnbText.class" WIDTH=580 HEIGHT=50>
<PARAM NAME="text"
 VALUE="H a w a ii's C o m p u t e r N e w s">
</APPLET>
```

The WIDTH and HEIGHT attributes do just what you'd expect them to—specify the dimensions of the region on the Web page that will contain the applet's output. The <PARAM> tag is used to supply any information that the specific applet needs to do its thing. The NAME identifies what information you're supplying to the applet, and VALUE is the actual information itself. In this example, the applet is designed to display some text, so you have to tell it what text to display.

Every applet will require different settings for the NAME and VALUE attributes, and most applets require more than one <PARAM> tag to set all their options. Whoever created the applet will tell you (usually in some kind of readme.txt or other documentation file) what NAME attributes you need to include and what sort of information to put in the VALUE attributes for each NAME.

Figure 22.2.

The <APPLET> *tags in Figure 22.1 insert a program to draw wiggly, colorful animated text on the page.*

Note that in Figure 22.1, the same applet is used twice on the page. This is quite efficient, because it will only need to be downloaded once, and the Web browser will then create two copies of it automatically. Figure 22.2 shows a still snapshot of the resulting animated Web page.

ActiveX Controls

For quite some time Microsoft Windows has included a feature called *object linking and embedding* (OLE), which allows all or part of one program to be embedded in a document that you are working on with another program. For example, you can use OLE to put a spreadsheet in a word processing document.

When the Internet explosion rocked the world in the mid-1990s, Microsoft adapted their OLE technology to work with HTML pages online and renamed it ActiveX. Everybody likes to invent their own jargon, so ActiveX programs are called *controls* rather than applets.

22

Though ActiveX is touted as the main competitor of Java, it actually isn't a specific programming language. It's a standard for making programs written in any language conform to the same protocols so that neither you, the Web page author, nor the people who view your pages need to be aware of what language the control was written in. It just works, whether the programmer used Visual Basic, VBScript (a simplified version of Visual Basic), C++, or even Java.

It's not surprising that support for the Microsoft ActiveX protocol is built into Microsoft Internet Explorer 3.0. For users of Netscape Navigator 2.0 and 3.0 to be able to see ActiveX controls, they need to download and install a plug-in from Ncompass Labs (`http://www.ncompasslabs.com`).

JUST A MINUTE

Note that ActiveX controls will only work on Windows and Macintosh computers. Also, ActiveX controls must be separately compiled for each different operating system.

Because ActiveX is the newest of the technologies discussed in this hour, you must use the new HTML 4.0 <OBJECT> tag to insert it into a page.

As Figure 22.3 shows, an ActiveX <OBJECT> tag looks rather different from other code you've seen in this book so far. Here's the relevant HTML from that page:

Figure 22.3.

The <OBJECT> *tag on this page embeds an ActiveX control.*

```
<HTML>
<HEAD><TITLE>Colour Calculator</TITLE></HEAD>
<BODY>
<A HREF="mailto:kencox@user.rose.com">kencox@user.rose.com</A>
<DIV ALIGN="center">
<BODY TOPMARGIN="4" BGCOLOR="white">
<OBJECT CLASSID="CLSID:812AE312-8B8E-11CF-93C8-00AA00C08FDF"
 ID="cntrl">
<PARAM NAME="ALXPATH" REF VALUE="cntrl.alx">
</OBJECT>
</DIV>
</BODY></HTML>
```

```
<OBJECT CLASSID="CLSID:812AE312-8B8E-11CF-93C8-00AA00C08FDF"
 ID="cntrl">
<PARAM NAME="ALXPATH" REF VALUE="cntrl.alx">
</OBJECT>
```

The unusual aspect is the CLASSID attribute, which must include a unique identifier for the specific ActiveX control you are including. If you use an automated program such as Microsoft's ActiveX Control Pad to create your ActiveX pages, it will figure out this magic number for you. Otherwise, you'll need to consult the documentation that came with the ActiveX control to find the correct CLASSID.

As if the long string of information in CLASSID isn't enough, the ID attribute must include another unique identifier, but this time you get to make it up. You can use any label you want for ID, as long as you don't use the same label for another ActiveX control in the same document. ID is used for identifying the control in any scripts you might add to the page.

JUST A MINUTE

> If you are something of a whiz with Windows, you can look in the Windows class Registry for the CLSID in HKEY_CLASSES_ROOT. If you don't feel comfortable about working in your Registry, you'll need to rely on the person who wrote the ActiveX control (or an automated Web page authoring tool) to tell you the correct CLASSID.

Microsoft's ActiveX is unique in using CLASSID in this manner. The attribute officially refers to the location (URL) of what the World Wide Web Consortium (W3C) quaintly calls a *rendering mechanism*—in other words, a program. HTML 4.0 objects are not nearly as complicated as this isolated example might lead you to believe. In the previous hour, I showed you a simple set of nested <OBJECT> tags that performs a rather complex failsafe mechanism, so if ActiveX seems complicated, focus on that earlier simplicity.

The <PARAM> tags work the same with <OBJECT> as discussed earlier in this hour with the <APPLET> tag. They provide settings and options specific to the particular ActiveX control you are placing on the Web page, with NAME identifying the type of information and VALUE giving the information itself. In the example from Figure 22.3, the REF attribute indicates that the <PARAM> tag is specifying the location of the ActiveX control itself. No other <PARAM> parameters are needed by this particular control. Notice that nothing in the HTML itself gives any clue as to what the ActiveX control on that page actually looks like or does. Only when you view the page, as in Figure 22.4, do you see that it is a nifty little program to mix custom colors by combining red, green, and blue brightness settings.

Neither Figure 22.3 nor Figure 22.4 reveals what language the person who created the ActiveX control used to write it. If you opened the cntrl.alx file itself, you'd see that Ken Cox used a version of VisualBasic specifically designed for Web page use, called VBScript. I'll spare you the rather lengthy source code listing here, but you can find this and other controls by Ken Cox at

```
http://www.rose.com/~kencox/index.html
```

22

Figure 22.4.

The ActiveX control on this page is a program for mixing custom colors, though you wouldn't know it by looking at the HTML in Figure 22.3.

22

Colour Calculator - Microsoft Internet Explorer

File   Edit   View   Go   Favorites   Help

Links   Address

kencox@user.rose.com

Colour Calculator

Red	Green	Blue
212	101	181

Sample Text

object.backcolor=#D465B5

Help

COFFEE BREAK

This and the previous hour have introduced a whirlwind of different options for adding cutting-edge multimedia and programming to your Web site. For an example of how to use multimedia and interactive elements with discretion (and, in some cases, gee-whiz abandon), meet the latest incarnation of the 24-Hour HTML Café at

`http://www.mcp.com/sites/1-57521/1-57521-366-4/`

You may find it difficult to distinguish the custom programming from the more traditional animation and HTML tricks, which is exactly as it should be in a well-balanced, integrated site. Always try to leave your audience free to experience the content of the site, rather than trying to awe them with your high-tech prowess.

To Do

Reading this hour will give you enough information to decide what types of programs or scripts might be best for your Web site. If you decide to take the leap into actually using some (or even creating your own) on your pages, you should look to the following resources:

1. You'll find a list of online sources for prewritten scripts and reusable program components in the 24-Hour HTML Café hotlist page at `http://www.mcp.com/sites/1-57521/1-57521-366-4/`

2. If you want to write your own interactive programming for Web pages, I recommend *Web Page Publishing Unleashed, Professional Reference Edition,* by Sams.net Publishing. You'll also find some online tutorials in the hotlist mentioned here. In the next hour, we'll introduce JavaScript, an easy-to-use scripting language that you can use to create your own programs or modify existing prewritten programs, to customize your Web site.

Summary

This hour has given you a brief outline of two of the three types of prewritten interactive programming that are easiest to add to your Web site: Java applets, ActiveX controls, and another mention of HTML 4.0 objects in passing. It also discussed the difference between these technologies and more traditional server-side scripting and Netscape plug-ins.

You didn't get enough technical stuff in this short hour to write your own programs and scripts, but you did learn the basic HTML to insert prewritten ones into your Web pages.

In Hour 23 you'll learn to write or modify some of your own simple JavaScripts to do some of the easiest and most useful tasks that scripting is commonly used for, covering the third type of interactive programming and introducing you to actual coding.

Table 22.1 summarizes the tags covered in this hour.

Table 22.1. HTML tags and attributes covered in Hour 22.

Tag	Attribute	Function
`<!-- ... //-->`		The standard way to create comments. Can also be used to hide JavaScript from browsers that do not support it.
`<SCRIPT>...</SCRIPT>`		An interpreted script program.
	`LANGUAGE="..."`	Currently only JavaScript is supported by Netscape. Both JavaScript and VBScript are supported by Microsoft.
	`SRC="..."`	Specifies the URL of a file that includes the script program.

22

Tag	Attribute	Function
`<APPLET>...</APPLET>`		Inserts a self-running Java applet.
	`CLASS="..."`	The name of the applet.
	`SRC="..."`	The URL of the directory where the compiled applet can be found (should end in a slash / as in `http://mysite/myapplets/`). Do not include the actual applet name, which is specified with the `CLASS` attribute.
	`ALIGN="..."`	Indicates how the applet should be aligned with any text that follows it. Current values are `TOP`, `MIDDLE`, and `BOTTOM`.
	`WIDTH="..."`	The width of the applet output area in pixels.
	`HEIGHT="..."`	The height of the applet output area in pixels.
`<PARAM>`		Program-specific parameters. (Always occurs within `<APPLET>` or `<OBJECT>` tags.)
	`NAME="..."`	The type of information being given to the applet or ActiveX control.
	`VALUE="..."`	The actual information to be given to the applet or ActiveX control.
`<OBJECT>...</OBJECT>`		Inserts images, videos, Java applets, or ActiveX OLE controls into a document.
	`CLASSID="..."`	The address of a Java applet, other program, or identification code for an ActiveX program.
	`ID="..."`	Gives an identifying name for a Microsoft ActiveX program.

continues

Table 22.1. continued

Tag	Attribute	Function
	DATA="..."	May be used in some situations to tell an applet or program where to find some data that it needs.
	TYPE="..."	May indicate the type of data referred to by a DATA attribute.
	STANDBY="..."	Lets you specify a text message to be displayed while an applet or program object is being loaded and initialized.

JUST A MINUTE

In addition to the standard <APPLET> attributes in Table 22.1, you can specify applet-specific attributes to be interpreted by the Java applet itself.

Q&A

Q So just what exactly is the difference between *scripting* and *programming* anyway?

A Usually, the word *scripting* is used for programming in relatively simple computer languages that are integrated directly into an application (or into HTML pages). However, the line between scripting and "real programming" is pretty fuzzy.

Q I've used Visual Basic before, and I heard I could use it in Web pages. Is that true?

A Yes, but only if you want to limit the audience for your pages to users of Microsoft Internet Explorer version 3.0 or higher. Microsoft has implemented LANGUAGE= "VBScript" as one of the language options in the <SCRIPT> tag, but so far the rest of the world is sticking to JavaScript. Visit the Microsoft Web site (http://www. microsoft.com) for details about the differences between VBScript and Visual Basic.

Q I've heard about ActiveX *scripting* and ActiveX *documents*. How are these different from ActiveX *controls*?

A In Microsoft-speak, *ActiveX scripting* means VBScript or JavaScript linking into a page as an ActiveX control. ActiveX documents are HTML pages that use an

ActiveX control to view a word processing document or spreadsheet within a Web page. (Career tip: If you want a job at Microsoft, consider listing your first name as *ActiveX* on the application form. They like that.)

Q Most of the Java applets I find on the Internet have two files, one ending with `.java` and one ending with `.class`. Which one do I put on my Web page, and what do I do with the other one?

A Put the file ending with `.class` on your Web page with the `<APPLET>` tag. The `.java` file is the actual Java source code, provided in case you are a Java programmer and you want to change it. You don't need the `.java` file to use the applet.

Quiz

Questions

1. What tag is used to distinguish JavaScript or VBScript from the rest of a Web page?

2. Suppose you found a cool Java game on the Internet and the documentation with it says it's free for anyone to use. It says you need to give the applet two parameters: the "speed" should be between 1 and 100, and the "skill" should be between 1 and 5. The applet itself is named `roadkill.class`. Write the HTML to display it in a 400×200-pixel area in the middle of a Web page.

3. From the Microsoft Internet Explorer Web site (`http://www.microsoft.com/ie/`), you can download the `IELABEL.OCX` control, which displays some text in any orientation you choose. Write the HTML to insert the ActiveX control in a Web page, given the following information:

   The class ID is:

   a. `clsid:{99B42120-6EC7-11CF-A6C7-00AA00A47DD2}`

      Confine the display area to 300×300 pixels.

   b. Specify the following parameter values:

      Caption: "New and Exciting!"

      Angle: 45

      FontName: Arial Black

      FontSize: 18

Answers

1. `<SCRIPT>`

2.
```
<APPLET CODE="roadkill.class" WIDTH=400 HEIGHT=200>
<PARAM NAME="speed" VALUE=50>
<PARAM NAME="skill" VALUE=2>
</APPLET>
```

3.
```
<OBJECT CLASSID="clsid:{99B42120-6EC7-11CF-A6C7-00AA00A47DD2}"
ID="label" WIDTH=300 HEIGHT=300>
<PARAM NAME="caption" VALUE="New and Exciting!">
<PARAM NAME="angle" VALUE="45">
<PARAM NAME="fontname" VALUE="Arial Black">
<PARAM NAME="fontsize" VALUE="18">
</OBJECT>
```

Activities

☐ Two of the most common uses of programming elements in a Web page are order forms that add up their own totals and marquees that scroll text across part of the page to draw attention to it. I've created a simple sample page to demonstrate both of these using Java and JavaScript. If you've had even a smattering of programming experience, you'll probably find it easy to modify my page to add up your own order form totals. The page is at

http://www.mcp.com/sites/1-57521/1-57521-366-4/

☐ You can also use the Marquee Java applet on the page for your own pages. The filename is marquee.class, and how to use it should be clear from the sample page.

☐ You'll find many more reusable scripts and applets by exploring the http://www.mcp.com/sites/1-57521/1-57521-366-4/ JavaScript and Java links.

22

Hour **23**

Using Scripts to Alter Elements

Scripting is a polite word for computer programming. Because it is obviously an enormous topic, you're not going to learn much about it in a one-hour chapter. Still, there are some awfully handy things that you can do in a snap with scripting—and which you can't do any other way. So with a spirit of bold optimism, this chapter aims to help you teach yourself just enough Web page scripting to make your pages stand out from the "non-de-script" crowd.

In this hour, you'll learn about

- ☐ Scripting languages
- ☐ A JavaScript example
- ☐ Interactive highlighting
- ☐ More JavaScript tricks
- ☐ Pre-written JavaScript
- ☐ JavaScript resources
- ☐ JavaScript problems
- ☐ How the `<OBJECT>` tag helps

Scripting Languages

A scripting language is a way to do complex things on the client side of your browser, things like changing the appearance of the page, displaying information, handling forms, frames, and other elements that might be difficult and time-consuming to code by hand, as well as requiring significant server power. Almost anything you can do with client pull can be done better and quicker with scripts, and you can do a lot more besides. In two words, they're *way cool.*

There are many script languages available: JavaScript (one of the first to be used on the Web), VBScript, JScript, and others. They have a lot in common and you can do a lot of different things with them. So let's concentrate on just one, JavaScript, and I'll teach you only one or two tricks. Believe me, it will be more than enough to interest you.

A JavaScript Example

During this hour, you will create a Web page using JavaScript. JavaScript was chosen because it is currently the best supported scripting language. JavaScript is currently supported in Netscape Navigator 3.0 and above, Microsoft Internet Explorer 3.0 and above, and a few lesser-known browsers floating around in cyberspace. Also, as with most scripting languages, if a browser doesn't support a scripting language, it will generally just gracefully ignore the script.

CAUTION

As you will soon discover, Microsoft's initial attempts at JavaScript left a few things to be desired. Certain features of the JavaScript language (such as Image, which you'll be using today) are missing in older versions of Internet Explorer. If you are using one of these versions of Internet Explorer, you will receive an error message. To avoid this error, you should be using at least Internet Explorer 3.0.1 for the Macintosh or Internet Explorer 4 for Windows. Of course, any version of Netscape Navigator 3.0 or above will do as well.

If the ease and power of the few JavaScript commands you use in this chapter whets your appetite for more (as I think it will), I encourage you to turn to a book such as Sams.net Publishing's *Teach Yourself JavaScript in a Week.*

Interactive Highlighting

At some time or another, you may have seen buttons that light up or change when your mouse passes over them in some software product or on a Web page. This not only looks cool, but it also gives you some visual feedback before you click on something, which research shows can reduce confusion and errors.

Right now you're going to create a Web page that does this very thing. For example, consider the page in Figure 23.1. Clicking on Prediction might take you to one page, while clicking on Fiction might take you to another. Wouldn't it be neat if the word Prediction lit up in bright yellow when your mouse passed over it, and turned back to dark blue when the mouse moved away? And, of course, then you'd want the word Fiction to light up when the mouse passed over it, too.

Unfortunately, as mentioned previously, you won't be able to see this effect if you're using an older browser. In fact, Microsoft IE 3.0 for Windows platforms will "choke" on the code because they implemented an early version of JavaScript that didn't really support images.

Figure 23.1.

Clicking on the left side of the graphical title takes you to a Prediction page. The right side of the title links to a Fiction page.

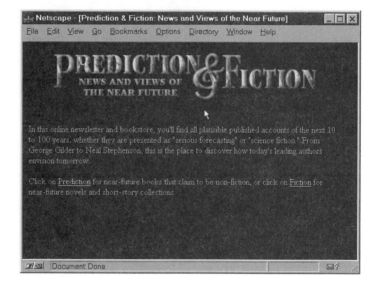

To create this effect, you will create two sets of each image: a normal image and a highlighted image. You will then use JavaScript to automatically swap images when the mouse passes over each given image.

The first step toward achieving that effect is to create the graphics for both the darkened and "lit up" words. Figure 23.2 shows the images used in my example in Paint Shop Pro. (Notice that I split each title into a left half and right half, so that I could use regular links instead of an image map. As discussed in Chapter 15, "Image Maps," the two halves will connect seamlessly as long as I make sure I don't put any spaces between the <IMG> tags in my HTML document.)

To make the bottom two images in Figure 23.2, I just made copies of the top images and colored the text bright yellow (using the magic wand tool and the Colors | Colorize menu option). Then I added a sparkle highlight to each word as an extra artistic touch.

Figure 23.2.

The top two images in this Paint Shop Pro window are the title shown in Figure 23.1. The bottom two images are a "lit up" version, with the words colored bright yellow and a sparkle added.

JUST A MINUTE

Surely you have a Web page or two that would look flashier or be easier to understand if the navigation icons or other images changed when the mouse passed over them? Try creating some highlighted versions of the images on them, and try modifying your own page as you read the following few paragraphs.

NEW TERM A *variable* is like a container that holds an object or a value in programming and scripting languages. In this example, each of our variables holds one of our images.

NEW TERM *Initializing* a variable is when you first declare what object or value will be contained within each variable. This is important because the object that is held by each variable can change. In our example, this initialization process also has the added benefit of downloading all the images.

Now for the magic part. The first thing you want to do as far as creating your Web page is to initialize the variables, which in this case are your images. You'll go ahead and do this in the Web page header so that your actual header should look something like this:

```
<HTML>
<HEAD>
<TITLE>
Prediction &amp; Fiction: News and Views of the Near Future
</TITLE>

<SCRIPT LANGUAGE="JavaScript">
<!--
```

23

```
        preBlue = new Image(280,100);
        preGold = new Image(280,100);
        ficBlue = new Image(220,100);
        ficGold = new Image(220,100);
        preBlue.src = "pre-blue.gif";
        preGold.src = "pre-gold.gif";
        ficBlue.src = "fic-blue.gif";
        ficGold.src = "fic-gold.gif";
// -->
</SCRIPT>

</HEAD>
```

23

Before you get too concerned about what it all means, let me explain. First of all, you should notice the <SCRIPT> tags. Like most other tags, these tell the browser where the script begins and where the script ends. The property LANGUAGE lets the browser know which scripting language you are using.

The next thing to look at is that it seems that all of my script is surrounded by comment tags (<!-- ... //-->). Yes, this is not a mistake: All scripts should be contained within comment tags; this hides the script from older browsers that do not support the <SCRIPT> tag. By the way, the fact that the comment tags are each alone on their own lines is important!

OK, now onto the actual scripting part. The first four lines of the script create four variables called preBlue, preGold, ficBlue, and ficGold; set up each of these variables to contain an image. The numbers in the parentheses are the width and height of the image. If you are not sure of the exact dimensions, you can just leave the parentheses empty.

TIME SAVER

Variables can be named just about anything using letters and numbers; however, it is generally best to give them names that make sense. In this example, the name of the variable is almost the same as the name of the image except the - was removed. Also, it is a common practice among programmers to use all lowercase letters in variables except when a variable contains more then one word. Then the first letter of each word after the first word would be capitalized. For example, thisVariable is made up of two words. Following such conventions helps you and others read scripts more easily.

CAUTION

Variables are case sensitive! aVariable and AVARIABLE represent two different variables.

The next four lines of the script actually tell what specific image gets contained in each variable. The `.src` extension refers to the actual source file or value of the variable. For example, `preBlue.src = "pre-blue.gif"` tells the Web browser that the source of the `preBlue` variable is the image file `pre-blue.gif`.

OK, so far, so good. The browser has now been given four variables, and has assigned an image to each of these variables. But, how do you use these variables?

In order for any action to happen, some event must take place. Each scripting language can respond to certain events. In this example, you will use two common events: `OnMouseOver` and `OnMouseOut`. `OnMouseOver` events occur when the mouse cursor enters a designated area. `OnMouseOut` events occur when the mouse cursor leaves that area.

NEW TERM *Events* are actions that scripts or programs "listen" for. When one of these events occurs, it usually triggers the script to cause something to happen. In this example, you will wait for the mouse to pass over a hyperlink; when this occurs, the Prediction or Fiction image will change. When the mouse leaves the link, the image will return to normal.

One of the easiest and most common ways to define an area is to use an anchor.

In this example, you want the first image on the Web page (`pre-blue.gif`) to change to `pre-gold.gif` when the mouse passes over the corresponding link, and change back to `pre-blue.gif` when the mouse moves away.

When the mouse passes over the second link, you want the second image on the page (`fic-blue.gif`) to change to `fic-gold.gif`. That image should change back to `fic-blue.gif` when the mouse moves away from the second link.

Here's what all that looks like in HTML and JavaScript:

```
<A HREF="predict.html" onMouseOver="predict.src=preGold.src"
onMouseOut="predict.src=preBlue.src"><IMG SRC="pre-blue.gif" NAME="predict"
ALT="Prediction" WIDTH="280" HEIGHT="100" BORDER="0"></A><A HREF="fiction.html"
onMouseOver="fiction.src=ficGold.src" onMouseOut="fiction.src=ficBlue.src"><IMG
SRC="fic-blue.gif" NAME="fiction" ALT="& Fiction" WIDTH="220" HEIGHT="100"
BORDER="0"></A>
```

CAUTION

Note that in the code there are no spaces between any of the tags. If you put a space between here, the two images will not line up correctly.

23

So, what did you do here? Well, let me explain. The first thing to notice are the <IMG> tags. For the most part they should be familiar; however, a new property called NAME was added to each of these tags. The first image tag is named predict, and the second image is named fiction. Giving the images good names makes the rest of our script writing much easier.

JUST A MINUTE

> If you choose not to name your images, you could also refer to them as document.images[0] and document.images[1]. document.images[0] refers to the first image listed in the current document (or Web page in this case), while document.images[1] refers to the second. It's important to note here that 0 refers to the first image, 1 is the second, 2 would be the third, and so on.

23

Finally, let's look at the <A> tag. This is where most of the actual action takes place. Looking at the first anchor, <A HREF="predict.html" onMouseOver="predict.src=preGold.src" onMouseOut="predict.src=preBlue.src">, you should already know what the A and the HREF mean. These are just parts of a basic anchor. Following these, though, are our events. The first event, onMouseOver="predict.src=preGold.src", tells us that when the mouse is over this link, the object or variable named predict, which is the name you have given to our first image, should equal the object or variable called preGold, which you defined in the header as pre-gold.gif. This effectively replaces our initial image with pre-gold.gif. The next event, onMouseOut="predict.src=preBlue.src", effectively switches the gold image back to the blue image when the mouse passes outside of the anchor. And that's it. The next anchor basically does the same thing, but using different images.

When you do this on your own Web pages, just follow my example closely, substituting your own names and images for the ones I've used. Figure 23.3 shows how my finished Web page looks.

Usually, you will want the image that the mouse is passing over to light up or change. But you aren't limited to doing it that way. For example, the page in Figure 23.3 includes two text-only links near the bottom, with JavaScript to make the title at the top of the page respond when the mouse moves over those text links. Figure 23.5 demonstrates the Fiction part of the title lighting up when the mouse cursor passes over the Fiction text link at the bottom of the page.

Figure 23.3.

The JavaScript-enhanced HTML for the page shown in Figures 23.1, 23.4, and 23.5.

```
<HTML>
<HEAD>
<TITLE>
Prediction &amp; Fiction: News and Views of the Near Future
</TITLE>

<SCRIPT LANGUAGE="JavaScript">
<!--
preBlue = new Image(280,100);
preGold = new Image(280,100);
ficBlue = new Image(220,100);
ficGold = new Image(220,100);
preBlue.src = "pre-blue.gif";
preGold.src = "pre-gold.gif";
ficBlue.src = "fic-blue.gif";
ficGold.src = "fic-gold.gif";
//-->
</SCRIPT>

</HEAD>
<BODY BACKGROUND="fadeblue.gif" BGCOLOR="#000000" TEXT="#CFCFCF"
LINK="#FFFF00" VLINK="#AFAFFF">
<DIV ALIGN="CENTER">

<A HREF="predict.html" onMouseOver="predict.src=preGold.src" onMouseOut="
predict.src=preBlue.src"><IMG SRC="pre-blue.gif" NAME="predict"
ALT="Preditction" WIDTH="280" HEIGHT="100" BORDER="0"></A><A
HREF="fiction.html" onMouseOver="fiction.src=ficGold.src"
onMouseOut="fiction.src=ficBlue.src"><IMG SRC="fic-blue.gif" NAME="fiction"
ALT="& Fiction" WIDTH="220" HEIGHT="100" BORDER="0"></A>

</DIV>
<P>
In this online newsletter and bookstore, you'll find all plausible publishe
accounts of the next 10  to 100 years, whethter they are presented as
"serious forcasting" or "science fiction." From George Gilder to Neal
Stephenson, this is the place to discover how today's leading authors
envision tomorrow.
</P>
<P>
Click on <A HREF="predict.html" onMouseOver="predict.src=preGold.src"
onMouseOut="predict.src=preBlue.src">Prediction</A> for near-future books
that claim to be non-fiction, or click on
<A HREF="fiction.html" onMouseOver="fiction.src=ficGold.src"
onMouseOut="fiction.src=ficBlue.src">Fiction</A> for near-future novels and
short-story collections.
</P>
</BODY></HTML>
```

COFFEE BREAK

You can also use the OnMouseOver and OnMouseOut attributes with image maps (which are covered in Chapter 15). For an example of a large interactive image map using no less than 24 separate images, move your mouse cursor around the pocket watch at the completed 24-Hour HTML Café site:

http://www.mcp.com/sites/1-57521/1-57521-366-4/

Peeking at the source code will show you exactly how to incorporate JavaScript commands into an image map.

23

Figure 23.4.

When the mouse passes over the word Prediction in Figure 23.1, the JavaScript in Figure 23.3 makes it light up.

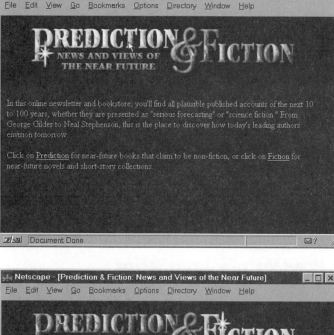

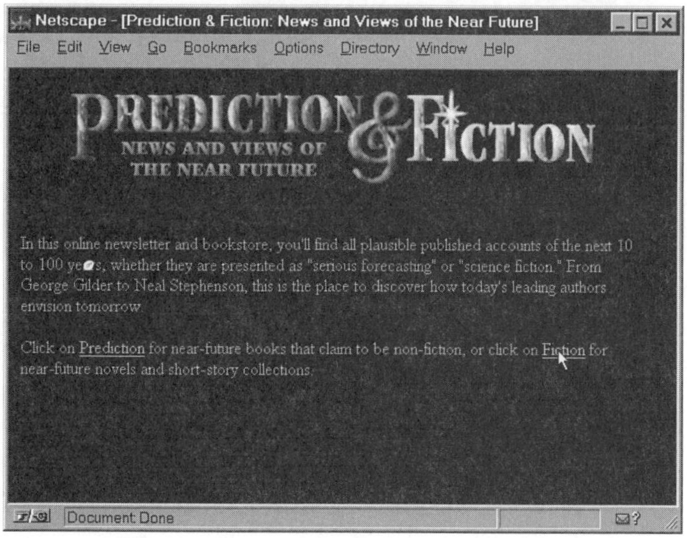

Figure 23.5.

Passing the mouse over a text link can affect graphics on a different part of the page. (This is the page listed in Figure 23.3.)

More JavaScript Hints

The techniques you've seen in this chapter so far are so simple that anyone can implement them, just by carefully following the examples in Figures 23.3 and 23.6. There are also a number of other JavaScript magic tricks that aren't much harder, because JavaScript lets you directly modify almost any element on your Web pages.

For instance, if your site uses frames (see Chapter 18, "Interactive Layout with Frames"), you can change the contents of a frame almost exactly the same way you change the contents of an image. Instead of `document.images[0].src`, you would say `top.frames[0].src`. The HTML to change the contents of the first frame in the window when the mouse passes over an image (which could be in any frame), would look like the following.

```
<A HREF="somewhere.htm"
onmouseover="top.frames[0].src='newbanner.htm'">
<IMG SRC="animage.gif"></A>
```

You can change a particular image in another frame by referencing `top.frames[0].document.images[0].src` with the frame number and image number you want in the square brackets.

Don't worry if you didn't quite follow that on the first read; Explaining these—and other nifty tricks like them—in more depth could obviously fill another whole book. (But don't be afraid to play around with the suggestions in the previous paragraph to see how they work, either!)

Pre-Written JavaScript

As you've seen above, JavaScript gives you a way to do a lot of interesting things. OK, so it's still programming. But it's the kind of programming you can learn in an afternoon, or in an hour if you've fooled around with BASIC or Excel macros before. It's programming for the rest of us, and the best thing about it is that you can often find JavaScript code on the Web that can be *tweaked* just a little to fit right in with the way your Web site operates (with the original author's permission of course). JavaScripts go right into the HTML of your Web pages, wherever you want something intelligent to happen.

Even if you don't immediately understand the exact syntax of each JavaScript statement, it should be obvious that it is much easier to learn than any other way to accomplish the same thing. Most programmers could probably customize and expand the page quite a bit without knowing anything whatsoever about JavaScript. What's more, this page works on any server and any JavaScript-enabled browser on any operating system.

If you don't do programming at all, you may find a JavaScript that can be incorporated into a Web page of your own with little or no modification. Generally, most JavaScripts go in the `<HEAD>` area, preceded by `<SCRIPT LANGUAGE="JavaScript">`, and followed by `</SCRIPT>`. The parts of the script that actually carry out the actions when the page is loaded go in the `<BODY>` part of the page, but still need to be set aside with the `<SCRIPT>` tag. Sections of script that respond to specific form entries go in the `<INPUT>` tag, with special attributes such as `ONCURSOR`.

JavaScript Resources

Now that you've learned enough in this chapter to have a head start on JavaScript and add some snazzy interaction to your Web pages, you've probably also gotten the idea that there's a lot more you can do, and it isn't as hard as you might have thought. By poking around at JavaScript reference sites on the Internet and playing with the examples you find there, you may find yourself able to create some amazing interactive pages without actually learning any serious programming. In fact, at most of these sites you can find lots of dandy little scripts that you can drop into your pages without any programming at all. Cool!

Here are four JavaScript sites to explore:

```
http://www.gamelan.com/pages/Gamelan.javascript.html
http://www.c2.org/~andreww/javascript
http://www.ce.net/users/ryan/java/
http://developer.netscape.com/
```

You'll also find links to JavaScript learning resources at `http://www.mcp.com/info/1-57521/1-57521-366-4/sitelist.htm`.

JavaScript Problems

OK, it was too good to be true. What about the problems you'll run into, and there are a few. I've mentioned some in passing above, but there is a general problem. JavaScript is a hot item, and different browser manufacturers are all competing to make their product the best. As a result, JavaScript varies from browser to browser.

Microsoft added to the confusion with JScript, which was based on an old version of JavaScript and left out a lot of functionality seen in more recent versions of the script. The trouble is that Microsoft IE identifies itself as being able to handle JavaScript, but it really only handles its own dialect. This can make your browser either choke or at least hiccup.

Here is a site that tracks the differences so you can decide for yourself what features to use:

```
http://gmccomb.com/javascript/
```

Is there light at the end of the tunnel? Well, yes and no. Microsoft and Netscape, as well as Sun Microsystems, IBM, and others, have been working out a common implementation of JavaScript, standardized as ECMA-262, which Microsoft implemented as JScript 3.0 and which is the version released with Microsoft IE 4.0. However, the ECMA standard does not actually enforce many rules about how objects communicate with each other, and both Microsoft and Netscape have said that their implementations will continue to innovate. This means that JavaScript will continue to be a mess from now until someday in the yet-to-be-seen future.

The safest course, if you want to use a scripting language, is to maintain two pages or very carefully restrict yourself to the features the various dialects have in common. As always, test your pages on several browsers and provide alternatives.

How the <OBJECT> Tag Helps

The World Wide Web Consortium (W3C) has been looking at these and other problems and came up with the <OBJECT> tag, which adds several layers of protection for your browser and is much more extensible than the jumble of extra tags that Microsoft and Netscape have been tossing at each other. We've talked about it before but it's worth considering again; HTML 4.0 <OBJECT> tags provide you with the capability to create built-in alternatives to any multimedia, interactive, or real-time enhancement you want to use. Using this tag, you can provide a fallback position for every advanced element you put on the page, so every visitor to your site is made to feel welcomed and comfortable. After all, isn't that what we really want to do?

Summary

In this chapter, you've seen how to use scripting to make the images on your Web pages respond to mouse movements. You've also seen how similar JavaScript commands can be used to change multiple images at once, and modify other elements such as frames and background colors, or much, much more.

None of these tasks requires any particular programming skills, though they may inspire you to learn the JavaScript language to give your pages more complex interactive features. Finally, you saw how HTML 4.0 is going to change the way you can add multimedia and new functionality to Web pages. Maybe that light at the end of the tunnel isn't a train after all!

Q&A

Q Are there other *secret* attributes besides OnMouseOver and OnMouseOut that I can use just as easily? Can I put them anyplace other than in an <A> tag?

A Yes, and yes. Each HTML tag has an associated set of JavaScript attributes, which are called *events*. For example, OnClick can be used within the <A> tag and some forms have tags to specify a command to be followed when someone clicks on that link or form element. The JavaScript references mentioned earlier in this chapter include complete listings of the events that you can use in each tag.

Q **Doesn't Microsoft use a different scripting language for Internet Explorer?**

A Yes, Microsoft recommends using a scripting language based on Visual Basic called VBScript, but Microsoft Internet Explorer version 3.0 or higher also supports a version of JavaScript. Many commands work slightly differently in the Microsoft implementation of JavaScript than they do in Netscape Navigator, however, and Microsoft left many features out of its version (called JScript), which is the case even with the simple commands covered in this chapter. The latest version of Microsoft IE 4.0 has fixed many of the problems so you can be slightly more confident that they will work exactly the same in both browsers, but there are still a lot of Microsoft IE 3.0 browsers out there. Drat!

Q **I tried using the tricks from this chapter with images that were arranged in a table, but it didn't work. Why?**

A There's a bug in Netscape Navigator 3.0 that causes problems when you dynamically change images in a table. The trouble was corrected in Netscape Navigator 4.0, and was never an issue with Microsoft Internet Explorer. Yet because so many people still use Navigator 3.0, it's safer to avoid changing any image within a table using JavaScript.

Q **You said it was `OnMouseOver`, but in the sample HTML file you used `onmouseover` instead. Doesn't the capitalization matter?**

A Nope. `ONMOUSEOVER` would do the same thing, too.

Quiz

Questions

1. Say you've made a picture of a button and named it `button.gif`. You also made a simple GIF animation of the button flashing green and white, named `flashing.gif`. How would you write the HTML and JavaScript to make the button flash whenever someone moves the mouse pointer over it, and link to a page named `gohere.htm` when someone clicks on the button? (Assume that it's the first image on the page.)

2. How would you modify what you wrote for question 1 so that the button starts flashing when someone moves the mouse over it, and keeps flashing even if they move the mouse away?

3. If you have ten images on a Web page, but the first and last images are both navigation icons linking to `homepage.htm`, how would you make them both change from `homedark.gif` to `homelite.gif` when the mouse cursor is over either one of them?

Answers

1. ```
   <A HREF="gohere.htm"

   onmouseover="document.images[0].src='flashing.gif';
   onmouseout="document.images[0].src='button.gif'">
   <IMG SRC="button.gif" BORDER=0></A>
   ```

2. ```
   <A HREF="gohere.htm"

   onmouseover="document.images[0].src='flashing.gif'">
   <IMG SRC="button.gif" BORDER=0></A>
   ```

3. Use the following HTML and JavaScript for *both* icons:

   ```
   <A HREF="homepage.htm"
   onmouseover="document.images[0]='homelite.gif';
                document.images[9]='homelite.gif'"
   onmouseout="document.images[0]='homedark.gif';
   onmouseout="document.images[9]='homedark.gif'">
   <IMG SRC="homedark.gif"></A>
   ```

Activities

☐ If you've enjoyed the information in this hour, and you're looking for more information, check out *Teach Yourself JavaScript in 24 Hours* or *Teach Yourself JavaScript in a Week* and take the next quantum leap in Web publishing!

23

Hour 24

Preparing for the Future of HTML

Any prognosticator who says that the Web, or any technology, is going to be the one and only force influencing the future is either fooling himself or trying to fool you. No matter what else may happen you can be sure that, as in the past, the future is going to look a whole lot different depending on where you're coming from, and many futures will look a lot like today.

In this hour, you'll learn about

- ☐ Where we are
- ☐ What's possible
- ☐ What's hot!
- ☐ Many roads, one journey
- ☐ Offices of the future
- ☐ From cubicles to conference rooms
- ☐ HTML: The universal GUI

☐ The digital media revolution
☐ Coming together
☐ Visions and dreams
☐ Be prepared!

Where We Are Now

Because of the way HTML was designed, new features largely haven't come into place at the expense of the old, so HTML code written to the original HTML standard still works just fine today. That's at least one less thing to worry about; everything you've learned in this book will work flawlessly with HTML-compatible software for many years, even generations to come. There are tens of millions of pages of information written in standard HTML, and even as that standard evolves, tomorrow's Web browsers and business software will retain the capability to view today's Web pages.

On the other hand, there are whole societies that have little or no access to the mass of information out there on the so-called World Wide Web because they have no facility in Western European languages, especially English, and perhaps even no knowledge of Roman alphabets, or alphabets of any kind, as well as telephone lines that end at the city limits of major urban centers.

Sub-Saharan Africa has little or no Internet connectivity outside of a few large cities. Asia has other problems, including at least a dozen major language groups that use ideographic or non-Roman alphabets. These alphabets have either had no computer representation or were so poorly standardized that written communication of any kind was difficult unless set down by hand. In China, for example, there are three competing machine-readable character sets vying for acceptance, as well as sub-classes of these.

Even in our own Western societies, there are groups who have been relegated to the information "have-nots," including persons with severe visual impairments, persons having limited dexterity or range of motion, and others for whom video monitors and keyboards are inappropriate means of interaction with a computer.

While you may be tooling along on a fast-paced and exciting information highway, it's important to remember that many people have been left by the side of the road.

What's Possible

It doesn't have to be that way. One of the primary thrusts of the HTML 4.0 study groups and committees has been to find ways to get more people on board the bus. Many of the new tags discussed have been created with the idea of making it easier for everyone to use the same Web and not be faced with pages full of cryptic symbols and nonsense codes when stumbling into a site in Japan, or impossible barriers when surfing into a page with frames or even tables using an audio or Braille browser. The current Web is a little like a house being built by a bunch of crazy carpenters, and sometimes when you walk into a room you fall through the floor.

HTML 4.0 puts a floor of basic capabilities into every conforming browser, so you will be able to surf into an Egyptian web site and either be drawn automatically to an English version of the page or have an Arabic font automatically downloaded to your browser, which will render the text properly from right to left, or even speak the words using an appropriate text-to-speech algorithm for that particular language.

With more processing power available on the desktop, it might even be possible to automatically translate a portion or all of the page, so you could at least understand what the page was about.

What's Hot!

Some of the most exciting capabilities of HTML, however, are still rapidly developing, driven by the twin desires of the manufacturers to distinguish themselves from the competition and of the world community to evolve HTML into a standard that supports everyone, not just those with the most money to spend. This hour stays away from tags and attributes and instead helps you to understand what these new HTML capabilities will enable you to do.

As a Web designer, you can use the new features of HTML 4.0 to help your pages stand out from the huge number of pages already on the Web, while maintaining compatibility with the millions of older browsers still in daily use by many people. Just because screaming video and booming multimedia sound makes your site the coolest place to be on Saturday night on either coast doesn't mean that you should ignore those who really want to be shown the sights without the eardrum-popping megawatt speakers thundering in the foreground.

The coolest feature of the new <OBJECT> tag is that it makes controlled alternatives possible, so that the dreaded "This feature requires a plug-in" message need no longer be a downer and a drag when you're hip-hopping through the sites. Don't have it? No problem! Try this instead. In time, this tag will come to be seen as basic to Web courtesy as it is to have non-alcoholic beverages available for designated drivers and others at even the wildest party.

To Do

When this hour was written, "now" meant mid-1997. Because you are living in "the future," you can check to make sure my crystal ball wasn't too cloudy.

1. Your best source for the latest HTML standards (and proposed future standards) is the World Wide Web Consortium site:

```
http://www.w3.org
```

2. To see how the standards are actually implemented in the latest Web browsers, and to see what nonstandard HTML extensions may be available, visit the Microsoft and Netscape Web sites:

   `http://www.microsoft.com`

   `http://home.netscape.com`

   You can also get copies of the latest Web browser updates from these two Web sites, as well as the Web Developers Virtual Library, at

   `http://www.wdvl.com/`

   and

   `http://www.browsers.com/`

Many Roads, One Journey

The intimate familiarity with HTML you've gained from this book will be one of the most important (and profitable) skills that anyone can have in the next few years. Yet most of the HTML pages you create in your lifetime will probably not be "Web pages," but rather ordinary business and personal documents created with your own word processor or mailing client.

To understand why, and to see the big picture of where HTML is headed, consider the following features of the latest HTML standard:

- ☐ Through style sheets and Web programming techniques such as JavaScript, you now have precise control over the appearance and functionality of virtually any textual and graphical information.

- ☐ All major programming languages, interactive media, and database formats can also be seamlessly integrated with HTML.

- ☐ HTML's extended character sets and fonts can now be used to communicate in the native script of any human language in the world.

- ☐ New tags and attributes, as well as advances in rendering technology, make it possible for documents to be accessible to everyone in the many different ways that people gather and comprehend information, including visual, audio, tactile, and immersive means.

- ☐ New data security standards are finally making it practical to carry out financial and other sensitive transactions with HTML.

- ☐ The proposed Platform for Internet Content Selection (PICS) standard provides a highly flexible way for the content of any HTML page to be rated according to any criteria that a rating authority or individual user might select. (Restricting access to adult-oriented or confidential information is one of many applications.)

24

☐ Future versions of the Microsoft Windows operating system will use HTML as a fundamental part of the user-interface, and other operating systems either have or are developing this capability today. Nearly all current versions of office productivity software also support HTML.

☐ Java, and other Web- and HTML-aware programming languages, will be embedded in smaller and smaller devices, until it will seem logical to plug your coffee-maker into your home network so that your house processor can turn it on in the morning, and necessary to plug your VCR and wall clock into the same network so your handy computer can set the time for you, neatly solving the problem of blinking 12:00 and daylight savings time at once.

In other words, the Web itself, in one form or another, will be ubiquitous in many people's homes, offices, and workplaces. Displays of any kind, from the clock on the wall to the speedometer and gauges in your car, will probably be driven by dedicated HTML engines. Mechanics will study automobile manuals on their palmtop diagnostic devices using HTML-driven screens. The Web TVs you're hearing so much about are in fact only the first of many such devices. Web toasters, Web refrigerators, Web elevators, Web golf carts, Web everything; the current Web TVs will seem primitive in a few years, as the video content itself is delivered directly to your home on the Web instead of being broadcast willy-nilly into the air.

24

All this adds up to a very near future where HTML will be a part of almost every daily activity, and used by almost everyone, whether they're fully aware of this or not. Of course, traditional computers and what is now thought of as the Web will without a doubt play a central role in the display and exchange of information across the computer networks on Earth, but not the only role. To understand how that can be so, take another step back to see an even bigger picture: the changing role of the computer itself in our society.

Offices of the Future

The computer was once considered a device for accounting and number crunching. Then it evolved into a device for dealing with a wide range of information, from words and numbers to graphics and sounds. Today and tomorrow, the computer is above all a communications device; its primary use is the transmission of information between people.

Two major trends are dragging HTML out of its niche as a Web page language:

☐ People from a wider variety of social, economic, and educational backgrounds are using information technology on a daily basis. Digital information is playing a greater role in all our lives.

☐ Physical location is no longer the primary factor in the market that most businesses serve. To find customers and do business in a global marketplace, even the smallest companies need to be able to gather and distribute many different types of information.

These large social trends may not seem at first glance to have much to do with HTML, except that they cause people and businesses to access the Web more often. However, they have led directly to two corresponding trends in technology:

☐ Entry-level information technology is getting—and must continue to get—both easier to use and less expensive.

☐ The distinctions between an individual computer, a local network, and the global Internet are blurring.

HTML is proving to be the dream technology that is enabling both of these trends to accelerate faster than anyone anticipated.

In many workplaces today, these two trends are already well established. You can use a computer to access business information every day without knowing much more than how to click on links and scroll down through long pages, and you can do so without being at all sure which information is coming from your computer, which is coming from the server down the hall, and which is coming from other servers, perhaps thousands of miles away.

The direction that these trends are taking us is also already clear: Users who become used to seeing highly readable and attractive pages of information (such as Figure 24.1) on their computer screens will lose the tiny bit of tolerance they have left for cryptic icons, unadorned text messages, and idiosyncratic menu mazes (Figure 24.2). They will soon expect their computer screens to *always* be as easy to read and interact with as the Web.

Figure 24.1.

HTML was designed to provide nicely formatted information that is easy to navigate.

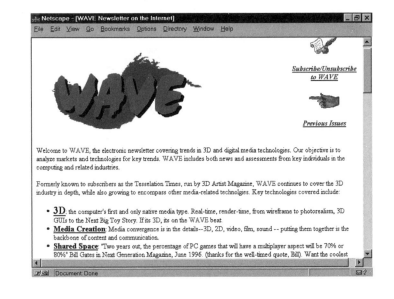

Figure 24.2.

Today's computer interfaces are simply too confusing and hard to learn for many of tomorrow's applications. (Note that the actual information content shown here is the same newsletter as in Figure 24.1.)

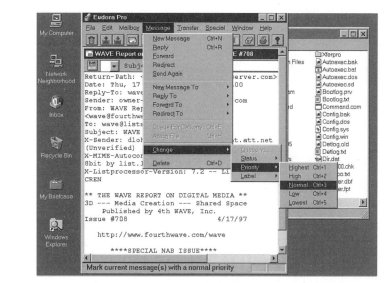

Those who make their millions supplying computer software are well aware of that expectation, and are expending an unprecedented amount of research and development effort toward fulfilling it. Along the way, the central metaphor for interacting with computers has changed from the window of the 1980s desktop to the page of the 1990s World Wide Web. It is in the process of changing even more radically to a metaphor focused on direct communication instead of old-fashioned paper shuffling.

From Cubicles to Conference Rooms

When personal computers first started appearing on desks, people bought them to help with the kind of tasks that take place on a desktop: reading, writing, calculating, and shuffling pages of information around. This reflected the business model of the mid-20th century: Isolated workers and companies spent most of their time processing information in their own little offices and a much smaller portion of their time directly communicating that information between individuals and companies.

As the century draws to a close, that business model is showing severe signs of strain. More and more time is spent in communication, and less and less in isolation. Workers who were trained in the older way of doing business complain that they now spend so much time attending meetings and conferences, or answering voice-mail and e-mail, that no time is left to get any work done. Those from the newer generation of employees and entrepreneurs, on the other hand, complain when co-workers or business associates create communication bottlenecks by being out-of-touch and hard to reach.

The old desktop metaphor is increasingly useless for doing the most crucial tasks in a communications-oriented business world. As the personal computer becomes more of an interpersonal communicator, the interface must be more of a conference table than a desktop. Like a conference room, your computer is now primarily a place to exchange textual and graphical documents, audio-visual presentations, and verbal interaction. Unlike most conference rooms, your computer allows you to directly exchange information with hundreds of millions of people all over the world.

HTML: The Universal GUI

As the role of the computer evolves, HTML is becoming more and more central to nearly everything we do with computers. HTML is *the* global standard for connecting all types of information together in a predictable and presentable way.

HTML gives you a painless and reliable way to combine and arrange text, graphics, sound, video, and interactive programs. And unlike older proprietary page layout standards, it was designed from the start for efficient communication between all kinds of computers worldwide. At this point, the likelihood of any other standard unseating it as king of the communications hill seems remote.

The prominence of HTML, however, does *not* mean that Web browsers will be a major category of software application in the coming years. In fact, the Web browser as a distinct program has already nearly disappeared. Microsoft Internet Explorer 4.0, for instance, does much more than retrieve pages from the World Wide Web. It lets you use HTML pages as the interface for organizing and navigating through the information on your own computer, including directory folders and the Windows desktop itself.

In conjunction with HTML-enabled software like Office 97, HTML becomes the common standard interface for word processing, spreadsheets, and databases, as well. Netscape Communicator 4.0 is also much more than a Web browser. It uses HTML to integrate all types of media into e-mail, discussion groups, schedule management, business documents, and collaborative project management (see Figure 24.3).

Meanwhile, HTML support is being included in every major software release so that every program on your computer will soon be able to import and export information in the form of HTML pages. In a nutshell, HTML is the glue that holds together all the diverse types of information on our computers and ensures that it can be presented in a standard way that will look the same to anyone in the world.

In a business world that now sees fast, effective communication as the most common and most important task of its workers, the information glue of HTML has the power to connect more than different types of media; it is the hidden adhesive that connects a business to its customers, and connects individual employees to form an efficient team. Knowing how to apply that glue—the skills you gain from this book—puts you in one of the most valuable roles in any modern organization.

24

Figure 24.3.

Netscape Communicator 4.0 offers a vision of the future by integrating HTML into e-mail, discussion groups, and other business communication.

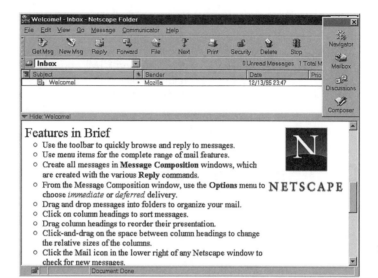

The Digital Media Revolution

The most important changes in the next few years may not be in HTML itself, but in the audience you can reach with your HTML pages. Many Web site developers hope that Internet-based content will have enough appeal to become the mass-market successor to television and radio. Less optimistic observers note that the global communications network has a long way to go before it can even deliver television-quality video to most users.

I won't pretend to have a magic mirror that lets me see how and when HTML becomes a mass-market phenomenon. But one thing is certain: All communication industries, from television to telephony, are moving rapidly toward exclusively digital technology. As they do so, the lines between communication networks are blurring. New Internet protocols promise to optimize multimedia transmissions at the same time that new protocols allow wireless broadcasters to support two-way interactive transmissions. The same small satellite dish can give you both high-speed Internet access and high-definition TV.

Add to this trend the fact that HTML is the only widely supported worldwide standard for combining text content with virtually any other form of digital media. Whatever surprising turns the future of digital communication takes, it's difficult to imagine that HTML won't be sitting in the driver's seat.

Over a million people can already access the Internet without a real computer through TV set-top boxes from WebTV Inc., cable TV companies, and digital satellite services. These devices are only the first wave of much more ubiquitous appliances that provide HTML content to people that wouldn't otherwise use computers.

JUST A MINUTE

The prospect of mass-market HTML access is obviously a great opportunity for HTML page authors. However, it can also present a number of challenges when designing HTML pages, because many people may see your pages on low-resolution TV screens or small hand-held devices. See the "Be Prepared!" section for some pointers on making sure your HTML pages can be enjoyed and understood by the widest possible audience.

Coming Together

So far in this hour, I've noted how HTML is in the right place at the right time to enable several key changes in business and interpersonal communication. As the people and companies of the world become more interconnected and interdependent, HTML's capability to make all information technology easier to use and less constrained by geography seems almost magical.

Even more magically, HTML has enabled an explosion of new media formats and incompatible file types, while at the same time providing the first truly universal format for exchanging all types of information.

But there is no secret mystical force behind this apparent paradox. The power of HTML comes from a very intentional (and seemingly mundane) aspect of its design. Quite simply, HTML standardizes the format of the most common types of information, while freely allowing unlimited special cases for proprietary formats and new technology. This means that you can both ensure complete compatibility between the widest variety of software and easily develop unique information formats to meet your individual needs.

Early multimedia Web sites were perhaps the first examples of how to meet these two (apparently conflicting) goals simultaneously. Text and graphics were visible to all visitors, while Shockwave movies, Java applets, or other formats were used to provide additional audio-visual or interactive content for those who had the necessary plug-ins or helper applications. Though multimedia formats have come a long way toward standardization, you can still freely include proprietary file formats in ordinary HTML pages and use the helper app, Netscape plug-in, ActiveX object, or Java program of your choice to handle them.

The capability to extend HTML pages with custom data types is far more than a way to embed a nifty movie or virtual reality scene into your Web page. To show how much more, the next section of this hour highlights some of the most exciting up-and-coming uses of HTML.

Visions and Dreams

The near-universal compatibility of HTML provides a big incentive to format any important document as a Web page—even if you have no immediate plans for putting it on the World Wide Web. You can create a single page that can be printed on paper, sent as an e-mail message, displayed during a board meeting presentation, and posted for reference on the company intranet. The traditional route of editing and reformatting the page separately for each of these applications—each with a different software program—when the information needs to be updated will soon be seen as a nonsensical waste of time and energy. Now that most business software supports the HTML standard, many organizations are trying to get employees to consistently use it for all important documents.

Yet the great migration to HTML goes beyond what you might have thought of as documents in the old days. Combined with Java, ActiveX, and other new technologies, HTML-based presentations can in many cases replace what was once done with proprietary data formats, specialized software, or more traditional programming languages. Here are a few of the other areas where HTML is finding application beyond the Web:

24

- [ ] Kiosks with HTML-based interactive content are popping up everywhere. They look like ATM machines on steroids, and they're helping sell records and theme park tickets, expand department store displays, and even automate the paying of parking tickets. The number of kiosks using intranet and/or HTML technology is projected to soar from under 90,000 today to over 500,000 by the end of 1998.

- [ ] Information-rich CD-ROM titles are migrating to HTML fast. Encyclopedia Britannica is already entirely HTML-based, which enables it to offer its content on CD-ROM, the Web, or a combination of both for maximum speed and up-to-the-minute currency. Because CD-ROM drives display multimedia so much faster than most Internet connections, dynamic HTML presentations become possible that just couldn't be done on today's World Wide Web. The new DVD-ROM drives will be even faster and will hold much more information, making them ideally suited to large multimedia sites.

- [ ] Corporate newsletters are now often created in HTML for the company intranet, and then printed on paper for delivery to employees or customers who wouldn't see them on the Web. The traditional difference between online and paper presentations was that graphics needed to be high-resolution black-and-white for printing and low-resolution color for computer screens. Today's inexpensive color printers, however, do a great job making low-res color images look great in an HTML-based newsletter.

☐ Teachers are finding that tests and educational worksheets are easier to administer as HTML pages, and can include many types of interactive content that wouldn't be possible on paper. Even for students that lack access to the Internet, simple HTML documents can be passed out on floppy disks.

☐ Vertical market users often buy a computer specifically to run a certain custom-designed application or set of applications. The VARs and systems integrators that provide these systems are delivering machines configured to start up displaying HTML pages. This helps walk users through the use of the machine, or replace old-fashioned "idiot menus" with a more attractive and sophisticated interface without sacrificing ease of use.

☐ There are already "haptic" (sensory) interfaces and devices which make it possible to touch objects that have no physical reality beyond the mind of the designer; when combined with immersive technologies such as VRML and the three-dimensional goggles now appearing in video games, it doesn't seem long until we'll be able to include realistic arm-wrestling and tiddlywinks, or other physical activities on our Web sites. How about touring an online version of the Musée Auguste Rodin sculpture garden where you could walk around and touch *Le Penseur*, or feel the anguish of *les Bourgeois de Calais*?

☐ Or how about a virtual palm reading, where the seer could send little tingles up your spine with the feathery touch of her finger on your palm as she traces your life line? When you start to think of what possibilities become possible when the power of the Web and high-bandwidth connections are combined, the mind truly boggles.

☐ Oh my gosh! Did I turn off the oven? Better surf on home using my satellite-linked palmtop and past my virtual front door (lucky I have my key!) so I can look. Of course, I could have switched the oven off if I had left it on, but, thank heavens, I remembered in spite of almost being late for my daughter's wedding.

Far from being the province of technophiles and guys wearing pocket protectors filled with multi-colored pens, the new Web is going to be a place where people do ordinary things for their own purposes in what are now extraordinary ways.

I could list many more creative and beneficial uses of HTML beyond run-of-the-mill Web pages, but the point should be clear: If you need to present any type of information, seriously consider HTML as an alternative to the specialized software or programming tools that you would have used a couple of years ago for the job.

Be Prepared!

If you've made your way through most of the hours of this book, you already have one of the most important ingredients for future success in the new digital world: a solid working knowledge of HTML.

Chances are that your primary reason for learning HTML at this time was to create some Web pages, but I hope this hour has convinced you that you'll be using HTML for far more than that in the future. Here are some of the factors you should consider when planning and building your Web site today, so that it will also serve you well tomorrow:

☐ The multimedia and interactive portions of your site are likely to need more revisions to keep up with technology than the text and graphics portions. When possible, keep the more cutting-edge parts of your site separate, and take especially good care to document them well with the <COMMENT> tag.

☐ Though new technologies such as Java and Shockwave may be the wave of the future, avoid them today except when developing for disk-based media or a fast local intranet. Even when everyone is using the new 33Kbps and 56Kbps modems, many people still will move on to a different site before they'll wait for an applet or interactive movie to download, initialize, and start working.

☐ Because style sheets give you complete control over the choice and measurements of type on your Web pages, it would be a good idea to study basic typography now if you aren't familiar with it. Understanding and working with concepts such as *leading, kerning, em-spaces,* and *drop caps* has long been essential for producing truly professional-quality paper pages. It will soon be essential for producing outstanding Web pages, too.

☐ One of the most popular and important features that will be added to many Web sites in the near future is interactive discussions and work groups. If you only have time to evaluate one new technology, that might be the one to pick. The new Netscape Communicator 4.0 package has especially strong support for group collaboration and communication.

☐ When you design your pages, don't assume that everyone who sees them will be using a computer. Televisions, video-telephones, game consoles, and many other devices may have access to them as well. Some of these devices have very low resolution screens (with as few as 320×200 pixels). Though it's difficult to design a Web page to look good at that resolution, you'll reach the widest possible audience if you do.

24

☐ As older Web browsers fall out of general use, you will be able to layer images and text on top of each other more reliably. That means that many things that you need large images for today you will be able to do much more efficiently with several small image elements tomorrow. Always keep copies of each individual image element that goes into a larger graphic, without any text. This will let you easily optimize the graphics later without recreating everything from scratch.

☐ Whenever you run into something that you'd like to do on a Web page, but can't with HTML as it stands today, include a comment in the page so you can add that feature when it becomes possible in the future.

COFFEE BREAK

The completed 24-Hour HTML Café site is located at

`http://www.mcp.com/sites/1-57521/1-57521-366-4`

In addition to providing an easy way to review all the sample pages and HTML techniques covered in this book, it offers many links to other great HTML resources and a few tricks and tips that this book didn't have room for.

As a way of refreshing your knowledge of all that you've learned in this book, you might walk through the development of the 24-Hour HTML Café site again. The pages named `cafe1.htm` through `cafe22.htm` show that development process, step by step.

Summary

This hour has provided a bird's-eye view of the future of HTML. It discussed the new roles that HTML will play in global communications. Finally, it offered some advice for planning and constructing Web pages today that will continue to serve you well into the future.

Q&A

Q So what is the difference between *digital communication* and other communication, anyway? Does *digital* mean it uses HTML?

A When information is transferred as distinct bits of information, which are essentially numbers, it's called digital. It's much easier to store, retrieve, and process information without losing or changing it when it is transferred digitally. Any information from a computer (including HTML) is by its nature digital, and in the not-too-distant future, telephone, television, radio, and even motion picture production will be digital.

24

Q **I've heard about this new kind of disk called DVD. Is it suitable for Web pages?**

A Yes. The new digital versatile disc (DVD) standard will provide a minimum of 4,700 megabytes (4.7 gigabytes) of storage, and can transfer data to a computer at least twice as fast as today's 6× CD-ROM drives. That will make DVD an excellent way to deliver multimedia Web pages.

Q **How soon can I start designing Internet Web pages that aren't limited by what I can transfer over a 28.8Kbps modem?**

A That depends on who you want to read your pages. There will be millions of 28.8Kbps modems (and the marginally faster 33.6Kbps and 56Kbps modems) in use for many years to come. But more and more people will have 128Kbps ISDN lines, 400Kbps satellite dishes, and 1Mbps (1,000Kbps) or faster cable, "copper-optic," and wireless connections, too. Before long, the number of 1.4Mbps users will just about match the number of 14.4Kbps users. That difference of 100× in speed will lead more and more Web page publishers to offer separate high-speed and low-speed sites.

24

Q **Man, I'm ashamed of you for not mentioning VRML in a hour about the future of the Internet! What gives?**

A Hey, didn't I mention that interactive, immersive three-dimensional worlds will be the future of the Internet? Virtual Reality Modeling Language (VRML) 2.0 is the current standard for making it happen, and it's compatible with your Web browser today. Unfortunately, VRML isn't quite ready for mass consumption and it's well beyond the scope of this book. But if you don't think it's going to change the world, think again. Go to `http://www.vrml.org` to read all about it.

Quiz

I want you to think about the use of HTML for *you* as an individual. How do you see yourself using HTML now—and in the future?

You've finished the book! Instead of a real quiz or defined activities, go ahead and treat yourself to something fun for a job well done!

PART

VII

Appendixes

Hour

A HTML Quick Reference

B HTML Learning Resources on the Internet

Appendix A

HTML Quick Reference

by Bob Correll

HTML 4.0 is an ambitious attempt to meet the needs of Web developers worldwide, both casual and professional. This appendix provides a quick reference to all the elements and attributes of the language.

JUST A MINUTE

> This appendix is based on the information provided in the *HTML 4.0 Specification W3C Working Draft 8-July-1997*, which can be found at `http://www.w3.org/TR/WD-html40/`.

In order to make the information readliy accessible, this appendix organizes HTML elements by their function in the following order:

- ☐ Structure
- ☐ Text phrases and paragraphs
- ☐ Text formatting elements
- ☐ Lists
- ☐ Links
- ☐ Tables
- ☐ Frames
- ☐ Embedded content
- ☐ Style
- ☐ Forms
- ☐ Scripts

Within each section the elements are listed alphabetically and the following information is presented:

- ☐ Usage—A general description of the element
- ☐ Start/End Tag—Indicates whether these tags are required, optional, or illegal
- ☐ Attributes—Lists the attributes of the element with a short description of their effects
- ☐ Empty—Indicates whether the element can be empty
- ☐ Notes—Relates any special considerations when using the element and indicates whether the element is new, deprecated, or obsolete

JUST A MINUTE

Several elements and attributes have been *deprecated*, which means they have been outdated by the current HTML version, and you should avoid using them. The same or similar functionality is provided using new features.

JUST A MINUTE

HTML 4.0 introduces several new attributes that apply to a significant number of elements. These are referred to as %coreattrs, %i18n, and %events and are explained in the last section of the appendix.

A

Following this, the common attributes (those with a % in front of them) and intrinsic events are summarized.

Structure

HTML relies upon several elements to provide structure to a document (as opposed to structuring the text within) as well as provide information that is used by the browser or search engines.

<BDO>...</BDO>

Usage	The bidirectional algorithm element is used to selectively turn off the default text direction.
Start/End Tag	Required/Required
Attributes	LANG="..."—The language of the document.
	DIR="..."—The text direction (ltr, rtl).
Empty	No
Notes	The DIR attribute is mandatory.

<BODY>...</BODY>

Usage	Contains the content of the document.
Start/End Tag	Optional/Optional
Attributes	%coreattrs, %i18n, %events
	BACKGROUND="..."—Deprecated. URL for the background image.
	BGCOLOR="..."—Deprecated. Sets background color.
	TEXT="..."—Deprecated. Text color.
	LINK="..."—Deprecated. Link color.
	VLINK="..."—Deprecated. Visited link color.
	ALINK="..."—Deprecated. Active link color.
	ONLOAD="..."—Intrinsic event triggered when the document loads.
	ONUNLOAD="..."—Intrinsic event triggered when document unloads.
Empty	No
Notes	There can be only one BODY and it must follow the HEAD. The BODY element can be replaced by a FRAMESET element. The presentational attributes are deprecated in favor of setting these values with style sheets.

Comments `<!-- ... -->`

Usage	Used to insert notes or scripts that are not displayed by the browser.
Start/End Tag	Required/Required
Attributes	None
Empty	Yes
Notes	Comments are not restricted to one line and can be any length. The end tag is not required to be on the same line as the start tag.

`<DIV>...</DIV>`

Usage	The division element is used to add structure to a block of text.
Start/End Tag	Required/Required
Attributes	`%coreattrs, %i18n, %events`
	`ALIGN="..."`—Deprecated. Controls alignment (`left`, `center`, `right`, `justify`).
Empty	No
Notes	Cannot be used within a `<P>` element. The `ALIGN` attribute is deprecated in favor of controlling alignment through style sheets.

`<!DOCTYPE...>`

Usage	Version information appears on the first line of an HTML document and is a Standard Generalized Markup Language (SGML) declaration rather than an element.

`<H1>...</H1>` through `<H6>...</H6>`

Usage	The six headings (`H1` is the uppermost, or most important) are used in the `BODY` to structure information in a hierarchical fashion.
Start/End Tag	Required/Required
Attributes	`%coreattrs, %i18n, %events`
	`ALIGN="..."`—Deprecated. Controls alignment (`left`, `center`, `right`, `justify`).
Empty	No
Notes	Visual browsers will display the size of the headings in relation to their importance, with `H1` being the largest and `H6` smallest. The `ALIGN` attribute is deprecated in favor of controlling alignment through style sheets.

A

\<HEAD>...\</HEAD>

Usage	This is the document header, and it contains other elements that provide information to users and search engines.
Start/End Tag	Optional/Optional
Attributes	%i18n
	profile="..."—URL specifying the location of \<META> data.
Empty	No
Notes	There can be only one \<HEAD> per document. It must follow the opening \<HTML> tag and precede the \<BODY>.

\<HR>

Usage	Horizontal rules are used to separate sections of a Web page.
Start/End Tag	Required/Illegal
Attributes	%coreattrs, %events
	ALIGN="..."—Deprecated. Controls alignment (left, center, right, justify).
	NOSHADE="..."—Displays the rule as a solid color.
	SIZE="..."—Deprecated. The size of the rule.
	WIDTH="..."—Deprecated. The width of the rule.
Empty	Yes

\<HTML>...\</HTML>

Usage	The HTML element contains the entire document.
Start/End Tag	Optional/Optional
Attributes	%i18n
	VERSION="..."—URL of the document type definition specifying the HTML version used to create the document.
Empty	No
Notes	The version information is duplicated in the \<!DOCTYPE...> declaration and therefore is not essential.

\<META>

Usage	Provides information about the document.
Start/End Tag	Required/Illegal

A

Attributes	%i18n
	HTTP-EQIV="..."—HTTP response header name.
	NAME="..."—Name of the <META> information.
	CONTENT="..."—Content of the <META> information.
	SCHEME="..."—Assigns a scheme to interpret the <META> data.
Empty	Yes

<SPAN>...</SPAN>

Usage	Organizes the document by defining a span of text.
Start/End Tag	Required/Required
Attributes	%coreattrs, %i18n, %events
Empty	No

<TITLE>...</TITLE>

Usage	This is the name you give your Web page. The <TITLE> element is located in the <HEAD> element and is displayed in the browser window title bar.
Start/End Tag	Required/Required
Attributes	%i18n
Empty	No
Notes	Only one title allowed per document.

Text Phrases and Paragraphs

Text phrases (or blocks) can be structured to suit a specific purpose, such as creating a paragraph. This should not be confused with modifying the formatting of the text.

<ACRONYM>...</ACRONYM>

Usage	Used to define acronyms.
Start/End Tag	Required/Required
Attributes	%coreattrs, %i18n, %events
Empty	No

<ADDRESS>...</ADDRESS>

Usage	Provides a special format for author or contact information.
Start/End Tag	Required/Required

A

Attributes	%coreattrs, %i18n, %events
Empty	No
Notes	The element is commonly used inside the <ADDRESS> element to break the lines of an address.

`<BLOCKQUOTE>...</BLOCKQUOTE>`

Usage	Used to display long quotations.
Start/End Tag	Required/Required
Attributes	%coreattrs, %i18n, %events
	CITE="..."—The URL of the quoted text.
Empty	No

`<BR>`

Usage	Forces a line break.
Start/End Tag	Required/Illegal
Attributes	%coreattrs, %i18n, %events
	CLEAR="..."—Sets the location where the next line begins after a floating object (none, left, right, all).
Empty	Yes

`<CITE>...</CITE>`

Usage	Cites a reference.
Start/End Tag	Required/Required
Attributes	%coreattrs, %i18n, %events
Empty	No

`<CODE>...</CODE>`

Usage	Identifies a code fragment for display.
Start/End Tag	Required/Required
Attributes	%coreattrs, %i18n, %events
Empty	No

`<DEL>...</DEL>`

Usage	Shows text as having been deleted from the document since the last change.
Start/End Tag	Required/Required

Attributes	%coreattrs, %i18n, %events
	CITE="..."—The URL of the source document.
	DATETIME="..."—Indicates the date and time of the change.
Empty	No
Notes	New element in HTML 4.0.

<DFN>...</DFN>

Usage	Defines an enclosed term.
Start/End Tag	Required/Required
Attributes	%coreattrs, %i18n, %events
Empty	No

<EM>...</EM>

Usage	Emphasized text.
Start/End Tag	Required/Required
Attributes	%coreattrs, %i18n, %events
Empty	No

<INS>...</INS>

Usage	Shows text as having been inserted in the document since the last change.
Start/End Tag	Required/Required
Attributes	%coreattrs, %i18n, %events
	CITE="..."—The URL of the source document.
	DATETIME="..."—Indicates the date and time of the change.
Empty	No
Notes	New element in HTML 4.0.

<KBD>...</KBD>

Usage	Indicates text a user would type.
Start/End Tag	Required/Required
Attributes	%coreattrs, %i18n, %events
Empty	No

A

`<P>...</P>`

Usage	Defines a paragraph.
Start/End Tag	Required/Optional
Attributes	%coreattrs, %i18n, %events
	ALIGN="..."—Deprecated. Controls alignment (left, center, right, justify).
Empty	No

`<PRE>...</PRE>`

Usage	Displays preformatted text.
Start/End Tag	Required/Required
Attributes	%coreattrs, %i18n, %events
	WIDTH="..."—The width of the formatted text.
Empty	No

`<Q>...</Q>`

Usage	Used to display short quotations that do not require paragraph breaks.
Start/End Tag	Required/Required
Attributes	%coreattrs, %i18n, %events
	CITE="..."—The URL of the quoted text.
Empty	No
Notes	New element in HTML 4.0.

`<SAMP>...</SAMP>`

Usage	Identifies sample output.
Start/End Tag	Required/Required
Attributes	%coreattrs, %i18n, %events
Empty	No

`<STRONG>...</STRONG>`

Usage	Stronger emphasis.
Start/End Tag	Required/Required
Attributes	%coreattrs, %i18n, %events
Empty	No

A

_{...}

Usage	Creates subscript.
Start/End Tag	Required/Required
Attributes	`%coreattrs, %i18n, %events`
Empty	No

^{...}

Usage	Creates superscript.
Start/End Tag	Required/Required
Attributes	`%coreattrs, %i18n, %events`
Empty	No

<VAR>...</VAR>

Usage	A variable.
Start/End Tag	Required/Required
Attributes	`%coreattrs, %i18n, %events`
Empty	No

Text Formatting Elements

Text characteristics such as the size, weight, and style can be modified using these elements, but the HTML 4.0 specification encourages you to use style instead.

<B>...</B>

Usage	Bold text.
Start/End Tag	Required/Required
Attributes	`%coreattrs, %i18n, %events`
Empty	No

<BASEFONT>

Usage	Sets the base font size.
Start/End Tag	Required/Illegal
Attributes	`SIZE="..."`—The font size (1–7 or relative, that is +3).
	`COLOR="..."`—The font color.
	`FACE="..."`—The font type.

A

Empty	Yes
Notes	Deprecated in favor of style sheets.

`<BIG>...</BIG>`

Usage	Large text.
Start/End Tag	Required/Required
Attributes	`%coreattrs, %i18n, %events`
Empty	No

`<FONT>...</FONT>`

Usage	Changes the font size and color.
Start/End Tag	Required/Required
Attributes	`SIZE="..."`—The font size (1–7 or relative, that is, +3).
	`COLOR="..."`—The font color.
	`FACE="..."`—The font type.
Empty	No
Notes	Deprecated in favor of style sheets.

`<I>...</I>`

Usage	Italicized text.
Start/End Tag	Required/Required
Attributes	`%coreattrs, %i18n, %events`
Empty	No

`<S>...</S>`

Usage	Strikethrough text.
Start/End Tag	Required/Required
Attributes	`%coreattrs, %i18n, %events`
Empty	No
Notes	Deprecated.

`<SMALL>...</SMALL>`

Usage	Small text.
Start/End Tag	Required/Required
Attributes	`%coreattrs, %i18n, %events`
Empty	No

A

`<STRIKE>...</STRIKE>`

Usage	Strikethrough text.
Start/End Tag	Required/Required
Attributes	%coreattrs, %i18n, %events
Empty	No
Notes	Deprecated.

`<TT>...</TT>`

Usage	Teletype (or monospaced) text.
Start/End Tag	Required/Required
Attributes	%coreattrs, %i18n, %events
Empty	No

`<U>...</U>`

Usage	Underlined text.
Start/End Tag	Required/Required
Attributes	%coreattrs, %i18n, %events
Empty	No
Notes	Deprecated.

Lists

You can organize text into a more structured outline by creating lists. Lists can be nested.

`<DD>...</DD>`

Usage	The definition description used in a `<DL>` (definition list) element.
Start/End Tag	Required/Optional
Attributes	%coreattrs, %i18n, %events
Empty	No
Notes	Can contain block-level content, such as the `<P>` element.

`<DIR>...</DIR>`

Usage	Creates a multi-column directory list.
Start/End Tag	Required/Required
Attributes	%coreattrs, %i18n, %events
	COMPACT—Deprecated. Compacts the displayed list.

A

Empty	No
Notes	Must contain at least one list item. This element is deprecated in favor of the `<UL>` (unordered list) element.

`<DL>...</DL>`

Usage	Creates a definition list.
Start/End Tag	Required/Required
Attributes	`%coreattrs, %i18n, %events`
	`COMPACT`—Deprecated. Compacts the displayed list.
Empty	No
Notes	Must contain at least one `<DT>` or `<DD>` element in any order.

`<DT>...</DT>`

Usage	The definition term (or label) used within a `<DL>` (definition list) element.
Start/End Tag	Required/Optional
Attributes	`%coreattrs, %i18n, %events`
Empty	No
Notes	Must contain text (which can be modified by text markup elements).

`<LI>...</LI>`

Usage	Defines a list item within a list.
Start/End Tag	Required/Optional
Attributes	`%coreattrs, %i18n, %events`
	`TYPE="..."`—Changes the numbering style (`1, a, A, i, I`), ordered lists, or bullet style (`disc, square, circle`) in unordered lists.
	`VALUE="..."`—Sets the numbering to the given integer beginning with the current list item.
Empty	No

`<MENU>...</MENU>`

Usage	Creates a single-column menu list.
Start/End Tag	Required/Required
Attributes	`%coreattrs, %i18n, %events`
	`COMPACT`—Deprecated. Compacts the displayed list.

A

Empty	No
Notes	Must contain at least one list item. This element is deprecated in favor of the `<UL>` (unordered list) element.

`<OL>...</OL>`

Usage	Creates an ordered list.
Start/End Tag	Required/Required
Attributes	`%coreattrs`, `%i18n`, `%events`
	`TYPE="..."`—Sets the numbering style (`1`, `a`, `A`, `i`, `I`).
	`COMPACT`—Deprecated. Compacts the displayed list.
	`START="..."`—Sets the starting number to the chosen integer.
Empty	No
Notes	Must contain at least one list item.

`<UL>...</UL>`

Usage	Creates an unordered list.
Start/End Tag	Required/Required
Attributes	`%coreattrs`, `%i18n`, `%events`
	`TYPE="..."`—Sets the bullet style (`disc`, `square`, `circle`).
	`COMPACT`—Deprecated. Compacts the displayed list.
Empty	No
Notes	Must contain at least one list item.

Links

Hyperlinking is fundamental to HTML. These elements enable you to link to other documents.

`<A>...</A>`

Usage	Used to define links and anchors.
Start/End Tag	Required/Required
Attributes	`%coreattrs`, `%i18n`, `%events`
	`CHARSET="..."`—Character encoding of the resource.
	`NAME="..."`—Defines an anchor.
	`HREF="..."`—The URL of the linked resource.

A

TARGET="..."—Determines where the resource will be displayed (user-defined name, _blank, _parent, _self, _top).

REL="..."—Forward link types.

REV="..."—Reverse link types.

ACCESSKEY="..."—Assigns a hotkey to this element.

SHAPE="..."—Enables you to define client-side imagemaps using defined shapes (default, rect, circle, poly).

COORDS="..."—Sets the size of the shape using pixel or percentage lengths.

TABINDEX="..."—Sets the tabbing order between elements with a defined TABINDEX.

Empty   No

`<BASE>`

Usage   All other URLs in the document are resolved against this location.

Start/End Tag Required/Illegal

Attributes   HREF="..."—The URL of the linked resource.

TARGET="..."—Determines where the resource will be displayed (user-defined name, _blank, _parent, _self, _top).

Empty   Yes

Notes   Located in the document `<HEAD>`.

`<LINK>`

Usage   Defines the relationship between a link and a resource.

Start/End Tag Required/Illegal

Attributes   %coreattrs, %i18n, %events

HREF="..."—The URL of the resource.

REL="..."—The forward link types.

REV="..."—The reverse link types.

TYPE="..."—The Internet content type.

MEDIA="..."—Defines the destination medium (screen, print, projection, braille, speech, all).

TARGET="..."—Determines where the resource will be displayed (user-defined name, _blank, _parent, _self, _top).

Empty   Yes

Notes   Located in the document `<HEAD>`.

Tables

Tables are meant to display data in a tabular format. Before the introduction of HTML 4.0, tables were widely used for page layout purposes, but with the advent of style sheets this is being discouraged by the W3C.

`<CAPTION>...</CAPTION>`

Usage	Displays a table caption.
Start/End Tag	Required/Required
Attributes	`%coreattrs`, `%i18n`, `%events`
	`ALIGN="..."`—Deprecated. Controls alignment (`left`, `center`, `right`, `justify`).
Empty	No
Notes	Optional

`<COL>`

Usage	Groups columns within column groups in order to share attribute values.
Start/End Tag	Required/Illegal
Attributes	`%coreattrs`, `%i18n`, `%events`
	`SPAN="..."`—The number of columns the group contains.
	`WIDTH="..."`—The column width as a percentage, pixel value, or minimum value.
	`ALIGN="..."`—Horizontally aligns the contents of cells (`left`, `center`, `right`, `justify`, `char`).
	`CHAAR="..."`—Sets a character on which the column aligns.
	`CHAROFF="..."`—Offset to the first alignment character on a line.
	`VALIGN="..."`—Vertically aligns the contents of a cell (`top`, `middle`, `bottom`, `baseline`).
Empty	Yes

`<COLGROUP>...</COLGROUP>`

Usage	Defines a column group.
Start/End Tag	Required/Optional
Attributes	`%coreattrs`, `%i18n`, `%events`
	`SPAN="..."`—The number of columns in a group.

A

WIDTH="..."—The width of the columns.

ALIGN="..."—Horizontally aligns the contents of cells (left, center, right, justify, char).

CHAR="..."—Sets a character on which the column aligns.

CHAROFF="..."—Offset to the first alignment character on a line.

VALIGN="..."—Vertically aligns the contents of a cell (top, middle, bottom, baseline).

Empty   No

<TABLE>...</TABLE>

Usage   Creates a table.

Start/End Tag   Required/Required

Attributes   %coreattrs, %i18n, %events

ALIGN="..."—Deprecated. Controls alignment (left, center, right, justify).

BGCOLOR="..."—Deprecated. Sets the background color.

WIDTH="..."—Table width.

COLS="..."—The number of columns.

BORDER="..."—The width in pixels of a border around the table.

FRAME="..."—Sets the visible sides of a table (void, above, below, hsides, lhs, rhs, vsides, box, border).

RULES="..."—Sets the visible rules within a table (none, groups, rows, cols, all).

CELLSPACING="..."—Spacing between cells.

CELLPADDING="..."—Spacing in cells.

Empty   No

<TBODY>...</TBODY>

Usage   Defines the table body.

Start/End Tag   Optional/Optional

Attributes   %coreattrs, %i18n, %events

ALIGN="..."—Horizontally aligns the contents of cells (left, center, right, justify, char).

CHAR="..."—Sets a character on which the column aligns.

CHAROFF="..."—Offset to the first alignment character on a line.

VALIGN="..."—Vertically aligns the contents of cells (top, middle, bottom, baseline).

Empty   No

`<TD>...</TD>`

Usage   Defines a cell's contents.

Start/End Tag   Required/Optional

Attributes   %coreattrs, %i18n, %events

AXIS="..."—Abbreviated name.

AXES="..."—axis names listing row and column headers pertaining to the cell.

NOWRAP="..."—Deprecated. Turns off text wrapping in a cell.

BGCOLOR="..."—Deprecated. Sets the background color.

ROWSPAN="..."—The number of rows spanned by a cell.

COLSPAN="..."—The number of columns spanned by a cell.

ALIGN="..."—Horizontally aligns the contents of cells (left, center, right, justify, char).

CHAR="..."—Sets a character on which the column aligns.

CHAROFF="..."—Offset to the first alignment character on a line.

VALIGN="..."—Vertically aligns the contents of cells (top, middle, bottom, baseline).

Empty   No

`<TFOOT>...</TFOOT>`

Usage   Defines the table footer.

Start/End Tag   Required/Optional

Attributes   %coreattrs, %i18n, %events

ALIGN="..."—Horizontally aligns the contents of cells (left, center, right, justify, char).

CHAR="..."—Sets a character on which the column aligns.

CHAROFF="..."—Offset to the first alignment character on a line.

VALIGN="..."—Vertically aligns the contents of cells (top, middle, bottom, baseline).

Empty   No

\<TH\>...\</TH\>

Usage	Defines the cell contents of the table header.
Start/End Tag	Required/Optional
Attributes	%coreattrs, %i18n, %events

AXIS="..."—Abbreviated name.

AXES="..."—axis names listing row and column headers pertaining to the cell.

NOWRAP="..."—Deprecated. Turns off text wrapping in a cell.

BGCOLOR="..."—Deprecated. Sets the background color.

ROWSPAN="..."—The number of rows spanned by a cell.

COLSPAN="..."—The number of columns spanned by a cell.

ALIGN="..."—Horizontally aligns the contents of cells (left, center, right, justify, char).

CHAR="..."—Sets a character on which the column aligns.

CHAROFF="..."—Offset to the first alignment character on a line.

VALIGN="..."—Vertically aligns the contents of cells (top, middle, bottom, baseline).

Empty	No

\<THEAD\>...\</THEAD\>

Usage	Defines the table header.
Start/End Tag	Required/Optional
Attributes	%coreattrs, %i18n, %events

ALIGN="..."—Horizontally aligns the contents of cells (left, center, right, justify, char).

CHAR="..."—Sets a character on which the column aligns.

CHAROFF="..."—Offset to the first alignment character on a line.

VALIGN="..."—Vertically aligns the contents of cells (top, middle, bottom, baseline).

Empty	No

\<TR\>...\</TR\>

Usage	Defines a row of table cells.
Start/End Tag	Required/Optional

Attributes	%coreattrs, %i18n, %events

ALIGN="..."—Horizontally aligns the contents of cells (left, center, right, justify, char).

CHAR="..."—Sets a character on which the column aligns.

CHAROFF="..."—Offset to the first alignment character on a line.

VALIGN="..."—Vertically aligns the contents of cells (top, middle, bottom, baseline).

BGCOLOR="..."—Deprecated. Sets the background color.

Empty   No

Frames

Frames create new "panels" in the Web browser window that are used to display content from different source documents.

<FRAME>

Usage	Defines a frame.
Start/End Tag	Required/Illegal
Attributes	NAME="..."—The name of a frame.

SRC="..."—The source to be displayed in a frame.

FRAMEBORDER="..."—Toggles the border between frames (0, 1).

MARGINWIDTH="..."—Sets the space between frame the border and content.

MARGINHEIGHT="..."—Sets the space between the frame border and content.

NORESIZE—Disables sizing.

SCROLLING="..."—Determines scrollbar presence (auto, yes, no).

Empty   Yes

<FRAMESET>...</FRAMESET>

Usage	Defines the layout of frames within a window.
Start/End Tag	Required/Required
Attributes	ROWS="..."—The number of rows.

COLS="..."—The number of columns.

ONLOAD="..."—The intrinsic event triggered when the document loads.

ONUNLOAD="..."—The intrinsic event triggered when the document unloads.

Empty	No
Notes	FRAMESETs can be nested.

`<IFRAME>...</IFRAME>`

Usage	Creates an inline frame.
Start/End Tag	Required/Required
Attributes	NAME="..."—The name of the frame.
	SRC="..."—The source to be displayed in a frame.
	FRAMEBORDER="..."—Toggles the border between frames (0, 1).
	MARGINWIDTH="..."—Sets the space between the frame border and content.
	MARGINHEIGHT="..."—Sets the space between the frame border and content.
	SCROLLING="..."—Determines scrollbar presence (auto, yes, no).
	ALIGN="..."—Deprecated. Controls alignment (left, center, right, justify).
	HEIGHT="..."—Height.
	WIDTH="..."—Width.
Empty	No

`<NOFRAMES>...</NOFRAMES>`

Usage	Alternative content when frames are not supported.
Start/End Tag	Required/Required
Attributes	None
Empty	No

Embedded Content

Also called inclusions, embedded content applies to Java applets, imagemaps, and other multimedia or programmatical content that is placed in a Web page to provide additional functionality.

<APPLET>...</APPLET>

Usage	Includes a Java applet.
Start/End Tag	Required/Required
Attributes	CODEBASE="..."—The URL base for the applet.
	ARCHIVE="..."—Identifies the resources to be preloaded.
	CODE="..."—The applet class file.
	OBJECT="..."—The serialized applet file.
	ALT="..."—Displays text while loading.
	NAME="..."—The name of the applet.
	WIDTH="..."—The height of the displayed applet.
	HEIGHT="..."—The width of the displayed applet.
	ALIGN="..."—Deprecated. Controls alignment (left, center, right, justify).
	HSPACE="..."—The horizontal space separating the image from other content.
	VSPACE="..."—The vertical space separating the image from other content.
Empty	No
Notes	Applet is deprecated in favor of the OBJECT element.

<AREA>

Usage	The AREA element is used to define links and anchors.
Start/End Tag	Required/Illegal
Attributes	SHAPE="..."—Enables you to define client-side imagemaps using defined shapes (default, rect, circle, poly).
	COORDS="..."—Sets the size of the shape using pixel or percentage lengths.
	HREF="..."—The URL of the linked resource.
	TARGET="..."—Determines where the resource will be displayed (user-defined name, _blank, _parent, _self, _top).
	NOHREF="..."—Indicates that the region has no action.
	ALT="..."—Displays alternative text.
	TABINDEX="..."—Sets the tabbing order between elements with a defined tabindex.
Empty	Yes

A

`<IMG>`

Usage	Includes an image in the document.
Start/End Tag	Required/Illegal
Attributes	`%coreattrs, %i18n, %events`

`SRC="..."`—The URL of the image.

`ALT="..."`—Alternative text to display.

`ALIGN="..."`—Deprecated. Controls alignment (`left`, `center`, `right`, `justify`).

`HEIGHT="..."`—The height of the image.

`WIDTH="..."`—The width of the image.

`BORDER="..."`—Border width.

`HSPACE="..."`—The horizontal space separating the image from other content.

`VSPACE="..."`—The vertical space separating the image from other content.

`USEMAP="..."`—The URL to a client-side imagemap.

`ISMAP`—Identifies a server-side imagemap.

Empty	Yes

`<MAP>...</MAP>`

Usage	When used with the `<AREA>` element, creates a client-side imagemap.
Start/End Tag	Required/Required
Attributes	`%coreattrs`

`NAME="..."`—The name of the imagemap to be created.

Empty	No

`<OBJECT>...</OBJECT>`

Usage	Includes an object.
Start/End Tag	Required/Required
Attributes	`%coreattrs, %i18n, %events`

`DECLARE`—A flag that declares but doesn't create an object.

`CLASSID="..."`—The URL of the object's location.

`CODEBASE="..."`—The URL for resolving URLs specified by other attributes.

DATA="..."—The URL to the object's data.

TYPE="..."—The Internet content type for data.

CODETYPE="..."—The Internet content type for the code.

STANDBY="..."—Show message while loading.

ALIGN="..."—Deprecated. Controls alignment (left, center, right, justify).

HEIGHT="..."—The height of the object.

WIDTH="..."—The width of the object.

BORDER="..."—Displays the border around an object.

HSPACE="..."—The space between the sides of the object and other page content.

VSPACE="..."—The space between the top and bottom of the object and other page content.

USEMAP="..."—The URL to an imagemap.

SHAPES=—Enables you to define areas to search for hyperlinks if the object is an image.

NAME="..."—The URL to submit as part of a form.

TABINDEX="..."—Sets the tabbing order between elements with a defined tabindex.

Empty	No

<PARAM>

Usage	Initializes an object.
Start/End Tag	Required/Illegal
Attributes	NAME="..."—Defines the parameter name.
	VALUE="..."—The value of the object parameter.
	VALUETYPE="..."—Defines the value type (data, ref, object).
	TYPE="..."—The Internet media type.
Empty	Yes

Style

Style sheets (both inline and external) are incorporated into an HTML document through the use of the <STYLE> element.

<STYLE>...</STYLE>

Usage	Creates an internal style sheet.
Start/End Tag	Required/Required
Attributes	%i18n
	TYPE="..."—The Internet content type.
	MEDIA="..."—Defines the destination medium (screen, print, projection, braille, speech, all).
	TITLE="..."—The title of the style.
Empty	No
Notes	Located in the <HEAD> element.

Forms

Forms create an interface for the user to select options and submit data back to the Web server.

<BUTTON>...</BUTTON>

Usage	Creates a button.
Start/End Tag	Required/Required
Attributes	%coreattrs, %i18n, %events
	NAME="..."—The button name.
	VALUE="..."—The value of the button.
	TYPE="..."—The button type (button, submit, reset).
	DISABLED="..."—Sets the button state to disabled.
	TABINDEX="..."—Sets the tabbing order between elements with a defined tabindex.
	ONFOCUS="..."—The event that occurs when the element receives focus.
	ONBLUR="..."—The event that occurs when the element loses focus.
Empty	No

<FIELDSET>...</FIELDSET>

Usage	Groups related controls.
Start/End Tag	Required/Required
Attributes	%coreattrs, %i18n, %events
Empty	No

`<FORM>...</FORM>`

Usage	Creates a form that holds controls for user input.
Start/End Tag	Required/Required
Attributes	%coreattrs, %i18n, %events

ACTION="..."—The URL for the server action.

METHOD="..."—The HTTP method (get, post). get is deprecated.

ENCTYPE="..."—Specifies the MIME (Internet media type).

ONSUBMIT="..."—The intrinsic event that occurs when the form is submitted.

ONRESET="..."—The intrinsic event that occurs when the form is reset.

TARGET="..."—Determines where the resource will be displayed (user-defined name, _blank, _parent, _self, _top).

ACCEPT-CHARSET="..."—The list of character encodings.

Empty	No

`<INPUT>`

Usage	Defines controls used in forms.
Start/End Tag	Required/Illegal
Attributes	%coreattrs, %i18n, %events

TYPE="..."—The type of input control (text, password, checkbox, radio, submit, reset, file, hidden, image, button).

NAME="..."—The name of the control (required except for submit and reset).

VALUE="..."—The initial value of the control (required for radio and checkboxes).

CHECKED="..."—Sets the radio buttons to a checked state.

DISABLED="..."—Disables the control.

READONLY="..."—For text password types.

SIZE="..."—The width of the control in pixels except for text and password controls, which are specified in number of characters.

MAXLENGTH="..."—The maximum number of characters that can be entered.

SRC="..."—The URL to an image control type.

ALT="..."—An alternative text description.

A

USEMAP="..."—The URL to a client-side imagemap.

ALIGN="..."—Deprecated. Controls alignment (left, center, right, justify).

TABINDEX="..."—Sets the tabbing order between elements with a defined tabindex.

ONFOCUS="..."—The event that occurs when the element receives focus.

ONBLUR="..."—The event that occurs when the element loses focus.

ONSELECT="..."—Intrinsic event that occurs when the control is selected.

ONCHANGE="..."—Intrinsic event that occurs when the control is changed.

ACCEPT="..."—File types allowed for upload.

Empty	Yes

<ISINDEX>

Usage	Prompts the user for input.
Start/End Tag	Required/Illegal
Attributes	%coreattrs, %i18n

PROMPT="..."—Provides a prompt string for the input field.

Empty	Yes
Notes	Deprecated

<LABEL>...</LABEL>

Usage	Labels a control.
Start/End Tag	Required/Required
Attributes	%coreattrs, %i18n, %events

FOR="..."—Associates a label with an identified control.

DISABLED="..."—Disables a control.

ACCESSKEY="..."—Assigns a hotkey to this element.

ONFOCUS="..."—The event that occurs when the element receives focus.

ONBLUR="..."—The event that occurs when the element loses focus.

Empty	No

<LEGEND>...</LEGEND>

Usage	Assigns a caption to a FIELDSET.
Start/End Tag	Required/Required
Attributes	%coreattrs, %i18n, %events
	ALIGN="..."—Deprecated. Controls alignment (left, center, right, justify).
	ACCESSKEY="..."—Assigns a hotkey to this element.
Empty	No

<OPTION>...</OPTION>

Usage	Specifies choices in a SELECT element.
Start/End Tag	Required/Optional
Attributes	%coreattrs, %i18n, %events
	SELECTED="..."—Specifies whether the option is selected.
	DISABLED="..."—Disables control.
	VALUE="..."—The value submitted if a control is submitted.
Empty	No

<SELECT>...</SELECT>

Usage	Creates choices for the user to select.
Start/End Tag	Required/Required
Attributes	%coreattrs, %i18n, %events
	NAME="..."—The name of the element.
	SIZE="..."—The width in number of rows.
	MULTIPLE—Allows multiple selections.
	DISABLED="..."—Disables the control.
	TABINDEX="..."—Sets the tabbing order between elements with a defined tabindex.
	ONFOCUS="..."—The event that occurs when the element receives focus.
	ONBLUR="..."—The event that occurs when the element loses focus.
	ONSELECT="..."—Intrinsic event that occurs when the control is selected.
	ONCHANGE="..."—Intrinsic event that occurs when the control is changed.
Empty	No

A

`<TEXTAREA>...</TEXTAREA>`

Usage   Creates an area for user input with multiple lines.

Start/End Tag   Required/Required

Attributes   `%coreattrs`, `%i18n`, `%events`

`NAME="..."`—The name of the control.

`ROWS="..."`—The width in number of rows.

`COLS="..."`—The height in number of columns.

`DISABLED="..."`—Disables the control.

`READONLY="..."`—Sets the displayed text to read-only status.

`TABINDEX="..."`—Sets the tabbing order between elements with a defined `tabindex`.

`ONFOCUS="..."`—The event that occurs when the element receives focus.

`ONBLUR="..."`—The event that occurs when the element loses focus.

`ONSELECT="..."`—Intrinsic event that occurs when the control is selected.

`ONCHANGE="..."`—Intrinsic event that occurs when the control is changed.

Empty   No

Notes   Text to be displayed is placed within the start and end tags.

Scripts

Scripting language is made available to process data and perform other dynamic events through the SCRIPT element.

`<SCRIPT>...</SCRIPT>`

Usage   The `<SCRIPT>` element contains client-side scripts that are executed by the browser.

Start/End Tag   Required/Required

Attributes   `TYPE="..."`—Script-language Internet content type.

`LANGUAGE="..."`—Deprecated. The scripting language, deprecated in favor of the TYPE attribute.

`SRC="..."`—The URL for the external script.

Empty   No

Notes   You can set the default scripting language in the `<META>` element.

`<NOSCRIPT>...</NOSCRIPT>`

Usage   The `<NOSCRIPT>` element provides alternative content for browsers unable to execute a script.

Start/End Tag   Required/Required

Attributes   None

Empty   No

Common Attributes and Events

Four attributes are abbreviated as `%coreattrs` in the preceding sections. They are

- ☐ `ID="..."`—A global identifier.
- ☐ `CLASS="..."`—A list of classes separated by spaces.
- ☐ `STYLE="..."`—Style information.
- ☐ `TITLE="..."`—Provides more information for a specific element, as opposed to the `<TITLE>` element, which entitles the entire Web page.

Two attributes for internationalization (i18n) are abbreviated as `%i18n`:

- ☐ `LANG="..."`—The language identifier.
- ☐ `DIR="..."`—The text direction (`ltr`, `rtl`).

The following intrinsic events are abbreviated `%events`:

- ☐ `ONCLICK="..."`—A pointing device (such as a mouse) was single-clicked.
- ☐ `ONDBCLICK="..."`—A pointing device (such as a mouse) was double-clicked.
- ☐ `ONMOUSEDOWM="..."`—A mouse button was clicked and held down.
- ☐ `ONMOUSEUP="..."`—A mouse button that was clicked and held down was released.
- ☐ `ONMOUSEOVER="..."`—A mouse moved the cursor over an object.
- ☐ `ONMOUSEMOVE="..."`—The mouse was moved.
- ☐ `ONMOUSEOUT="..."`—A mouse moved the cursor off an object.
- ☐ `ONKEYPRESS="..."`—A key was pressed and released.
- ☐ `ONKEYDOWN="..."`—A key was pressed and held down.
- ☐ `ONKEYUP="..."`—A key that was pressed has been released.

A

Appendix **B**

HTML Learning Resources on the Internet

General HTML Information

The 24-Hour HTML Café (the online companion to this book)

`http://www.mcp.com/sites/1-57521/1-57521-366-4/`

Microsoft Internet

`http://www.microsoft.com/internet`

Netscape Communications

`http://home.netscape.com`

The Developer's JumpStation

`http://oneworld.wa.com/htmldev/devpage/dev-page.html`

The HTML Writer's Guild

`http://www.hwg.org/`

The Web Developer's Virtual Library

`http://WWW.Stars.com/`

Netscape's HTML Assistance Pages

`http://home.netscape.com/assist/net_sites/index.html`

The World Wide Web FAQ

`http://www.boutell.com/faq/`

Tim Berners-Lee's Style Guide

`http://www.w3.org/hypertext/WWW/Provider/Style/Overview.html`

Web Pages that Suck

`http://www.webpagesthatsuck.com/`

The HTML Guru

`http://members.aol.com/htmlguru/index.html`

Carlos' Forms Tutorial

`http://robot0.ge.uiuc.edu/~carlosp/cs317/cft.html`

B

Recommended Software

Paint Shop Pro (a highly recommended Windows graphics editor)

http://www.jasc.com

GIFTool (UNIX)

http://www.homepages.com/tools/

Perl Library to Manage CGI and Forms

http://www.bio.cam.ac.uk/cgi-lib/

MapEdit (a tool for Windows and X11 for creating imagemap files)

http://www.boutell.com/mapedit/

HotSpots (a Windows image map tool)

http://www.cris.com/~automata/index.html

Software Archives

Shareware.com (best source for almost any type of free or inexpensive software for all types of computers)

http://www.shareware.com

The Ultimate Collection of Winsock Software

http://www.tucows.com/

Dave Central Software Archive

http://www.davecentral.com/

Cool Helpers Page

http://www.teleport.com/~alano/coolhelp.html

WinSite Windows Software Archive

http://www.winsite.com/

B

Graphics

Graphics Wonderland

http://www.geocities.com/SiliconValley/Heights/1272/index.html

Kira's Icon Library

http://fohnix.metronet.com/~kira/icongifs/

Anthony's Icon Library

http://www.cit.gu.edu.au/~anthony/icons/index.html

Barry's Clip Art Server

http://www.barrysclipart.com

256 Color Square

http://www59.metronet.com/colors/

Color Triplet Chart

http://www.phoenix.net/~jacobson/rgb.html

Imaging Machine

http://www.vrl.com/Imaging/

Frequently Asked Questions About JPEG

http://www.cis.ohio-state.edu/hypertext/faq/usenet/jpeg-faq/faq.html

Frequently Asked Questions from comp.graphics

http://www.primenet.com/~grieggs/cg_faq.html

Dick Oliver's Nonlinear Nonsense Netletter

http://netletter.com/

Multimedia and Virtual Reality

RealAudio

http://www.realaudio.com

Streamworks

`http://www.xingtech.com`

QuickTime

`http://quicktime.apple.com`

VDOLive

`http://www.vdolive.com`

Macromedia's Shockwave

`http://www.macromedia.com/`

NCompass Plug-in for Netscape Navigator

`http://www.ncompasslabs.com/`

Multimedia Authoring Languages

`http://www.mcli.dist.maricopa.edu/authoring/lang.html`

The VRML Repository

`http://www.sdsc.edu/vrml/`

JavaSoft

`http://www.javasoft.com/`

Gamelan (Java resource registry)

`http://www.gamelan.com/`

TechWeb's ActiveXpress

`http://www.techweb.com/activexpress/`

Standards and Specifications

The Home of the WWW Consortium

`http://www.w3.org/`

Secure HTTP Information

`http://www.eit.com/projects/s-http/`

B

Secure Sockets Layer (SSL) Information

`http://www.netscape.com/info/security-doc.html`

Current List of Official MIME Types

`ftp://ftp.isi.edu/in-notes/iana/assignments/media-types/media-types`

HTML Validators

HTML Validation Service

`http://www.webtechs.com/html-val-svc/`

Htmlchek

`http://uts.cc.utexas.edu/~churchh/htmlchek.html`

Lvrfy (link checker)

`http://www.cs.dartmouth.edu/~crow/lvrfy.html`

Weblint

`http://www.unipress.com/cgi-bin/WWWeblint`

Directories with HTML Information

Yahoo! World Wide Web

`http://www.yahoo.com/Computers/Internet/World_Wide_Web/`

HotWired's WebMonkey

`http://www.webmonkey.com/`

Cool Site of the Day

`http://cool.infi.net/`

HTML and WWW Tools Index

`http://www.w3.org/hypertext/WWW/Tools/`

Internet Resources Meta-Index

`http://www.ncsa.uiuc.edu/SDG/Software/Mosaic/MetaIndex.html`

B

Web Service Providers List

`http://union.ncsa.uiuc.edu/HyperNews/get/www/leasing.html`

Lycos Web Publishing Index

`http://a2z.lycos.com/Internet/Web_Publishing_and_HTML/`

InfoSeek HTML Index

`http://www.infoseek.com/Internet/HTML`

TechWeb's HTML Authoring Tools

`http://www.techweb.com/tools/html/`

B

INDEX

Teach Yourself Web Publishing with HTML 4 in a Week, Fourth Edition

Laura Lemay

Teach Yourself Web Publishing with HTML 4 in a Week, Fourth Edition is a thoroughly revised version of the shorter, beginner's softcover edition of the best-selling book that started the whole HTML/Web publishing craze.

Now covers the new HTML Cougar specifications, the Netscape Communicator and Microsoft Internet Explorer 4 environments, as well as style sheets, dynamic HTML and XML.

This title teaches Web publishing in a clear, step-by-step manner with lots of practical examples of Web pages. Still the best HTML tutorial on the market!

Price: $29.99 US/$42.95 CDN   *User Level:New—Casual*
1-57521-336-2   *720 pp.*

Teach Yourself Web Publishing with HTML in 14 Days, Second Professional Reference Edition

Laura Lemay and Arman Danesh

A thoroughly revised version of the best-selling book that started the whole HTML/Web publishing phenomenon, *Teach Yourself Web Publishing with HTML in 14 Days*, Second Professional Reference Edition is easy enough for the beginner yet comprehensive enough that even experienced Web authors will find it indispensable for reference.

Includes 16 more chapters than the softcover edition, plus a 300-page HTML reference section

Covers the new Cougar specification for the next version of HTML and the new Netscape and Microsoft technologies such as style sheets, absolute positioning, and dynamic HTML.

The CD-ROM includes an electronic version of the reference section, plus additional Web publishing tools for Windows and Macintosh platforms.

Price: $59.99 USA/$84.95 CDN   *User Level: New—Casual—Accomplished*
1-57521-305-2   *1,176 pp.*

Teach Yourself to Create a Home Page in 24 Hours

Rogers Cadenhead

This book is a carefully organized tutorial that is divided into 24 short, one-hour chapters that teach the beginning Web page author what he needs to know to make a Web page operational in the shortest time possible.

The quickest and easiest way to learn how to create your own Web pages with a WYSIWYG editor.

No HTML required—the book steps the reader through the process using Claris Home Page, a leading entry Web page editor for novices.

Truly a starter kit, the Windows and Macintosh CD-ROM includes a full working copy of Claris Home Page Lite and a collection of examples from the author.

Price: $24.99 US/$35.95 CDN　　　*User Level:New—Casual*
1-57521-325-7　　　*305 pp.*

Secrets of Successful Web Sites

David Siegel

Much of the book consists of visual case studies that give information that most sites won't give out—what worked for them, why, and exactly how. Readers learn the insider secrets of successful business planning, budgeting, and collaboration. Each case study explores both the client and developer points of view, so readers can see for themselves what works and what doesn't. This book gives clients everything they need to guarantee a successful site and gives Web developers everything they need to guarantee a successful Web business.

Explore visual case studies revealing the insider secrets of managing a Web project.

Never-before-revealed expert advice on cost/benefit analysis, contracts, rights issues, and marketing.

Price: $49.99 US/$70.95 CDN　　　*User Level:Intermediate—Expert*
1-56830-382-3　　　*304 pp.*

Add to Your Sams.net Library Today
with the Best Books for Internet Technologies

ISBN	Quantity	Description of Item	Unit Cost	Total Cost
1-57521-336-2		Teach Yourself Web Publishing with HTML 4 in a Week, Fourth Edition	$29.99	
1-57521-305-2		Teach Yourself Web Publishing with HTML in 14 Days, Second Professional Reference Edition (Book/CD-ROM)	$59.99	
1-57521-325-7		Teach Yourself to Create a Home Page in 24 Hours (Book/CD-ROM)	$24.99	
1-56830-382-3		Secrets of Successful Web Sites	$49.99	
		Shipping and Handling: See information below.		
		TOTAL		

Shipping and Handling: $4.00 for the first book, and $1.75 for each additional book. If you need to have it NOW, we can ship product to you in 24 hours for an additional charge of approximately $18.00, and you will receive your item overnight or in two days. Overseas shipping and handling adds $2.00. Prices subject to change. Call between 9:00 a.m. and 5:00 p.m. EST for availability and pricing information on latest editions.

201 W. 103rd Street, Indianapolis, Indiana 46290

1-800-428-5331 — Orders   1-800-835-3202 — FAX   1-800-858-7674 — Customer Service

1-57521-366-4

MACMILLAN COMPUTER PUBLISHING USA
A VIACOM COMPANY

Technical ---- **Support:**

If you need assistance with the information in this book or with a CD/Disk accompanying the book, please access the Knowledge Base on our Web site at **http://www.superlibrary.com/general/support**. Our most Frequently Asked Questions are answered there. If you do not find the answer to your questions on our Web site, you may contact Macmillan Technical Support **(317) 581-3833** or e-mail us at **support@mcp.com**.